Institutionalization of Entrepreneurship Research

The institutionalization of entrepreneurship is undeniably a good thing for the members of the research community, as it implies the legitimization of particular research topics and research practices; the emergence of norms for developing and publishing this research; and the creation of structures that provide employment opportunities and a conducive environment for pursuing research. However, we can also question if this institutionalization is such a good thing when it comes to producing critical, innovative, contextualized, and complex research or when considered from the point of view of non-academic entrepreneurship stakeholders and society in general.

The objective of this book is to challenge the main research streams, theories, methods, epistemologies, assumptions and beliefs dominating the field of entrepreneurship. In order to achieve this objective, this book comprises six conceptual and empirical contributions, each one unorthodox, controversial, inspiring and challenging.

This book was originally published as a special issue of the *Journal of Entrepreneurship & Regional Development*.

Alain Fayolle is Professor of Entrepreneurship at the Emlyon Business School, Lyon, France.

Hans Landström is Professor at the Sten K. Johnson Center for Entrepreneurship at Lund University, Sweden.

William B. Gartner is Professor of Entrepreneurship at Babson College, MA, USA.

Karin Berglund is Professor of Business at Stockholm Business School at Stockholm University, Sweden.

Institutionalization of Entrepreneurship Research

Edited by
**Alain Fayolle, Hans Landström,
William B. Gartner and Karin Berglund**

Routledge
Taylor & Francis Group

LONDON AND NEW YORK

First published 2018 by Routledge

2 Park Square, Milton Park, Abingdon, Oxfordshire OX14 4RN
52 Vanderbilt Avenue, New York, NY 10017

Routledge is an imprint of the Taylor & Francis Group, an informa business

First issued in paperback 2020

British Library Cataloguing in Publication Data
A catalogue record for this book is available from the British Library

ISBN 13: 978-1-138-57619-3 (hbk)
ISBN 13: 978-0-367-51919-3 (pbk)

Typeset in Myriad Pro
by RefineCatch Limited, Bungay, Suffolk

Publisher's Note
The publisher accepts responsibility for any inconsistencies that may have
arisen during the conversion of this book from journal articles to book chapters,
namely the possible inclusion of journal terminology.

Disclaimer
Every effort has been made to contact copyright holders for their permission to
reprint material in this book. The publishers would be grateful to hear from any
copyright holder who is not here acknowledged and will undertake to rectify
any errors or omissions in future editions of this book.

Contents

Citation Information

The chapters in this book were originally published in the *Journal of Entrepreneurship & Regional Development*, volume 28, issues 7–8 (September 2016). When citing this material, please use the original page numbering for each article, as follows:

Chapter 1
The institutionalization of entrepreneurship
Alain Fayolle, Hans Landström, William B. Gartner and Karin Berglund
Journal of Entrepreneurship & Regional Development, volume 28, issues 7–8 (September 2016), pp. 477–486

Chapter 2
A bureaucrat's journey from technocrat to entrepreneur through the creation of adhocracies
R. Duncan M. Pelly
Journal of Entrepreneurship & Regional Development, volume 28, issues 7–8 (September 2016), pp. 487–513

Chapter 3
A CULTure of entrepreneurship education
Steffen Farny, Signe Hedeboe Frederiksen, Martin Hannibal and Sally Jones
Journal of Entrepreneurship & Regional Development, volume 28, issues 7–8 (September 2016), pp. 514–535

Chapter 4
A theoretical and methodological approach to social entrepreneurship as world-making and emancipation: social change as a projection in space and time
Nicolina Montesano Montessori
Journal of Entrepreneurship & Regional Development, volume 28, issues 7–8 (September 2016), pp. 536–562

Chapter 5
Destituent entrepreneurship: disobeying sovereign rule, prefiguring post-capitalist reality
Pascal Dey
Journal of Entrepreneurship & Regional Development, volume 28, issues 7–8 (September 2016), pp. 563–579

Chapter 6
Entrepreneurial Orientation: do we actually know as much as we think we do?
Kathleen Randerson
Journal of Entrepreneurship & Regional Development, volume 28, issues 7–8 (September 2016), pp. 580–599

For any permission-related enquiries please visit:
http://www.tandfonline.com/page/help/permissions

Notes on Contributors

Karin Berglund is Professor of Business at Stockholm Business School at Stockholm University, Sweden.

Pascal Dey is Associate Professor at the People, Organizations and Society Department at Grenoble Ecole de Management and a Senior Research Fellow at the Institute for Business Ethics at the University of St. Gallen.

Steffen Farny is a Postdoctoral Researcher in the School of Business at Aalto University, Helsinki, Finland.

Alain Fayolle is Professor of Entrepreneurship at the Emlyon Business School, Lyon, France.

Signe Hedeboe Frederiksen is Assistant Professor in the Department of Management at Aarhus University, Denmark.

William B. Gartner is Professor of Entrepreneurship at Babson College, MA, USA.

Martin Hannibal is Associate Professor in the Department of Marketing and Management at the University of Southern Denmark, Odense, Denmark.

Sally Jones is a Reader in Entrepreneurship and Gender Studies at Manchester Metropolitan University, UK.

Hans Landström is Professor at the Sten K. Johnson Center for Entrepreneurship at Lund University, Sweden.

Nicolina Montesano Montessori is Associate Professor in the Faculty of Education at the HU University of Applied Sciences, Utrecht, The Netherlands.

R. Duncan M. Pelly is Assistant Professor in the Department of Management at California State University, Los Angeles, CA, USA.

Kathleen Randerson is Associate Professor in the Department of Business and Society at Audencia Business School, Nantes, France.

The institutionalization of entrepreneurship

Questioning the status quo and re-gaining hope for entrepreneurship research

Alain Fayolle, Hans Landström, William B. Gartner and Karin Berglund

ABSTRACT
In this article, we briefly identify three main challenges/issues that should be taken into consideration in the institutionalization of entrepreneurship research: (1) recognizing the complexity of the phenomenon under study; (2) producing interesting, relevant and useful research results for all stakeholders; and (3) developing a critical posture in research. Following the discussion of these challenges/ issues we introduce the five contributions to the Special Issue that, in different ways, problematize and challenge mainstream research and approaches. These articles use 'dissensus discourses', apply critical, ideological and paradigmatic stances and in some cases underline the importance of contextual factors.

1. Introduction

Putting this Special Issue in context, we are writing this introduction during Summer 2016. The RENT (Research in Entrepreneurship and Small Business) Conference is 30 years old. It is also the year that the Academy of Management Entrepreneurship Division celebrates its 30-year anniversary. Entrepreneurship as a social and economic phenomenon, has, then, over these past 30 years, become a field of inquiry, and gained significant interest from policy-makers, 'practitioners' (to be more loosely defined later on this article), and in society more generally (Berglund, Johannisson, and Schwartz 2012). During this period, entrepreneurship research has grown remarkably and is, today, a well-established scholarly field with its own endowed chairs, faculty positions, academic associations, scientific journals and conferences (Aldrich 2012; Fayolle and Riot 2016). In this respect, entrepreneurship research has become more and more institutionalized (Fligstein 1997; Lamont 2012; Scott 2001) and, as such, entrepreneurship research has received greater academic legitimacy.

We can argue that this institutionalization is undeniably a good thing for the members of the research community, as it implies the legitimization of particular research topics and research practices, the emergence of norms for developing and publishing this research, and last but not least, the creation of structures that provide employment opportunities and a conducive environment for pursuing research (Riot and Fayolle 2016). However, we can also question if this institutionalization is such a good thing when it comes to producing critical, innovative, contextualized and complex research or when considered from the point of view of non-academic entrepreneurship stakeholders and society in general (Tedmanson et al. 2012).

Yet, entrepreneurship is also a multidisciplinary field having attracted researchers in, for example, economics, sociology, psychology, history, philosophy and management (Aldrich 2016; Gartner 2004). In line with these multidisciplinary academic interests and in an attempt to address social needs and problems, entrepreneurship has also unfolded in new societal areas. This is discernible by the increasing (and sometimes questionable) use of such prefixes as 'social', 'green', 'sustainable' or suffixes such as entrepreneurial learning, culture, intention, orientation and management. The use of 'entrepreneurial' is thus diffused, but does that mean that entrepreneurial practices also are diffused, in the better way? Is entrepreneurship becoming institutionalized in a society that cherishes and strives for diversity when it comes to the entrepreneurial? Is entrepreneurship scholarship calcifying and 'thereby beset by an increasing number of assumptions, even myths' (Rehn et al. 2013), while society acts entrepreneurially in different ways with different meanings? Assumptions and myths concern both the focus, i.e. the main research objects/topics, and the ways (theories, methods) we should use to study entrepreneurship as a historical, cultural, social and economic phenomena (Berglund and Johansson 2007). Finally, have society's ideas about entrepreneurship also become institutionalized in ways that have made its conception and practice hollow?

All these questions highlight the fact that the institutionalization of entrepreneurship as a field of research and a domain of practices has important consequences at different levels. Discussing the institutionalization of entrepreneurship is something relatively new in a way where researchers are invited to attend workshops and research projects[1] which clearly focus on the topic (i.e. Fayolle and Riot 2016; Landstrom et al. 2016).

The objective of this Special Issue of *Entrepreneurship & Regional Development* is to challenge the main research streams, theories, methods, epistemologies, assumptions and beliefs dominating the field of entrepreneurship. In order to achieve this objective, we have selected five conceptual and empirical papers based on their unorthodox, controversial, inspiring and challenging contributions.

This introduction to the Special Issue is organized as follows. We briefly identify three main challenges/issues that should be taken into consideration in the institutionalization of entrepreneurship research: (1) recognizing the complexity of the phenomenon under study; (2) producing interesting, relevant and useful research results for all stakeholders; and (3) developing a critical posture in research. Following the discussion of these challenges/issues we introduce the five contributions to the Special Issue that, in different ways, problematize and challenge mainstream research and approaches. These articles use 'dissensus discourses' (Alvesson and Deetz 2000), apply critical ideological and paradigmatic stances and in some cases underline the importance of contextual factors.

2. Three main challenges in entrepreneurship institutionalization

In order to maximize (or at least to try to maximize!) the positive effects of institutionalizing entrepreneurship and in the same time reduce the impact of its negative consequences, we believe that research communities in the entrepreneurship field should think about the better ways to: deal with the complexity of the phenomenon (Bruyat and Julien 2001; Fayolle 2003; Gartner 1985); produce interesting research (Frank and Landström 2016) and, develop a more reflective and critical posture in research activities (Fayolle and Riot 2016; Landstrom et al. 2016).

2.1. Dealing with complexity

Entrepreneurship can be understood as a complex, process-based and multidimensional phenomenon (Bruyat and Julien 2001; Fayolle 2007; Gartner 1985). We could also add that entrepreneurship as a field of research is fragmented (Fayolle 2007) and multidisciplinary (Aldrich 2016). Complexity comes from the diversity/variety of entrepreneurship forms/situations and the context in which they emerge and develop (new venture creation, corporate entrepreneurship, social entrepreneurship, sustainable entrepreneurship, etc.), the multidimensionality of the phenomenon, itself (i.e. individual, environment, process and organization [Gartner 1985]), and the key roles that temporal and contextual variables play in the process (that is, entrepreneurship is a context-based and dynamic phenomenon). The context of entrepreneurship, then, can be seen and studied in different ways and dimensions: spatial, industry, market, temporal, social and institutional (Welter 2011; Zahra and Wright 2011). As a result, a great number of variables should be taken in consideration to understand how different research streams try to capture, or destabilize, the 'true essence' of the phenomenon. There is today an increasingly widespread recognition that there is a great variety of entrepreneurial situations, new venture creations and profiles of entrepreneurs. Entrepreneurs and their entrepreneurial projects are different from one another (Gartner 1985, 2016). Complexity also comes from the nature of the phenomenon. For some scholars (e.g. Gartner, Steyaert, Hjorth and Johannisson), entrepreneurship is a matter of emergence and/or becoming. For Gartner (2014), as an example, entrepreneurship can be conceptualized as organizing emergence. By 'organizing emergence', Gartner suggests 'a commonality in phenomena (both theorized and studied) that involve situations where something develops from one state to another and that within that development there is a process in which the phenomena becomes more "organized"' (2014, 14). Entrepreneurship as 'organizing emergence' can be studied and theorized from a wide range of disciplines. These disciplines, such as sociology, psychology philosophy and so on, can bring value to the concept of entrepreneurship, but the opposite is true, entrepreneurship can also add value to other the disciplines which study the phenomena. Thinking in this stream, Gartner offers interesting thoughts to deal with the complexity of the phenomenon notably by looking at the ways disciplines are informed by and informing entrepreneurship. Another example is offered by Johannisson (2014) in that the notion of 'entrepreneuring' seems well appropriated to qualify a phenomenon, entrepreneurship, that is generically associated with movement and process (Steyaert 2007). Johannisson sees 'entrepreneurship as a collective phenomenon, as creative organizing – of thoughts, actions and people in projects which accumulate for the individual into an existential endeavour, as an approach to and way of life' (2014, 63). His main goal is to offer 'conceptual ideas of entrepreneurship as a phenomenon that is made comprehensive through encounters between theory, art and practice' (2014, 64). In this way, he shows that entrepreneuring can be understood as a process of becoming whereby children become natural born entrepreneurs because they live in a world of becoming where they experience new things, learn from mistakes and where failures are essential components of their life. Based on this analogy (which can be seen as way to deal with complexity), a convincing argumentation is offered, highlighting the interrelationships among theory, art and practice (three modes that are suggested to capture entrepreneurship as a phenomenon). For other scholars (Bruyat and Julien 2001; Fayolle 2007), the field of entrepreneurship might be envisaged through the dialogic relation between the individual/entrepreneur (the subject) and the value he or she contributes to create (the object). The dialogic principle means that two or several perspectives are bound into a unity, in a complex way (complementary, concurrent and opposing) without the duality being lost in the unity. The subject–object dialogic relationship can be seen as being part of an entrepreneurial system interacting with its environment and engaged in a dynamic of change under the influence of time. So, using system-based approaches, theories, models and metaphors can be seen as a way to deal with the complexity of entrepreneurship phenomenon. Finally, complexity comes from the level of uncertainty and the unpredictableness of entrepreneurial processes or events. In this case, getting knowledge about specific mechanisms of entrepreneurial action like effectuation, causation, bricolage and improvization (Fisher 2012) could be an insightful way to deal with such complexity.

In conclusion, dealing with complexity implies notably adopting holistic and systemic views, combining qualitative and quantitative research methods, designing longitudinal research, doing context-based research and using analogies and metaphors as relevant alternatives to 'established' theories and methods.

2.2. Producing interesting research

In recent decades, the entrepreneurship field has grown significantly with the development of an international community of scholars (Aldrich 2012) who have made extensive advances in our knowledge of entrepreneurship (Landström, Harirchi, and Åström 2012). One explanation for these successes is that entrepreneurship has been regarded as an 'interesting' field of research (Davis 1971). Interesting contributions have been published that have opened up new research paths and challenged old beliefs that have turned conventional wisdom upside down. Yet, in an increased institutionalization of the field (including, for example, a growing number of highly ranked journals, a stronger focus on journal citations, a reasonable coherent set of research questions and methodologies that favour scientific rigor) there is always a risk that individual scholars will become embedded in a culture and incentive system that makes their contributions less and less interesting.

How do theories that are generally considered 'interesting' differ from those that are considered 'non-interesting?' When it comes to theoretical work, Murray Davis (1971) suggested that theories that tend to challenge certain assumptions of the audience were more likely to stand out and capture attention. A theory will be regarded as interesting if it challenges accepted truths and questions the taken-for-granted world of the audience. If a theory merely confirms taken-for-granted beliefs the audience will reject its value and the response will be: 'Of course!' 'That's obvious!' or 'Everybody knows that!'. On the other hand, if a theory challenges too many of our assumptions, the audience will seldom regard it as interesting, but rather as 'absurd'. It is in this 'in between' space of the obvious (what everyone already knows) and the 'absurd' (it is too strange and different to be considered plausible) that the 'interesting' has the possibility of challenging and changing assumptions and beliefs.

When it comes to empirical contributions, the perception of what is regarded as interesting is much more diverse, for example, depending on the characteristics of the research field and the context in which the contribution occurs. In management studies, interesting work seems to be linked to the scientific quality and rigour of the study (Bartunek, Rynes, and Ireland 2006; Das and Long 2010): well-crafted theory, good fit between the data and theory, engaging data analyses, generalizability, and good writing that is well-crafted with a clear and engaging story. However, interesting work in family business studies are markedly different, and family business works are perceived as interesting when it describes family-specific issues, such as processes and structures of the family business (Salvato and Aldrich 2012).

While what is perceived as interesting could be regarded as a matter of taste, something personal and subjective – what one scholar regards as interesting in entrepreneurship research does not necessarily attract another scholar – we can't relate interestingness only to a matter of individual taste. There are collectively held assessments regarding, for example, popular research topics and methodological approaches that over time are regarded as interesting within a research field (Alvesson and Sandberg 2013). Thus, what is regarded as interesting is dependent on the audience the article addresses.

As Davis points out, a field of knowledge typically begins with both scholars and practitioners having the same set of facts, insights and values as to what is 'interesting.' As a field develops, this initial cohesion between scholars and practitioners eventually bifurcates into two separate groups, with scholars developing knowledge and insights that are not 'interesting' to practitioners. In entrepreneurship scholarship, this presents us with a conundrum. Frank and Landström (2016) found that many entrepreneurship scholars regarded 'relevance' as a key criterion for entrepreneurship scholarship to be interesting. Indeed, since the inception of entrepreneurship as a research field in the 1980s, entrepreneurship research has had a focus on a practice-oriented scholarship (see, for example, early issues of the *Journal of Business Venturing* that required Executive Summaries with practice implications, and, obviously the 'practice' in the title of: *Entrepreneurship Theory and Practice*). Obviously, there are many reasons for this development towards a focus on what appears to be academic issues of rigour rather than issues of what constitutes value to other stakeholders (Frank and Landström 2016). For example, there is a strong incentive and career system in academia, supported by different indicators to measure scholarly impact that influence the behaviour of entrepreneurship scholars. When citation counts or publication in certain journals become the measure of value, then, writing to other audiences in other venues (which could be relevant and interesting to those audiences) is de-incentivized. Institutional theory at play: Yes?

The challenge, then, in an attempt to be interesting to academics and other stakeholders is to develop an 'applicative knowledge' that reaches beyond the knowledge generated by means of more dominant approaches in entrepreneurship research. This requires a close connection and exchange with 'others'.

2.3. Becoming more critical and self-reflecting

Institutionalized behaviours and practices are 'widely followed, without debate, and exhibit permanence' (Tolbert and Zucker 1983, 25). Institutionalization also refers to 'more or less taken for granted repetitive social behaviour that is underpinned by normative systems and cognitive understandings that give meaning to social exchange and thus enable self-reproducing social order' (Greenwood et al. 2008, 4–5). We believe, that, implicit in the nature of entrepreneurship (by whatever definition one might use, so, for purposes of this sentence, let's suggest it be: doing things differently) the consequences of institutionalization cannot be considered entirely positive for research on entrepreneurship. Can the study of phenomena that are different be studied in similar ways with similar theories? In the spirit of the sense of 'requisite variety' (Weick 1979, 2012), to reduce the possible negative effects of entrepreneurship institutionalization, there would be a necessity to develop critical and self-reflecting settings and postures both at individual and collective levels.

Fletcher and Selden (2016) discuss the different meanings of the term 'critical' in entrepreneurship. At the researcher level, critical thinking refers to a posture which adopts a critical stance towards extant research positions, validate the evidence bases used and 'strive to avoid speculative arguments and erroneous conclusions' (Alvesson and Ashcraft 2009). For example, Fayolle (2013) claims there is a lack of critical thinking and approach in entrepreneurship education. To a certain extent, this sub-domain appears as a 'taken for granted' professional domain. At the community of research level, being 'critical' would mean 'a search for alternative ways of knowing and understanding what constitute entrepreneurial activity and how these activities/practices may be studied' (Fletcher and Selden 2016). One example here is given by the creation, several years ago, of a special interest group in critical studies, the Entrepreneurship Studies Network, who connects together scholars who share a common interest in alternative approaches to entrepreneurship research. This group has secured a permanent track (Critical Perspectives in Entrepreneurship) at the RENT Conference and benefits from the advice and guidance of an advisory board including pioneers in such alternative approaches to entrepreneurship research such as Chris Steyaert, Daniel Hjorth, Bengt Johannisson and Denise Fletcher.

Fletcher and Selden (2016) have identified, in their literature review of critical perspectives in entrepreneurship research, four different approaches characterizing the use of critical research tactics in entrepreneurship: (1) critical review of a theme/topic/sub-domain; (2) critical study of a 'standpoint' issue to overcome marginalized experiences/contexts; (3) critical entrepreneurship; and (4) critical research practices. What could be done to becoming more (and better) critical and self-reflecting in the field of entrepreneurship both at the individual and collective levels? A plurality of ways, previously suggested by some entrepreneurship scholars, could be considered. Fletcher and Selden (2016), for example, are suggesting a substantial list of what we should do engaging in critique-inspired research practices. They emphasize notably the importance of contextualization processes (Buchanan and Bryman 2009) and entrepreneurial contexts. They suggest to take into consideration process, time and context relativity. Fletcher and Selden (2016) also recommend alternative and pluralistic ways of understanding the world and finally they think making explicit the emotions, politics and ethics of research practice would be a relevant posture in this way.

It should be pointed out that, in the above development, some elements fit with the 'complexity' and 'interesting research' challenges underlying the point that our three challenges are interrelated.

Riot and Fayolle (2016) voice similar arguments claiming that there is a need for pushing towards the frontiers of the field, finding inspiration from other disciplines, challenging the dominant epistemological posture and developing critical reflection about the myths of entrepreneurship and their hidden economic and political dimensions. Looking more specifically at entrepreneurship education, Fayolle (2013, 8) is suggesting that a way to developing a reflexive and critical posture could be to regularly question the main research streams, theories, methods, epistemologies, assumptions and beliefs dominating the field and the educational practices of entrepreneurship education. It can be achieved by adopting a critical and constructive attitude towards the questions raised and the issues covered and by breaking down the silos between thinking and acting, the world of academia and that of practice, and between disciplines looking at entrepreneurship education.

As an aside, then, all these suggestions should probably lead us to reconsider the way we are educating PhD students in entrepreneurship. We believe that there is a need to include

Table 1. Summary of the five papers accepted in the Special Issue.

Author(s)	Research question(s)	Theoretical perspective	Data and methods	Key findings
Farny et al.	How are values and beliefs about entrepreneurship institutionalized in entrepreneurship education?	Religious theoretical lens	Qualitative research interviews of entrepreneurship educators in European countries: UK, Denmark, Finland	Offering new lenses and a critical perspective to analyse the institutionali-zation of entrepreneurship in entrepreneurship education as a value/belief system
Pelly	How we understand entrepreneurship as a function of the story we tell?	The 'cult' Process theory	Qualitative research	New understanding of entrepreneurship through story weaving
		Philosophical background	Auto-ethnography storytelling	Entrepreneur viewed as a master storyteller in the context of a large organization with a high level of bureaucracy
Montesano Montessori	How can a new methodology be developed that allows for the analysis of social movements in the light of social entrepreneur-ship as emancipation and world-making?	Political theory	Qualitative and longitudinal research	Offering a new methodology to analyse social entrepreneurial movements in the light of both emancipation and world-making
		Discourse theory	Three Dutch cases Critical discourse analysis Narrative analysis	
Dey	How and why to study entrepreneurship in time of crisis?	Destituent power theory	Qualitative research	Entrepreneurship under conditions of crisis as an opportunity to redefine realm of economic practice by one's own practice
		Theories of prefigurative praxis	Worker-occupied enterprises in Argentina as an illustrative example	
Randerson	What behaviours other than innovation, pro activeness and risk-taking can be considered to be entrepreneurial?	Entrepreneurial orientation theoretical framework	Conceptual paper based on a literature review on entrepre-neurial orientation	Offering five distinctive conceptualizations of entrepreneurial orientation
	How can other research modes or philosophies of science shed light on firm-level entrepre-neurship?			Offering new ways perspectives, and alternative philosophies rooted in the European tradition of research to do research on entrepreneur-ial orientation

doctoral courses focusing explicitly on critical thinking and critical perspectives both at researcher and research-community levels.

3. Contribution of the Special Issue to the institutionalization of entrepreneurship

The call for papers resulted in 15 submissions. We asked eight authors or teams to revise and resubmit their work. From these revisions, five papers were accepted for publication. Each submission was reviewed according to standard double-blind evaluation procedures. Table 1 summarizes those that successfully, after (at least) two rounds of review and revision, negotiated this process.

The selected papers in this Special Issue expose unusual cases, try out original and/or untested perspectives, and pose new questions: unwrapping the nature of firm level entrepreneurship (Randerson 2016); exploring new ways to study social changes in societies (Montesano Montessori 2016); reflecting on entrepreneurship 'in crisis' through the occupy enterprise movement in Argentina (Dey 2016); retelling the story of entrepreneurship through a study of a US Military post office in Korea (Pelly 2016); and recasting the roles and beliefs of entrepreneurship education in the Western world through a sense of 'cult' (Farny et al. 2016).

All papers are strongly embedded in the European tradition of research (Down 2013). In terms of the three main challenges to the institutionalization of entrepreneurship research outlined earlier (complexity, interesting, critical), these Special Issue articles push the boundaries of the three criteria in the ways we hoped for when the call for papers was posted.

4. Conclusion

The articles in this Special Issue are reminders of the ways that entrepreneurship takes new alternative positions, meanings and routes. Entrepreneurship is a phenomenon that, by its nature, creatively destructs (and constructs) itself. Taking this perspective seriously, it becomes impossible to shackle entrepreneurship to unchanging definitions, theories and methodologies. To study entrepreneurship requires that we follow how it moves and multiplies and, therefore, scholars need to stay open to how previous relevant definitions, theories and methodologies must be altered. This requires that the field of entrepreneurship scholarship frees itself to study entrepreneurship in unorthodox empirical contexts, try out new research approaches and perspectives, and pose new questions. We re-approach entrepreneurship by going beyond assumed boundaries of what the phenomenon is and how it should be studied. We hope that scholars continue to re-ignite their curiosity and seek to follow the phenomenon in ways that interest them. Confronting the challenges and issues raised by the process of entrepreneurship institutionalization offers fantastic possibilities for entrepreneurship scholars to invent (or reinvent) the futures of entrepreneurship research while capitalizing on the benefits (robustness, quality, intellectual rigor) generated by the process itself.

Note

1. Several workhops have been organized on the topic, since 2012, as pre-conference workshop of the *BCERC* and PDWs of *Academy of Management Entrepreneurship Division*. A book series, *Rethinking Entrepreneurship Research*, is actually running by Routledge.

Disclosure statement

No potential conflict of interest was reported by the authors.

References

Aldrich, H. E. 2012. "The Emergence of Entrepreneurship as an Academic Field: A Personal Essay on Institutional Entrepreneurship." *Research Policy* 41 (7): 1240–1248.

Aldrich, H. E. 2016. "Dimly through the Fog: Institutional Forces Affecting the Multidisciplinary Nature of Entrepreneurship." In *Rethinking Entrepreneurship. Debating Research Orientations*, edited by Alain Fayolle and Philippe Riot, 12–27. New York: Routledge.

Alvesson, M., and K. L. Ashcraft. 2009. "Critical Methodology in Management and Organization Research." In *The Sage Handbook of Organizational Research Methods*, edited by D. Buchanan and A. Bryman, 61–77. London: Sage.

Alvesson, M., and S. Deetz. 2000. *Doing Critical Management Research*. London: Sage.

Alvesson, M., and J. Sandberg. 2013. *Constructing Research Questions. Doing Interesting Research*. Thousand Oaks, CA: Sage.

Bartunek, J. M., S. L. Rynes, and R. D. Ireland. 2006. "What Makes Management Research Interesting, and Why Does It Matter?" *Academy of Management Journal* 49 (1): 9–15.

Berglund, K., and A. W. Johansson. 2007. "Constructions of Entrepreneurship: A Discourse Analysis of Academic Publications." *Journal of Enterprising Communities: People and Places in the Global Economy* 1 (1): 77–102.

Berglund, K., B. Johannisson, and B. Schwartz. 2012. *Societal Entrepreneurship: Positioning, Penetrating, Promoting*. Cheltenham: Edward Elgar.

Bruyat, C., and P. A. Julien. 2001. "Defining the Field of Research in Entrepreneurship." *Journal of Business Venturing* 16: 165–180.

Buchanan, D., and A. Bryman. 2009. *The Sage Handbook of Organizational Research Methods*. London: Sage.

Das, H., and B. S. Long. 2010. "What Makes Management Research Interesting? An Exploratory Study." *Journal of Managerial Issues* 22 (1): 127–144.

Davis, M. S. 1971. "That's Interesting! towards a Phenomenology of Sociology and a Sociology of Phenomenology." *Philosophy of the Social Sciences* 1 (2): 309–344.

Dey, P. 2016. "Destituent Entrepreneurship: Disobeying Sovereign Rule, Prefiguring Post-capitalist Reality." *Entrepreneurship and Regional Development* (this issue).

Down, S. 2013. "The Distinctiveness of the European Tradition in Entrepreneurship Research." *Entrepreneurship and Regional Development* 25 (1–2): 1–4.

Farny, S., S. Hedoboe Frederiksen, M. Hannibal, S. Jones. 2016. "A culture of Entrepreneurship." *Entrepreneurship and Regional Development* (this issue)

Fayolle, A. 2003. "Research and Researchers at the Heart of Entrepreneurial Situations." In *New Movements in Entrepreneurship*, edited by Chris Steyaert and Daniel Hjorth, 35–50. Cheltenham: Edward Elgar.

Fayolle, A. 2007. *Entrepreneurship and New Value Creation: The Dynamic of the Entrepreneurial Process*. New York: Cambridge University Press.

Fayolle, A. 2013. "Personal Views on the Future of Entrepreneurship Education." *Entrepreneurship and Regional Development* 25 (7–8): 692–701.

Fayolle, A., and P. Riot. 2016. *Rethinking Entrepreneurship. Debating Research Orientations*. New York: Routledge.

Fisher, G. 2012. "Effectuation, Causation and Bricolage: A Behavioral Comparison of Emerging Theories in Entrepreneurship Research." *Entrepreneurship Theory & Practice* 36 (5): 1019–1051.

Fletcher, D., and P. Selden. 2016. "Navigating the Growing Field of Entrepreneurship Inquiry: Successionist and Relational Modes of Theory Development." In *Rethinking Entrepreneurship. Debating Research Orientations*, edited by Alain Fayolle and Philippe Riot, 100–122. New York: Routledge.

Fligstein, N. 1997. "Social Skill and Institutional Theory." *American Behavioral Scientist* 40 (4): 397–405.

Frank, H., and H. Landström. 2016. "What Makes Entrepreneurship Research Interesting? Reflections on Strategies to Overcome the Rigour-relevance Gap." *Entrepreneurship and Regional Development* 28 (1–2): 51–75.

Gartner, W. B. 1985. "A Conceptual Framework for Describing the Phenomenon of New Venture Creation." *Academy of Management Review* 10 (4): 696–706.

Gartner, W. B. 2004. "Achieving 'Critical Mess' in Entrepreneurship Scholarship." In *Advances in Entrepreneurship, Firm Emergence, and Growth*, edited by J. A. Katz and D. Shepherd, 199–216. Greenwich: Emerald Publishing.

Gartner, William B. 2014. "Organizing Entrepreneurship (Research)." In *Handbook of Research in Entrepreneurship*, edited by Alain Fayolle, 13–22. Cheltenham: Edward Elgar.

Gartner, William B. 2016. *Entrepreneurship as Organizing: Selected Papers of William B. Gartner*. Cheltenham: Edward Elgar.

Greenwood, R., C. Oliver, K. Sahlin, and R. Suddaby. 2008. "Introduction." In *The Sage Handbook of Organizational Institutionalism*, edited by Royston Greewood, Christine Oliver, Ray Suddaby, and Kerstin Sahlin-Anderson, 1–46. London: Sage.

Johannisson, B. 2014. "Entrepreneurship: Theory, Art and/or Practice ?" In *Handbook of Research in Entrepreneurship*, edited by Alain Fayolle, 63–85. Cheltenham: Edward Elgar.

Lamont, M. 2012. "Toward a Comparative Sociology of Valuation and Evaluation." *Annual Review of Sociology* 38 (1): 201–221.

Landström, H., G. Harirchi, and F. Åström. 2012. "Entrepreneurship: Exploring the Knowledge Base." *Research Policy* 41 (7): 1154–1181.

Landstrom, H., A. Parhankangas, A. Fayolle, and P. Riot. 2016. *Challenging Entrepreneurship Research*. London: Routledge.

Montesano Montessori, N. 2016. "A Theoretical and Methodological Approach to Social Entrepreneurship as World-making and Emancipation. Social Change as a Projection in Space and Time." *Entrepreneurship and Regional Development* (this issue).

Pelly, D. 2016. "A Bureaucrat's Journey from Technocrat to Entrepreneur through the Creation of Adhocracies." *Entrepreneurship and Regional Development* (this issue).

Randerson, K. 2016. "Entrepreneurial Orientation: Do We Actually Know as Much as We Think We Do?" *Entrepreneurship and Regional Devlopment* (this issue).

Rehn, A., M. Brännback, A. Carsrud, and M. Lindahl. 2013. "Challenging the Myths of Entrepreneurship?" *Entrepreneurship and Regional Development* 25 (7–8): 543–551.

Riot, P., and A. Fayolle. 2016. "Conclusion. Final Thoughts and Perspectives." In *Rethinking Entrepreneurship. Debating Research Orientations*, edited by Alain Fayolle and Philippe Riot, 179–185. New York: Routledge.

Salvato, C., and H. E. Aldrich. 2012. "'That's Interesting!' in Family Business Research." *Family Business Review* 25 (2): 125–135.

Scott, W. R. 2001. *Institutions and Organizations*. London: Sage.

Steyaert, C. 2007. "'Entrepreneuring' as a Conceptual Attractor? A Review of Process Theories in 20 Years of Entrepreneurship Studies." *Entrepreneurship and Regional Development* 19 (6): 453–477.

Tedmanson, D., K. Verduyn, C. Essers, and W. B. Gartner. 2012. "Critical Perspectives in Entrepreneurship Research." *Organization* 19 (5): 531–541.

Tolbert, P. S., and L. G. Zucker. 1983. "Institutional Sources of Change in the Formal Structure of Organizations: The Diffusion of Civil Service Reform, 1880–1935." *Administrative Science Quarterly* 28: 22–39.

Weick, K. E. 1979. *The Social Psychology of Organizing*. 2nd ed. New York: McGraw Hill.

Weick, K. E. 2012. "Organized Sensemaking: A Commentary on Processes of Interpretive Work." *Human Relations* 65 (1): 141–153.

Welter, F. 2011. "Contextualizing Entrepreneurship – Conceptual Challenges and Ways Forward." *Entrepreneurship Theory & Practice* 35 (1): 165–184.

Zahra, S. A., and M. Wright. 2011. "Entrepreneurship's Next Act." *Academy of Management Perspectives* 25 (4): 67–83.

A bureaucrat's journey from technocrat to entrepreneur through the creation of adhocracies

R . Duncan M. Pelly

ABSTRACT

How we understand entrepreneurship is a function of the stories we tell. This article uses insights from process theory to explore the ways in which an entrepreneur can employ a story to mobilize others to shed conflicting viewpoints to converge with the abstract. In this story, regulation as a reification of past procedures did not fully account for organizational realities of mailroom inspections conducted by the military post office, so an appeal to foundational values was adopted to alter the shared vision of future potentiality and overcome bureaucratic barriers through the creation of adhocracies. As a result of overcoming interorganizational boundaries, a technocrat became an entrepreneur by changing the view of stakeholders from a fixed audience to active co-authors during the spawning of adhocracies. The creation of adhocracies in this story is explored through an autoethnographic layered account, which is a storytelling approach that mirrors the co-construction of the narratives found within this paper's vignettes. The understanding of entrepreneurship provided in this paper challenges commonly held assumptions of entrepreneurship, in addition to corporate, organizational and public service entrepreneurship, as well as the methods and writing styles to explore these concepts.

Introduction

So many times we have all been confronted by, or perhaps played the part of the hostile bureaucrat. Whether it is a public health official making threats over a late payment for treatment received, or local tax authorities making the customer wait hours in line for the privilege of paying them, we have all felt victimized by public employees who use regulations as a justification for their behaviour. While I am not proud to say it, I too may have been one of those tyrannical bureaucrats who adopted regulation as a sacred object (Durkheim 1915; Eliade 1958) in an attempt to alter the behaviour of those in my periphery. This autoethnography is a story of my transition from the classic bureaucrat (Bennis 1966; Dugger 1980; Thompson 1969; Weber 1958) to a public service entrepreneur (Gore 1994; Llewellyn and Jones 2003; Teske and Schneider 1994) who traded the limitations of regulation for shared norms as a means to break down organizational barriers and alter the course of the future.

As the vignettes of this story unfold, I will illustrate by what means this transformational mindset assisted my colleagues and me to realize novel forms of entrepreneurship via co-constructed stories and their subsequent adhocracies within the context of a large, highly bureaucratic organization: the United States Army.

In order to better understand the power of stories in this paper, it is important to review the theoretical roots supporting the incorporation of stories. After the introduction, this work will describe some of the basic tenants of process theory. The paper will explore the nature of abstractions as described by Whitehead (1978) and Plato (2012), organizations as actual entities (Whitehead 1978), and the role of integration (Follett 1919, 1924, 1940) in organization formation, in particular of adhocracies (Autier 2001; Johannisson and Olaison 2007; Toffler 1970), and relate these concepts to entrepreneurial storytelling.

It may appear at first glance that these philosophical ideas have little bearing on entre-preneurship, but this paper will embrace these metaphors from process theory as a means to provide a new perspective in entrepreneurship. This paper will explore entrepreneurship in large bureaucratic organizations without a profit motive, or in other words, public service entrepreneurship (Gore 1994; Llewellyn and Jones 2003; Mandell and Steelman 2003). The key is to shift the entrepreneurial manager's role from a storyteller focusing on a fixed audi-ence to a story weaver who views his context as a co-author seeking new possibilities. The theoretical impetus behind the integrative and narrative framework may be found by incor-porating metaphors from process theory. Abstractions or eternal objects serve as the over-arching principles guiding any organization, especially in the case of the United States Army and the military post office. Similar to abstractions, the omnipresence of values dictates how an organization may behave. In the case of this paper, the abstractions of army values are reified through regulations, which served as both an enabler and constrainer of our daily behaviour, since regulations represent the validation of past practices. Actual entities serve as a proxy for adhocracies, and the process of concrescence is broken down into two steps – co-constructed narration, followed by co-constructed adhocracies.

After presenting the theoretical background, there will be a discussion of the method used in this paper: autoethnography. Because this autoethnography is about the storytelling processes of entrepreneurship, I felt that a storytelling methodology was appropriate. Autoethnography is an embodied approach that interweaves the perspectives of the author and the environment, which when combined with *post hoc* theoretical explanations in mov-ing vignettes, serves as a robust sensemaking device. The first vignette describes my expe-riences as a traditional bureaucrat. The second through fifth vignettes describe my moving from a traditional bureaucracy to a peripheral organization and its accompanying challenges. The sixth and seventh vignettes describe my overcoming the challenges of serving in a peripheral organization while simultaneously honouring my traditional duties. The discus-sion situates the formation of adhocratic organizations within the military bureaucracy with respect to extant entrepreneurship literature, as well as explains its broader implications. Following the vignettes, the conclusion addresses contributions of the paper.

This paper makes a number of contributions. First, through its theoretical orientation, it provides a new understanding of entrepreneurship through story weaving. Second, it paints entrepreneurs as master storytellers who are not heroic (Schumpeter 1934) but are rather perfectly flawed individuals who must view their context as a series of co-authors instead of as audience members. Third, it provides an empirical example of the power of stories in promoting entrepreneurship in the context of a larger organization. Lastly, through this storytelling perspective it also contributes to the power of future potentiality in articulating entrepreneurship. This perspective supplements existing ideas from corporate entrepreneurship, organizational entrepreneurship and public service entrepreneurship.

Theoretical section

It is fairly simplistic to classify entrepreneurs as storytellers (Johansson 2004; Lounsbury and Glynn 2001; Garud, Schildt, and Lant 2014), or even indicate that rhetoric and stories are the bridge between the abstract and the actual (Hernes 2014; Lyotard 1979; Smith and Anderson 2004). However, the specific mechanisms of storytelling, as well as the assumptions that drive stories, deserve attention. This section will overview process theory in a general sense. This review will discuss eternal objects (Whitehead 1978) or abstractions (Plato 2012), and their role as proxies for values in organizations. This work will then discuss organizations from a process-orientated perspective, by using the actual entity (Whitehead 1978) as a proxy for organizations, specifically adhocracies (Autier 2001; Mintzberg 1981). This section will explain how entrepreneurs, to include public service entrepreneurs, can use story-based articulation to manipulate the flow of time, and more importantly, its respective potentiality.

Process theory is interesting both from a philosophical and entrepreneurial perspective because of its ability to bridge the objective and subjective aspects of reality. In order to clarify the relationship between process theory and entrepreneurship, a discussion of the objective aspects of nature is necessary. Eternal objects (Whitehead 1978) or forms (Plato 2012) are the basic rules of the universe. Forms define the purest of possibilities and epitomize ideas rooted in literature on potentiality (Heiddegger 1927; Hernes 2014). If reality were a game, then forms would represent the basic rules, the roles of the pieces and the area of play. Examples of forms are objects of moral, mathematical or logical thought (Griffin 2006). Everything we understand in reality is an attempt to mimic these perfect forms. However, like Tantalus, who could never drink the water beneath him nor reach the grapes within arm's reach, forms by nature are abstract – they are everywhere and yet are unreachable through human sensory perception (Plato 2012). The harder we try to appreciate the full nature of a form, the more objects we incorporate into our agency, and hence embrace more ambiguity. In this work, organizational norms, in particular the army values, serve as a metaphor for forms. Like forms, they are ideals that are unreachable, yet every soldier does his or her best to embody them. For example, as an eternal object, the army value of selfless service is preached to all soldiers. Yet no one can provide perfect definitions of any of these values, and can only provide examples of what they are and are not, much like Socrates was unable to provide a perfect definition of virtue from Meno, due to the duality of the general and particular (Plato 2013).

While the objective forms the background – the subjective and constructed occur in response to attempts to derive meaning from or prehend the abstract. The mechanism used to reach these abstractions, forms, or values is the actual entity (Whitehead 1978). Actual entities are collated when an actual subject coordinates the processes of any number of actual objects. Actual entities form the building blocks of reality as it makes ever increasing attempts to reach an eternal object, and the agency that an actual entity exercises is proportional to the number and size of actual subjects it controls. Another interesting point is that even as actual entities increase in size, they must incorporate ever greater numbers of actual objects, and hence embrace ever greater ambiguity, and divergent goals and agency.

Actual entities are used as a proxy for adhocracies (Autier 2001; Toffler 1970). Unlike the bureaucratic organizational view (Bennis 1966; Thompson 1969; Weber 1958), actual entities are not assumed to be static or spatial (Burgelman 1983b). Instead, they are ever in a state of perishing and being reborn. Actual entities only last in a given state for an infinitesimally small moment, after which they must be reborn to survive. This work operates under this assumption of organizations and consequently utilizes the vignettes to develop the concepts of adhocracies in greater detail, which like actual entities, are abstraction-bound and fleeting. To build on the discussion of selfless service mentioned above – specific examples of this value are derived from the formation and interactions of and within actual entities. In the struggle to define a form, such as any of the army values, an actual entity could be formed. The interactions within the actual entity such as discussions, disagreement, work, and the co-authoring of stories represent stages in the quest to understand the extra sensory, or that which man knew in a previous form (Plato 2013). After a discussion or series of actions, the actual entity dissipates, leaving its members with a clearer, albeit more complex understanding of an eternal object.

The link between these two worlds of the actual and the abstract are processes. The first process is ingression (Whitehead 1978). Ingression is of passive nature where abstractions impose themselves into reality. The simple presence of abstractions dictates their influence into the way the game of reality is played. The second process is concrescence (Whitehead 1978), where actual entities choose an abstraction, or series of abstractions to imitate, and as a result attracts other actual objects and entities into their influence. In contrast to ingression, concrescence is an active process and at some point a choice is made as to which abstraction to imitate. Furthermore, since concrescence is reliant on subscription of interpretation from elements of the nexus, it requires active engagement from the context.

In terms of entrepreneurship, the process of ingression and concrescence has two parallels: storytelling and narrative co-construction. When the entrepreneur perceives a form or abstraction via ingression, the entrepreneur serves as a vector for the virtualization of the abstract via a story. The entrepreneur's story is part of entrepreneurship because it is full of potentiality (Gartner 2007) and may focus on a lack of alignment with a present and future state, which may be embodied in an anomaly (Spinosa, Flores, and Dreyfus 1999). If a context believes a story, then they will buy into the story and exercise concrescence, and contribute to and change the story to create a co-constructed narrative. The co-constructed narrative is then reified into an actual entity, or adhocracy. While process philosophers discuss the general struggle to understand the abstract, stories, the follow-up co-constructed narratives, and adhocracies represent the specific process-based mechanisms used by entrepreneurs as they attempt to change their environment.

While bureaucratic organizations, especially the post office and the army, are seen as rigid, room for entrepreneurship nonetheless exists. In accordance with precepts from public service entrepreneurship, entrepreneurship in the government sectors can occur when regulations or procedures are interpreted, circumvented, supplemented or executed in novel ways (Gore 1994; Llewellyn and Jones 2003; Mandell and Steelman 2003). The type of entrepreneurship relative to bureaucracies occurs via actual entities. In the vignettes, adhocratic organizations are formed to respond to a situation that regulation, and hence past precedent, did not specifically address. Adhocracies, like actual entities, are temporary in nature (Autier 2001; Mintzberg 1981; Toffler 1970) and adhere to a certain or a series of abstractions, or use narratives to derive their legitimacy as actions in conformity with basic, underlying beliefs

(Suchman 1995) that are blended and supplemented to match a given situation (Follett 1919, 1940; O'Connor 2000).

As emerging organizations, adhocracies are built on stories that potentialize future or past states of existence (Boutaiba 2004; Foss 2004; Gartner, Bird, and Starr 1992) to reinterpret a given or series of eternal objects. Adhocracies, as organic organizations (Miller 1983) operate in heterogeneous environments, have diffused power through the nexus, experience ingression, or scan the environment for underlying values, and complexify reality through projects during concrescence. The entrepreneurship in this case resulted from a novel type of concrescence, or in other words, reinterpreting abstractions in a way that ran parallel to regulation, but may have represented a more faithful understanding of the spirit of the regulations and the values they embody. This story will emphasize concrescence as a two-part process: first a narrative is co-constructed with stakeholders, and second, an adhocracy is co-constructed. After the disappearance of the adhocracy, remnants of those narratives integrate themselves into larger bureaucratic dialogues.

Furthermore, stories, narratives, and their vehicle of adhocracies, configure space and time and employ cohesive devices to create relationality across scenes (Fletcher 2011) or a larger process called articulation (Deleuze and Guattari 2004; Hernes 2014; Pierce 1998). Articulation is not about creating or discovering, but about explaining processual and temporal convergence. Articulation implies interpreting the significance of any given set of forms and then explaining that interpretation to a given context or group of stakeholders, for example, through a story. The ability to explain an abstraction's alignment with the contextual is what differentiates an entrepreneur as merely a knower of forms or philosopher as in Plato (2012) or someone who understands the abstract through prayer (Aurelius 2008).

Instead of individual-centric articulation as mentioned within Plato or Aurelius, the entrepreneur or entrepreneurial organization tells a story. Stories are the seed of potentiality (Hjorth 2007) for organizations and can be used to facilitate greater possibilities for articulation. Through the use of a story, the processes of concrescence can be altered, which as the resulting practices are modified, the future can be changed and the past reinterpreted (Garud, Schildt, and Lant 2014; Hernes 2014; Spinosa, Flores, and Dreyfus 1999). Since practices, which mark the passage of time, are a result of interpretations of abstractions and relaying these abstractions to the nexus, then a good story can likewise provide novel interpretations of values, and alter the behaviour of the nexus and its future (Borup et al. 2006; Emirbayer and Mische 1998; Gartner 2007; Spinosa, Flores, and Dreyfus 1999), and alter the course of history. In this way, stories and narratives are processes that link the abstract and the real (Cornelissen and Clarke 2010; Trope and Liberman 2003). Through a skilful narrative, conflicting elements, such as organizational boundaries, can be shed (von Burg and Kenney 2000; Follett 1919, 1924, 1940; Lampel 2001) and purer forms of an abstraction may be better interpreted through an adhocracy.

This understanding of entrepreneurship represents an ontological split from the bureaucratic view of organizations. A bureaucracy has as competencies execution and stability. Yet bureaucracies are not entirely static but rather are slower moving organizations (Nayak and Chia 2011). The middle core of bureaucracies do not experience ingression; their respective eternal objects and values as well as their interpretations are already provided. The core of the bureaucracy experiences a single iteration of concrescence, and its behaviours are stuck in a continuous feedback loop within that actual entity. The bureaucracy has but one storyteller and an assumed fixed audience; hence two-way communication is limited. But these aspects of a bureaucracy are not negative; they do provide a degree of stability, and a sense of spatial certainty (Burgelman 1983a, 1983b) in a world so full of processes that it may be a boundless anarchy.

But in the fringes or lowest levels of an organization, there is a border that is shared with the chaotic outside world. Hence there are always new situations not accounted for in the systematic and bureaucratic world, resulting in 'cracks', 'spaces for play', and hence a zone where the processual-based outside world seeps in and allows for entrepreneurship. It is this zone where entrepreneurial storytelling has a 'place loose' (Foss 2004), temporally flexible and co-constructed character.

The next section of this paper will explain the methodology used – autoethnography. The narrative in this story has two meanings. Since stories are told, narratives are both a method and a meaning system (Smith and Anderson 2004). As a meaning system, the narrative is an umbrella term that groups different forms of articulation. In a broader theoretical sense, the narrative represents a grouping of both concrescence and ingression. On the ingression side, stories represent an elegant way to transmit values (Buckler and Zien 1996). Just as in concrescence, narratives continue to select underlying values and in the process create new ones). So the legitimacy of actions, such as adhocracy's formation derived from narratives, must support underlying beliefs in order to be considered legitimate (Suchman 1995).

Narratives also serve as a method, and in this paper it is autoethnography. The use of autoethnography is appropriate because a life lived is essentially a life told, or humans are inherent storytellers, and use narratives to make sense of life, and this is particularly true of entrepreneurs (Foss 2004; Lindh de Montoya 2004). A narrative approach to studying entrepreneurship is particularly appropriate to this theoretical orientation, since narratives can pull people into a created space, such as in an adhocracy, to harness the potentiality of the past and future (Boutaiba 2004). Following the discussion of autoethnography, this paper will proceed directly into the vignettes, which blend theory and empirics into a first-person narrative.

Methodology – autoethnography

The methodology chosen to illustrate entrepreneurship in large organizations is coherent with the empirical setting and process theory. The autoethnography will unfold in the upcoming vignettes; however, the following paragraphs will highlight the methodology used. Since I am examining my own experience in the United States Army as the basis for describing entrepreneurship in large bureaucratic organizations, I completed this work in a manner consistent with academic research methods while maintaining an evocative flavour, yet avoided composing a glorified autobiography. Therefore, I chose autoethnography, which is a self-narrative that critiques the relationships of self with others. Autoethnography is a method and a set of diverse interdisciplinary practices (Spry 2001). Ellis (1999) and Johannisson (2011) also indicate that autoethnography is not necessarily a rigid set of methods but rather is a methodological orientation.

Sparkes (2000) adds that autoethnography includes personalized accounts that benefit from the experience of the author or researcher for the purposes of extending theoretical understanding. Autoethnography seamlessly blends the researcher, context, the abstract and their respective interactions in such a way that may blur the lines between self and other

(Atkinson 2006; Ellis, Adams, and Bochner 2011; Rambo 2005; Spry 2001), and further stipulates that the individual is thoroughly implicated in the phenomenon he or she investigates (Atkinson 2006; Ellis, Adams, and Bochner 2011; Engstrom 2012). The process of retrospective inquiry enables the researcher to benefit from a deeper level of understanding (Ellis 1999; Ellis, Adams, and Bochner 2011; Rambo 2005).

This paper will utilize insights from analytical autoethnography to create a work that is personal, theoretically supported and benefits from my unique position (Anderson 2006). It is different from a traditional ethnography in that the researcher is a full participant in the research setting, in contrast to an outsider who observes a process. As a researcher I was an opportunistic complete member researcher, meaning that I acquired my knowledge through occupational and lifestyle participation, which is a theme reflected in entrepreneurial autoethnographic literature (Fletcher 2011; Steyaert 2011). I maintain analytic reflexivity, since as a first-line leader in the army, I was intimately aware of my connection with the environment and my impact upon it (Johannisson 2011; Johannisson, Ramirez-Pasillas, and Karlsson 2002), which required a significant amount of self-conscious introspection as part of my professional development. This approach is in contrast to that of a conventional researcher who may only observe the research environment in lieu of attempting to change it. I will validate that my participation provides transparency and allows others to draw their own conclusions as to the case's ability to provide a different perspective on the articulatory power of narrative entrepreneurship. There will be significant dialogues with external stakeholders. The goal is to illustrate porous institutional borders that facilitated the interactions among groups and individuals both internal and external to the post office who recognized mutually critical abstractions. This case will apply the findings of this study to broader theoretical understandings (Anderson 2006) and provide a practice-based example (Ellis, Adams, and Bochner 2011; Fletcher 2011) of adhocracies in action (Autier 2001).

The use of autoethnography may provide insights overlooked using more conventional research methods when examining entrepreneurship in large institutions. Sørensen (2007) invites a greater understanding of the specific avenues of prior bureaucratic behaviour suppressing new venture creation. Greenwood and Suddaby (2006) indicate that in corporate entrepreneurship, the embeddedness of an individual or organization is difficult to extrapolate through the use of data. Scholars in entrepreneurship (Engstrom 2012; Fletcher 2011; Hjorth 2007; Johannisson 2011; Steyaert 2011) also believe that the best way to understand entrepreneurship is to be actively engaged. Furthermore, this work explores entrepreneurial epiphany. In other words, my prior beliefs based on more mainstream theories of bureaucracy and entrepreneurship were challenged due to new circumstances, a phenomenon best studied through autoethnography (Doloriert and Sambrook 2012; Ellis, Adams, and Bochner 2011).

The structure of this autoethnography was inspired by Rambo (2005), and Doloriert and Sambrook (2012). In lieu of a more formal academic structure, I interwove theory with the story to form a more powerful sensemaking device. This structure is described as a 'layered account' which builds on Derrida's (1978) characterization of consciousness as a mystic writing pad. Simplified, consciousness may appear as a blank slate but what was previously on the pad partially remains. Thus, this layered account contains seven vignettes that blend theory with experience to capture this rich tradition and accommodates the belief that enactive research traditions such as autoethnography should incorporate the biography of the researcher (Engstrom 2012; Fletcher 2011; Hjorth 2007; Johannisson 2011).

A layered account autoethnography combines storytelling with *post hoc* theoretical analyses that acknowledges multiple selves within the individual (Humphreys 2005; Rambo 2005). In this story, I am blending feelings of myself as a first lieutenant with analysis of those experiences retrospectively as a researcher. While the line between these selves is not a clear-cut boundary, this composite storytelling technique is more holistic than would be either my present or previous self in abstraction.

The structure of the autoethnography furthermore marks a change in the way that scholars write about entrepreneurship. Many entrepreneurships fail to survive in the long term, and the success stories are certainly outliers (Martin de Holan 2014). While many methods are not suited to study outliers, these outliers nonetheless have a story to tell, which may be used as a significant sensemaking device, since perhaps stories are a natural vehicle for relating events (Buckler and Zien 1996); but at the minimum, narratives communicate and explore ambiguity (Foss 2004) and represent a means for understanding the practice of entrepreneurship (Rae and Carswell 2000). This autoethnography envisions the role of the entrepreneur as a master storyteller, and upon acceptance of this shift in role, then perhaps a storytelling approach to understanding how stories are told is appropriate. The entrepreneur uses a story to convince an audience, or uses rhetoric to bring the abstract into the real (Hernes 2014; Lyotard 1979; Smith and Anderson 2004), whereas I will use a story to integrate the real into the abstract. In both cases, we explain alignment, but the bridge is constructed along different slopes. So this autoethnography marks a departure from conventional techniques of describing entrepreneurship and reveals a novel way to explore the role of the entrepreneur.

One of the precepts of the layered account is that every event exists in a continuum, and in accordance with autoethnography, this infers that every story has a prequel and a sequel and understanding what transpires before and after an event is key to understanding why sequences take place in a specific way (Fletcher 2011; Hjorth 2007; Johannisson 2011; Rambo 2005). To merely describe what occurred during a period of study is insufficient and assumes an evacuation of time (Langley and Tsoukas 2010). Consequently, Part I depicts the events that occurred before moving to the post office and presents a contrast of my norms of behaviour requiring alteration in order to understand the relevance of finding joint interests. Parts II through V transition to the early days of my tenure at the post office that transformed my perspectives on entrepreneurial behaviour and organizational creation.

Postal evocative narrative part I: before the post office

I received my commission as an Adjutant General officer in June 2006, and like many newly minted officers, I felt I knew everything for a successful career in the army. During my Adjutant General Officer Basic Course, we were constantly reminded that as lieutenants, we should inherently understand everything from tactics to doctrine better than subordinates – namely, we enjoyed a high degree of metacognition (Hayward, Shepherd, and Griffin 2006). When confronted with the unknown, we were trained to search manuals, which embodied the best of past practices, and we always relied on regulation as a black and white guide to illustrate that we, as adjutants (which is a blend of administrator and human resource officer), could trump most authorities through our exclusive understanding of doctrine.

This implied that regulations and the past practices they represented were sacred objects (Durkheim 1915; Eliade 1958). This domination of regulation suppresses opportunity recognition and achievement (Burgelman 1983a), which inhibited our ability to develop new theories and retarded productive dialogue with peers within our units and administrative fields (Sørensen 2007).

I was no exception to the stereotype of the overconfident Lieutenant. In April 2007, I rotated to my first unit on Osan Air Force base in the Republic of Korea, with an overwhelming self-confidence that bordered on arrogance, combined with a lack of any real experience, a characteristic of lieutenants that is simultaneously irritating and comical, analogous to poorly performing actors' inability to identify the absurdity of their demeanour (Hayward, Shepherd, and Griffin 2006). I assumed a position as an assistant brigade adjutant devoted to training the battalion staff sections, in particular their adjutants, in the management of an administrative section. A common theme in this first unit was that only one way of thinking was acceptable, reinforcing the stereotype that bureaucracies suppress entrepreneurship and new organizational creation.

What I, and so many of my peers failed to realize at the time, was that regulations are designed to service the values upon which they are built, and are supposed to represent the best of past precedent (Burgelman 1983a), not reflect bureaucratic power or convenience (Emerson 2004). The basic army values – Loyalty, Duty, Respect, Selfless Service, Honor, Integrity and Personal Courage – are the abstract principles upon which our army is built. These principles are a starting point; however, they are generally insufficient for the daily functions of an organization. Regulations guide us in our history and our future (Burgelman 1983a) and are the path to success. My understanding of regulation when I had the mentality of a bureaucrat however, focused on the regulation, word for word, and not necessarily the values that should have been embodied in those regulations. I mentally lacked the flexibility to cope with situations outside the prevue of a regulation, or ones that were novel to me. Essentially, I exercised control over the interpretation of forms and enforced an inflexible version of concrescence. I was a storyteller, and my captive audience would listen and obey. This mentality was soon challenged as I transitioned to my next unit.

Part II: moving to the post office and out of a central organization

In April 2008, I was assigned to be a platoon leader at the military post office in Camp Humphreys, Republic of Korea (Korea). In this new position, I managed the equivalent of three United States Postal Service (USPS) mail distribution centres. Every morning mail was delivered from Incheon Airport by truck to each distribution centre. In the mail distribution centre, mail was processed and provided to more than 30 unit mailrooms, all of which were responsible for delivering mail to the service members in their unit. The customer base was diverse, including military units, civil service organizations and government contracting firms. A secondary mission was customer-focused, and involved accepting packages, processing money orders and selling postage/philatelic items.

An additional duty, and one that will serve as the subject of the autoethnography, was to ensure the proper handling of mail in all unit mailrooms located within my area of Korea. This was accomplished by conducting quarterly postal inspections and providing a pass/fail rating to any mailroom in my area of operations according to the standards set forth by the Deputy G-1 (Eighth Army-level personnel/administration officer) for postal affairs. The inspection checklist was exhaustive since its author was the Deputy G-1 for Postal Affairs, and passing a mailroom inspection was difficult. In the first quarter, more than half of all mailrooms failed their initial inspection. Upon failure, under the guidance of the Deputy G-1 for Postal Affairs, I provided the results of the failed mailroom inspection to the first Lieutenant Colonel in that unit's chain of command. Repeated failures eventually resulted in a formal notification to the first General Officer in the unit's chain of command and potential closure of the mailroom.

The command structure was another anomaly of the Military Postal Service. Unlike most units of the military, which are based on a matrix style organization, the postal platoons maintained a diffuse power structure. The majority of the employees were uniformed service members (approximately 20 per platoon), and each platoon had a Custodian of Postal Effects (COPE) who was a civilian employee working directly for the platoon leader, with allegiance to the Deputy G-1 for Postal Affairs – a civil servant with a military title. Additionally, the COPE informally managed all other Korean and American civil servants in each post office. Each platoon was on a different base in Korea, but the formal military chain of command was headquartered at Youngsan Garrison in Seoul, which was two hours by train from my main post office. An additive layer of command included the garrison, an equivalent to a military municipal authority. All equipment except computers, firearms and specialized postal equipment belonged to the garrison, including the post office building, vehicles, electricity and water services, and furniture.

With this overlapping and amorphous command structure, the post office bridged several organizations (Greenwood and Suddaby 2006). Although the postal platoon's facilities belonged to the garrison, its standards were derived from the USPS, and owed formal loyalty to its military chain of command. This duality (Janssens and Steyaert 1999) was intertwined with the army values and overlaid with the nuances of civilian employees. The following organizational descriptions illustrate several points. First, it is possible for organizations to exist without clear demarcation of beginning and ending, illustrating that a purely open and proactive organization versus a closed and non-entrepreneurial bureaucracy is merely an abstraction. Furthermore, change can be effectuated by internal and external stakeholders because authority is derived from standards of multiple organizations, which required my adherence to several groups' organizational values (Greenwood and Suddaby 2006).

This ability to cause change outside any single domain also implies that entrepreneurial impetus lies in a system dictated by universal norms modified to meet the demands of a situation and context, not in any particular manager interpreting an omnipotent regulation (Follett 1924). In other words, through using common and abstract values, an entrepreneurial manager may serve as a bridge between his organization, the abstract and the context, or craft a value-laden story to articulate alignment and highlight an avenue for collaboration. This lack of emphasis on formal authority is especially evident given my low rank as a platoon leader and the lack of support my chain of command provided when dealing with garrison or postal authorities. Additionally, the system of interactions between different isolated organizations is rarely precedented, ergo undescribed by regulation and outside the prosaics of the bureaucracy. The lack of previous practice means that each new interaction is full of potentiality, is at a temporally novel stage and solutions can be left to the imagination and storytelling ability of a public service entrepreneur to manage norms and relationships in new and creative ways (Gore 1994; Hales 2002; Mandell and Steelman 2003). These stories within the post office were co-constructed with my interorganizational co-constituents. We all had different antecedents, and my role was more of an integrative facilitator (Follett 1919) in a jointly constructed, co-authored story.

Part III: initial mail room inspection failures

My confidence from previous unit experiences and my complacency with the simplicity of the postal mission were challenged after my first 60 days as I began inspecting unit mailrooms under my purview. As in my prior mission, I understood the regulations and this appeared to be a straightforward obligation. Following the advice of one of my sergeants, I inspected mailrooms that historically had outstanding records during the quarterly inspections, which confirmed my belief that the task was clear-cut, the sanctity of regulations would always be respected, and only one correct way to manage a mailroom existed. These simple inspections solidified my belief that the post office was a central organization, and partner organizations were on the periphery, rendering me completely unaware that other perceptions of the importance of mail were possible (Greenwood and Suddaby 2006).

I inspected multiple mailrooms in the first quarter that quickly proved that although regulations were objective, the importance any individual would place on regulations related to outside tasks and timelines could prove to be problematic, contradicting the monolithic precepts of the traditional bureaucracy, and certainly dethroning me as the king or writer of the story. Three failures in particular illustrate this point. The first involved an abysmal mailroom attached to a logistics unit and its accompanying motor pool. The mailroom clerk had misplaced multiple pieces of registered mail, which could have resulted in a federal prison sentence if the recipients of the packages had chosen to press charges; classified mail was open and strewn on the floor; one of the clerks had been arrested that month for attempting to use the military post office to smuggle contraband; and, most disappointingly, the mailroom clerk was not distributing mail to his customers, instead leaving it in bags partially emptied on the mailroom floor.

The second mailroom that proved equally disappointing was attached to our base hospital. In this mailroom, accountable mail was left unsecured, which could have facilitated theft and was in violation of regulation; the mailroom did not have administrative paperwork updated; and, the clerk came to the mail distribution centre infrequently.

The final delinquent mailroom belonged to a quartermaster unit that managed a series of supply warehouses. The most serious violation was the clerk's not distributing mail to customers; instead, mailbags were hidden in the ceiling tiles. Her predecessor was equally irresponsible – I located mail with postmarks from a prior decade. Furthermore, if customers did not pick up their catalogues, the clerk would place this mail in a bin labelled 'free mail' outside the mailroom, encouraging anyone to take mail addressed to others.

Part IV: a bureaucrat with no regulation upon which to stand

My approach to these problems was initially identical to violations of regulation in my previous job. I understood the regulation more thoroughly than others, and I was empowered to provide a failure rating to any mailroom that did not respect my interpretation of the standard. It was my story or no story, reinforcing my thinking as described while serving as a conventional bureaucrat. Unfortunately, I encountered two major obstacles in my plan. First of all, many mailrooms, including the three examples cited above, were staffed by individuals who did not care if mail was handled properly. Secondly, I did not have the support of my chain of command.

The first hurdle was highlighted in the three commanders' responses to failing mailroom inspections. The commander from the logistics unit initially threatened me; then blamed his battalion's adjutant for the deficiencies, he then explained 'I am a seeker of new experiences, I enjoy exploring ideas and systems, and I am a lifelong student; but I certainly don't give a half of a (deleted explicative) about mail'. In accordance with guidance from the Deputy G-1 for postal affairs I informed his battalion commander of the failure which elicited an epic spot in my inbox:

> Do not email my superiors ever again. If you want to email your smarmy, 'federally mandated' comments to your chain of command, Lieutenant, that's fine, but you will not email them to mine. I will personally rip your (deleted explicative) head off if this happens again.

He then instructed his soldiers to remove parts from the postal platoon's vehicles in the middle of the night from our shared motor pool. The commander of the hospital stated that mail was not his priority, and he would not make any changes to his operations, stating, almost jokingly in the spirit of Star Trek 'Lieutenant, I'm a doctor, not a mailman!'. The quartermaster commander replaced the mail clerk and postal officer, but did not send the new clerk or the postal officer to my training classes. I began to realize that to these organizations, mail was the periphery, and they were the central organization, and these units did not consider the delivery of mail as an important part of their professional standards or mission. This divergent understanding illustrated a number of inconsistencies vis à vis the bureaucratic organizational view. Not all units acknowledged the same vertical source, but horizontal communication did occur, albeit it was significantly retarded. I felt like a bad comedian in an audience full of hecklers.

What is interesting about our conflicts is that each unit, despite membership in larger macro-level organizations, existed within its own bubble. Each bubble, or actual entity, had its own timeline, preferred set of regulations, and given interpretations of the army values it chose to honour. These bubbles highlighted the cracks in micro- and macro-level bureaucracies, which were the source of our differences. There was a conflict between our actual entities because we had our own stories. Under the mindset of a rigid bureaucrat, these obstacles of conflicting timelines, regulations and values were impossible to overcome, which lead to my dilemma.

In addition to these spectacular failures, there were fifteen mailrooms that failed inspections; however, none had the same number of deep-rooted problems, glaring deficiencies, or the accompanying hostility as the three aforementioned cases. I felt these mailrooms did not have any major violations of federal law; and therefore, I decided to focus on my haemorrhages before my smaller leaks.

I was visibly upset when confronted with a situation outside the scope of my training and experience, and I realized that deficient mailrooms could result in my failure when the Deputy G-1 visited my distribution centre. I found myself unable to coerce others, yet if I could not effectuate change in targeted units I would suffer the consequences. With a sense of desperation and urgency, I solicited the help of my commander. She explained that our unit and those I inspected did not share common chains of command; therefore, coercion through the use of rank was impossible. Her response to the logistics unit commander's behaviour was that 'Professionally, he is a jerk, and personally he is (insert you favourite explicative here), he has threatened both me and your predecessor before'. She then told me to 'keep failing the hospital commander and eventually change will occur'. Finally, her suggestion regarding the third commander was to train that clerk when she was working in the mailroom and correct the violations myself if the clerk was unable to do so. Nonetheless, she reminded me that

> If the Deputy G-1 inspected these mailrooms during one of his visits to your area, and if they are not up to standard, and if you embarrass this company irrespective of the reason, including unacceptable performance of mail rooms, I will make you suffer before I take away your platoon.

This was a classic case of corporate management not understanding the specific challenges facing middle managers (Burgelman 1983a).

I was devastated – suddenly the confidence, tools and authority I previously enjoyed vanished into thin air. For the first time in my short career, I did not have all the answers. Federal law remained important, and my job was still in jeopardy if I did not enforce the precepts of regulation. Yet these same regulations did not appear to have any meaning to those I inspected. My chain of command was unable to assist me and offered advice that was not beneficial. My regulatory structures were embedded in a distant geographical location and, therefore, unable to understand the complexity of my dilemma (Greenwood and Suddaby 2006). I was accountable to regulations, so my capacity to compromise on certain principles was limited. It seemed that I was stuck, with no clear route of escape. I was bound to adhere to a certain bureaucratic story, but others did not entirely share my position.

In many ways, I found myself in an organization frequently stereotyped as the world's most bureaucratic – the USPS. At the same time, it appeared that bureaucratic artifacts, such as regulations and their respective past precedents had no real meaning for peer organizations. I had been spoiled before, having worked in a planning firm (Miller 1983) with a plethora of slack resources, a stable environment and operational orientation that placed a high value on the power of the technocrat. Now I realized I was adrift, and it seemed that I was little more than a slave to my environment, and outside the administrative systems I understood based on my previous learning (Burgelman 1983a). I was a bureaucrat in a bureaucracy that was not bureaucratic, which was the epitome of an individual juxtaposed among base suppositions. I had been trained so long to rely on precedents shown in regulation, and I was crippled when I could no longer lean on the support of the past and its practices. I needed in some way to carve out a future with no past from which to jump.

Part V: deep thought, a visit to the past and a reexamination of the present and future

With a sense of impending doom, facing a chain of command who was unwilling to help, knowing my career and reputation were on the line, and dealing with stakeholders who were indifferent in the best case, I could only think of one thing to do at the end of my week – I went home, opened up a bottle of bourbon, and in the words of the Statler brothers (Dewitt 1965), I counted flowers on the wall, played solitaire 'till dawn with a deck of 51, and watched episodes of Captain Kangaroo (but I didn't smoke any cigarettes). For one, I needed a laugh and wanted to blow off some steam. In all seriousness, I thought, I thought and I thought, perhaps aided by the bourbon, or driven by a sense of purpose, it is hard to say. I asked myself what the army had come to that a regulation did not have value, and how far had we strayed.

I thought for a moment about my time in college as a cadet, and I remembered a frigid winter training exercise at Fort Indiantown Gap, Pennsylvania. That particular weekend had been cold, sleeting, and muddy. All of the cadets were freezing, tired and hungry. Any one of us would have killed for a cup of hot soup, or even five minutes inside a warm tent. Instead, we stood in formation, in the sleet, when a warm barracks stood directly behind us. Our professor of military science, or the lieutenant colonel in charge of cadets, came to inspect the formation. One cadet had lost a glove during the exercise and therefore was only wearing one glove. That lieutenant colonel proceeded to belittle and humiliate that cadet, but not before making all of us in the platoon remove our gloves. His standard operating procedure, or his way of meeting regulatory standards or the army values, was that everyone had to be uniform, irrespective of the cold. We then shivered in the wind and frozen rain for another two hours while our lieutenant colonel 'inspected' us. My knuckles were turning blue, and the morale of all of the cadets was crushed. I remember thinking at that time, that I would never be such a stickler for standard operating procedures if it meant abusing others.

I woke up from my stupor, and realized that maybe I was the problem. I had standards that reflected regulation, and I aimed to act like the petty bureaucrat to impose these standards. Perhaps I, unaware, was making others shiver in the cold without gloves, when it was all really unnecessary. Regulations are specific interpretations of values, and unlike values, they are not an anti-teleological alpha and omega, but the endpoint is relatively clear. However, the path needed to reach those endpoints is very rarely specified, which provides spaces for play, where alternate possibilities may be discussed (Hjorth 2004). In the case of the freezing cadets, it is true that everyone in a unit needs to be in the same uniform, but we could have gone inside the warm barracks for our inspection, that gloveless cadet could have been given a spare pair of gloves, or the inspection could have been conducted at a later time. Any of these solutions would have better reflected the army values and regulation than what actually happened. The gloveless cadet story is empirically different than mail room inspections; yet no process is truly novel (Bickham 2009; Deleuze 1994; Whitehead 1978) even if it is without direct precedent. Powerful narrative analogies can be drawn from dissimilar situations that are consequently used to drive a very unique future path (Bartel and Garud 2003; Cornelissen and Clarke 2010).

Perhaps ultimately, I was the source of noncompliance. Perhaps I was the problem. Perhaps a 'gut check' was required and I needed to ask myself if my enforcement of a certain way of doing things was really in line with the army values. What if, in the spirit of Follett (1919, 1924, 1940) I practiced 'integration'; namely, what if I attempted to understand why mail rooms were unable or unwilling to comply with regulation, and we would jointly discover alternative strategies to attack these problems, and in the process meet the ends specified in regulation and appreciate our joint interpretations of the army values. In the case of the post office, this way of dealing with non-compliant mail rooms was without precedent, and so somehow I would have to step out of normal behaviour and think about how to compose a future that was both convincing and valuable for myself and my stakeholders.

I couldn't help but wonder if I could find a common ground to unite others with a very divergent set of interests. As my glass became empty I wondered if I too could compose a convincing narrative based on values as a way to 'make others move' (Hjorth and Gartner 2014) or express entrepreneurship within a public organization by perhaps putting regulations aside and focusing on a shared set of abstractions, such as army values, and explaining or articulating an alignment of interests, which would then feed back into solutions that matched the regulation. Since the out-of-left-field gloveless cadet story was so powerful to my individual-level sensemaking, could I not compose a similar story to be used for sensegiving between organizations in a vein akin to Gioia and Chittipedi (1991)? Ironically, it was a few glasses of bourbon that represented the spark to light the fire, that helped me begin to understand how to bridge the abstract and the actual, not prayer (Aurelius 2008) or philosophy (Plato 2012).

Part VI: an anecdotally successful co-constructed narrative

The next morning, I decided that I would not begin by revamping the mailroom from the logistics company or the hospital, but I would concentrate on training the new postal clerk and postal officer in the quartermaster unit. I determined that I could work with a blank slate easier than with a stick in the mud. I also realized that I needed to become a tabula rasa and derive new methods to accomplish my mission and remain faithful to regulation and federal law. I, therefore, took the first entrepreneurial step by deciding to abandon previous practices (Stopford and Baden-Fuller 1994), and empty to the best of my ability, my previous bureaucratic stance. I began by calling the postal officer of that mailroom, who was also a lieutenant, to meet for lunch. I suggested a restaurant off post that was known for excellent Korean barbecue. Much to my surprise he answered 'No way, I don't eat Korean food, it isn't clean – how about Subway in the food court?'. While I am not personally a fan of Subway, I decided that I would need to make a few compromises, and this would be a good start. This interaction was the starting point for my transformation from bureaucrat to public service entrepreneur. During this exchange, we had a sincere and open dialogue about our personal and professional priorities; and, despite our differences, we were remarkably similar. While the most memorable discovery during this meal was that this lieutenant could somehow force two-foot-long sandwiches down his throat without chewing them in a fashion similar to the Coneheads, a more important discovery with regards to this paper was that in many ways we were like the bees in Plato's bee metaphor; namely, that we were different but similar in ways that mattered most (Plato 2013). It was on these similarities that I decided to focus in order to achieve an integration of common interests.

His major concern with his mailroom was that neither he nor his postal clerk had adequate time to perform their postal duties because it was a part-time extra assignment. As he explained

> Look bro, I know mail is important, I know there are federal consequences associated with this duty, but I am also running a platoon, serving as the company voting assistance officer, public affairs liaison, range officer in charge, and distinguished visitor coordinator. I have so many things on my plate and at some point, something has got to give.

He had a genuine interest in doing a good job but did not have the time to do so. Like me, he feared punishment for failing a myriad of duties, and the unit mailroom was just one among his many jobs. I, too, had an interest in ensuring his success; likewise, I could not devote an inordinate amount of time to just one mailroom. It was at this point I realized that the idea of a peripheral or central organization (Greenwood and Suddaby 2006) was merely a construction, or a function of the identity of any story's narrator, and that I had a tremendous opportunity before me. I knew my organization was not fully embedded in the military or civil service, and my position as a bridge between multiple organizations when I conducted mailroom inspections exposed me to alternate conventions, and could allow me to benefit from, instead of conflict with, the different strengths of the units I inspected (Greenwood and Suddaby 2006), highlighting the duality (Janssens and Steyaert 1999) between the network of abstractions (Plato 2013) or eternal objects (Whitehead 1978) and the diversity of praxis.

The strengths of the organizations to which I was exposed, both internal and external, combined with the lack of any directly analogous precedents, meant that together we could compose a new future revolving around the army values and how they equally applied to the post office and unit mail rooms. Previously all of our units had operated within their own bubbles, so neatly inscribed on spatial organization charts (Burgelman 1983b), and each with a centrally imposed, yet slightly disparate narrative. Yet neither regulation nor the army values mandated organizational structure. My plan was to compose temporally based organizations, specifically focused on creating productive future pathways.

I, therefore, used my bridge analogy to appreciate multiple abstractions and this experience forced me to realize that I would have to shift from a planning firm to an organic firm mentality, meaning that I would need to create an adhocratic organization, or one that thrived in a heterogeneous environment with new and complex innovative managing mechanisms to effectuate change (Miller 1983). Because I had no resources other than my technocratic knowledge, I knew I would need to build social ties to effectuate entrepreneurial coordination (Hayward, Shepherd, and Griffin 2006). The total disconnect between my chain of command and the environment further facilitated entrepreneurship, because it required me to scan and understand my surroundings, plan for additional flexibility, reduce my dependence on centralized power and derive the rewards of creative processes (Barringer and Bluedorn 1999). Furthermore, the disconnect liberated me from the few irrelevant and binding precedents of my military chain of command.

The result of this shift in thinking was that our (as in my and the unit postal officer's) fundamental, general and objective interests were the same, but the execution of specificities was divergent. However, divergent interests are not necessarily conflicting (Follett 1919, 1924, 1940) and we agreed to derive a solution that would provide mutual maximum benefit. Instead of specifics of each unit's standard operating procedures, we began to appreciate our common and abstract interests derived from army values, which are a metaphor for eternal objects, representing a shift from a spatial bureaucratic to a temporal entrepreneurial mindset.

Regulations may represent an immediate form of past precedent (Burgelman 1983a; Emerson 2004), such as in my previous bureaucratic job where there was so much past precedent that tasks were routine. These precedents are the stories that guide organizational daily functions. In fact, from a temporal and processual lens, it could be argued that time passes very slowly in bureaucracies because processes repeat themselves with little variation, especially when variations are used to mark the passage of time. In order to create a new future and embrace its potentiality, my stakeholders and I would have to leave the somewhat slower moving processes of spatially bound bureaucracies (Burgelman 1983a) and move into the world of temporally focused adhocracies. By forming repeated albeit different organizational interactions that continually reinterpreted shared abstractions based on the demands of the situation, my stakeholders and I were able to speed up the passage of kairological or process-based time (Orlikowski and Yates 2002; Tsoukas and Hatch 2001), and charge into a future of our own design so we could achieve a mutually beneficial temporal position that reflected shared abstractions and better articulated our interests.

The postal officer, the clerk from the mailroom, and I jointly took the first step in articulating our shared goals. Because his commander would not permit him to visit the post office for postal training, I decided to follow my commander's advice to conduct the training in their mailroom. I moved the post office from a centralized, controlling and bureaucratic organization, to a customer oriented, co-constructed viewpoint by physically moving the adhocracy to the customer's place of work. I began the writing of our new story with a series of questions. First I asked 'Given the current way this unit mail room functions, does it support the army values? Does the current mail room service support the morale of the soldiers?' We both answered no for two different reasons. On my part simply failing a mail room did support regulation, but did nothing for anyone except explain their deficiencies and did not support the army values or promote customer service. From his point of view, perhaps working more efficiently with a given set of resources could increase the quality of unit mail room operations. However, we both agreed that our procedures needed to change.

I then asked 'What is the maximum amount of resources that you can provide on a daily basis to support the mail room?' He then provided me with a spreadsheet showing the manpower and time he had available to dedicate to the mail room. I then asked 'Would you like to achieve passing ratings on your inspections consistently?' and 'Are you willing to provide resources if I provide a similar commitment to help us reach passing inspections together?' He responded in the affirmative to both questions, hence confirming the desirability of future potentiality. These questions and the discussion that followed formed the basis of our narrative and paved the way for the real work of the adhocracy to begin. The second step was to use this narrative as an anchor for the manpower we contributed to the adhocracy. The post office contributed manpower and technical expertise in the form of three postal staff. My colleague contributed his own manpower and expertise via himself, his alternate postal officer, and his two mail clerks. For the next two days, we devoted our efforts to fixing all of the deficient administrative paperwork in the unit mail room. This task with their resources alone would have taken weeks, but with our added manpower and expertise, and their singular focus on the mission, it was accomplished in 48 h. The end state on how a form should look was relatively black and white, but in the spirit of cooperation, combined with a healthy dose of humour, we jointly derived novel solutions based on our unique competencies, which is the epitome of integration (Follett 1919, 1924, 1940).

The remaining tasks required a little more co-construction. That unit's soldiers would not come to the post office to pick up their mail, which was why their clerk was hiding mail in the ceiling tiles, which was not only illegal, but was not good for unit morale, as especially my fellow lientenant explained 'The rumor mill is full of stories about mail, booze, and dead bodies in the ceiling'. Of course neither he nor I had the authority to force anyone to come to the mail room given our low rank, but he suggested 'Can I distribute mail at close of business formation?' To which I answered in the affirmative, and was thrilled that he had suggested something I would have never considered, illustrating a co-constructed aspect of the narrative. His idea then eliminated a vast majority of the unit's remaining problems. By delivering the majority of mail to colleagues at formation, mail no longer accumulated in the unit mailroom, and the clerk did not have to spend as much time in the mailroom with regards to customer service, and could instead focus unit mailroom administration. In fact, the clerk's work day went from overwhelming, to having plenty of time to spare. Once the basics were in place, at the end of the adhocracy her duties focused on maintenance instead of improvement. After the adhocracy, a few of us went out for drinks that night. My friend, the lieutenant from the quarter master unit, remarked 'We got months' worth of work done in just a couple of days – I still can't believe it!'. In retrospect, I realize this was because of the fact that chronologically the adhocracy lasted only a couple of days, but kairologically, it launched this unit mail room far into the future to better appreciate our shared goals.

In lieu of my previous mentality of pointing out flaws and the regulation that explained deficiencies, the narrative and adhocracy focused on illustrating what the end state should be, and how to achieve this opportunity. To avoid conflicts, we created temporary or joint organizational interactions that ebbed and flowed, in parallel, yet in step with our dynamic environment (O'Connor 2002). We jointly composed a story around how to reach a mutually beneficial end state, which emphasizes an entrepreneurial and theme-based approach (Stopford and Baden-Fuller 1994). This joint discovery process was something that was unexplained in a regulation; instead, it was the result of exploring broad principles and using a shared narrative to apply them to specific situations (Garud, Schildt, and Lant 2014; Mandell and Steelman 2003). Through our shared collaboration we had an almost perfect inspection for the quartermaster mailroom in the next quarter, and an important lesson was learned. These adhocracies reflected, and were tailored to interpretations of our needs, the demands of regulation, and the relational affordances and constraints of the environment. While working within the context of these temporary organizations or adhocracies, we operated in an isolated bubble that used a shared narrative to jointly craft its own interpretations of values, contexts and used accelerated kairological timelines. What occurred in the adhocracy was separate from, but not in conflict with the outside environment, and yet crafted solutions tailored to meet external criteria. It was in this spirit that I conducted mailroom inspections for the next three quarters.

Part VII: postal inspection 2.0: a new start

The first quarter of mailroom inspections challenged my previous mindset. I realized that as a first lieutenant, I maintained no formal authority over other lieutenants and captains I was training as postal officers. Second, despite the fact that non-commissioned officers and junior soldiers I trained as postal clerks were technically obligated to follow my orders, their commanders could easily override any order from postal personnel. In essence, I had no military authority to obligate any service member on the installation to submit to my training or follow my edicts. Even failing a unit multiple times in a quarter was difficult, because I was required to provide a 14-day pause between inspections. In theory, severe violations of federal law could potentially result in criminal liability, as in the case of lost registered mail, but these mishaps could be concealed by unit commanders.

The question remains, how was I able to direct others without any formal authority, and impact the actions of others in seemingly separate systems outside my purview? The answer was through an appeal to a shared and co-constructed narrative, which involved articulating to commanders a common opportunity – promoting the morale of soldiers through the use of mail service, which supports the abstractions of army values, as well as federal and postal regulations. In lieu of coercion or compromise, the bureaucracy-independent story was the tool we used to craft a small bubble with abstractions to which we were all equally subordinate, and within this adhocracy we learned not only how to adhere to the postal guidelines and promote unit morale, but also to reach our shared abstractions more efficiently so that their designated mailroom clerks and postal officers could use the time gained for other endeavours. We explored abstractions, and in the process of adhocratic organization creation we increased our agency to reach a future state.

Fortunately, I was able to duplicate the model of the quartermaster unit mailroom across the garrison. However, I did have some help from an unexpected source. Three of the companies in the garrison – the logistics unit, the quarter master unit and their headquarters company (which also had historically failed inspections) belonged to the same battalion. The company commander of the quartermaster unit, or the supervisor of the lieutenant with whom I worked to create the first adhocracy, could not help but gloat about his perfect unit mail room inspection at a weekly training meeting to his peers across the peninsula. He used this newfound expertise to ingratiate himself to his supervisor, while also using it as an opportunity to embarrass the commander of the logistics unit, who was just as nasty to him as he was to me. The quartermaster company commander then sent his lieutenant to these sister companies in their battalion to help them pass their next mail room inspections. Even now, I can't help but chuckle at the thought of a lieutenant from one company providing a session of professional development to a company commander, especially one with such a large ego as the logistics company commander. Due to my friend from the quartermaster unit's efforts, the other unit mail rooms representing that battalion began making improvements to their operations before I began working with them on an adhocratic level. Granted, they did not have perfect inspection records as did the quarter master unit, but their efforts certainly reduced the amount of work that needed to be done during the adhocracy and facilitated the building of a co-constructed narrative.

A similar phenomenon occurred in the hospital. When the commanding general of the medical command found out about the hospital's deficiencies, he added his personal touch to the narrative and rendered mail service a basic standard for units under his command. When I inspected a sister unit of the hospital, I was surprised to discover that they transitioned from marginally passing the previous quarter to having built an entirely new mail room and an almost perfect inspection. After reviewing the inspection items on the checklist, I congratulated the lieutenant from that mail room. With a chuckle he told me 'Ya, the commanding general saw your inspection failures for the hospital and several junior soldiers complained to him via the open door policy. Uhh, ya it made a ripple throughout the medical command to put it gently'. Similar strengthened inspection successes occurred with a military police company, which had two mail rooms serving two different platoons – a platoon with a very strong mail room assisted a platoon with a significantly weaker mail room.

The examples illustrate the effect of narratives on a larger bureaucracy. Adhocracies are indeed temporary in nature, but the narratives they construct are not. An echo of the narrative remains (Boutaiba 2004), even after the dissipation of the adhocracy. One reason for the echo remaining is because there was a large degree of 'buy in' or co-construction of the narratives. Because stakeholders were able to participate in the construction of the narrative, they assumed partial ownership. This means implies that when the unit mail rooms were not being inspected, they continued to adhere to the narrative we created, and with rare exception, once the new integrated processes were created that incorporated the best of postal regulations combined with individual needs, very few updates were required, and the need to reform an adhocracy was negligible because even though the adhocracies had dissipated, the narrative's echo remained and became integrated into the larger context (Garud, Schildt, and Lant 2014; O'Connor 2002; Tripsas and Gavetti 2000). Using these methods, the number of mailrooms that failed their inspections dropped from more than fifteen in a quarter to all mailrooms except two passing on the fourth quarter's inspection. According to Spinosa, Flores, and Dreyfus (1999), this change in practices embodies entrepreneurship as a form of history making. The co-constructed narratives became integrated into the larger bureaucratic narrative and changed the way stakeholders viewed the mail, and hence altered the process of handling the mail.

Discussion

My experiences in the post office provided an insightful example of a significant reward of the narrative and integrated approach to managing mailrooms. With minimal formal authority, I was able to use a storytelling approach to communicate and realize the achievement of joint interests. As a result, the majority of mailrooms passed their inspections in the fourth quarter. The close interactions fostered through the process of identifying joint opportunities via shared narratives created temporary organizations, a form of corporate entrepreneurship in accordance with Greenwood and Suddaby (2006), but also of organizational entrepreneurship (Hjorth 2003, 2004, 2007, 2014; Massumi 2002), and public service entrepreneurship (Gore 1994; Llewellyn and Jones 2003; Teske and Schneider 1994). These adhocracies (Mintzberg 1981) shared a remarkable degree of similarity with actual entities as described by Whitehead (1978). Adhocracies, like actual entities, contributed to the experiences of the self, other and whole. As an example, the unit mailroom and the post office benefitted themselves, one another and the army.

My goal as a public service entrepreneur was to serve as a link between the abstractions we shared and our respective organizations, in essence behave as an actual subject that was consequently able to articulate shared interests. The specific mechanism I used to achieve this end was entrepreneurial storytelling, and I began to view my colleagues as co-authors of a novel. Like a good storyteller I began by understanding my audience (Follett 1919, 1924, 1940; Warren 2004) – I had to understand what activated their interest (Barnard 1938). I also needed to comprehend the basic rules of the army game – the abstractions of army values – and how I could best link the shared values with our respective, and seemingly conflicting interests. Once I was able to formulate this link, my task was then to create an interactive narrative binding us together, which formed the basis for the adhocracy. The need to incorporate and build on the desires and interests of stakeholders represents a shift in the storytelling orientation. Instead of viewing my stakeholders as a captive audience, which failed miserably, I had to view them more holistically. I not only had to understand my audience, but through accommodating their interests they evolved into co-authors of a story where their voices were heard loud and clear, and they greatly influenced the practices spawned from such stories. Because the narrative was jointly composed, there was stakeholder 'buy in' (von Burg and Kenney 2000; van Lente 2012), and my colleagues were more amenable to incorporating the changes discovered during their adhocracy into their larger, external narrative.

The experiences in the vignettes offer several implications. First, entrepreneurship can assume many forms, not only the creation of a new business ex nihilo. Understanding that authority may be embodied in situations (Follett 1919), and not exclusively in any particular individual, may avoid the conflicts that interfere with a manager's ability to lead, thereby increasing the entrepreneurial impetus. Furthermore, focusing on the joint needs of a situation may reveal truths or opportunities that were outside the abilities of an entrepreneur or actual subject to perceive them, as was the case of the successful collaboration with unit mailrooms. Finally, adhocracies may be an ideal pathway to realizing entrepreneurial possibilities because they are built around forms, require little upfront investment, perish when a given interpretation of an eternal object becomes irrelevant, and thrive in the same timeline as their respective opportunity.

Managers in large firms can adopt the same perspective and become entrepreneurs through a similar shift in assumptions from story givers to story weavers. While any given firm may have explicitly stated rules and regulations, a shift in behaviour may pave the way for articulation through novel interpretations of joint interests. Instead of a prefabricated regulation of behaviour with a fixed audience as shown in bureaucracies, process theory integrates the interests of stakeholders into co-authors through co-construction of stories. Additionally, due to their limited duration and investment, adhocracies formed from shared narratives may prove to be a useful vehicle for entrepreneurial experimentation and conflict resolution. Further research into this entrepreneurial mindset would require academics to abandon currently accepted research traditions in favour of narratives, work in the firms they study and examine the birth of adhocracies and their effectiveness in organizations.

Conclusion

This autoethnography examined a context in which entrepreneurship thrived despite a high level of bureaucracy. Mainstream literature professes that high levels of organizational rigidity suppress entrepreneurship, but this empirical setting illustrated a context in which a highly structured institution, the United States Army, achieved proactive and new organization forming behaviour (Greenwood and Suddaby 2006). The internal need for entrepreneurship resulted in a shift from thinking based on centralized authority to one grounded in abstractions, narratives and the subsequent creation of adhocracies.

With regards to the advancement of the understanding of entrepreneurship, this paper makes a number of contributions. It illustrates the use of a fundamentally divergent perspective in the study of entrepreneurship, one that decomposes Whitehead's process of concrescence (Whitehead 1978) into two steps. The first step is the co-construction of a narrative around a given understanding of a, or a series of abstract values. The second step involves the creation of an adhocracy, or temporary organization in which the kairological timeline is greatly accelerated towards the alignment of interests. Once this alignment is achieved, the adhocracy perishes, but echoes of the narratives upon which the adhocracy was built remain.

The postal case addresses multiple concepts from corporate entrepreneurship literature. First, it shatters stereotypes that bureaucracies suppress entrepreneurship. For one, neither the army nor USPS are private firms. The Department of Defense is America's largest employer and is among its oldest and most established. However, there still remained pockets for entrepreneurship through shared narratives. While my manager provided me with no real support, which in many ways decreased my prospects for success, she did not suppress my creativity, which fostered an entrepreneurial spirit (Burgelman 1983a), and allowed me to search for abstractions and shared, yet localized narratives. The extreme adversity I encountered with respect to these inspections highlighted the need to learn, surmount the impossible, resolve immediate dilemmas and eliminate my previous behaviours (Stopford and Baden-Fuller 1994) – in short, create a new organizational form, which is also a type of entrepreneurship (Greenwood and Suddaby 2006). Furthermore, according to Zahra (1991) corporate entrepreneurship is informal or formal behaviour that seeks to create new bureaucracies via innovation within established firms. However, this adhocratic organization was designed to skirt bureaucracies, and their accompanying restrictive narratives, which were seen as obstacles to our joint underlying values. Sharma and Chrisman's (1999) emphasis on organization renewal may not be relevant because renewal implies inherent novelty, yet this paper is about returning to the roots of the organization. However, the idea from corporate entrepreneurship literature that small teams can foster entrepreneurship within a bureaucracy is supported (Stopford and Baden-Fuller 1994).

There are also some similarities between organizational entrepreneurship literature and the establishment of adhocracies. A common definition of organizational entrepreneurship is the establishment of separate spaces within an organization designed to subvert established orders such as in a bureaucracy (Hjorth 2003, 2004, 2007, 2014; Massumi 2002). It is certainly true that the creation of adhocracies is the result of narratives spawning in separate spaces. However, I would differ on the discussion of subverting established orders. The established order in this case was not the bureaucracy, but rather the values the bureaucracy was designed to embody. In this sense, both the values and the bureaucracy are mutually supportive, but the formation of the adhocracy was designed to grasp future potentiality and speed up processes in the context of a slower moving bureaucracy. After the death of the adhocracy, the narratives were incorporated into the larger bureaucratic dialogue. This paper illustrates a novel form of adherence, not dissent.

This work also contributes to the study of public service entrepreneurship. While the formation of adhocracies represents a novel way to manage relationships and alter procedures for the greater public good (Llewellyn and Jones 2003), even perhaps in spite of regulation, this body of literature focuses on the tactical mechanisms of public service entrepreneurship that may be represented via material objects (Gore 1994), innovative leadership (Currie et al. 2008) or operational improvements such as Lean Six Sigma (George and George 2003). I have seen very little on crafting of alternative narratives, or the formation of adhocracies. So while this paper confirms the spirit of public service entrepreneurship, it also extends its letter, or the specific mechanisms used in this type of entrepreneurship.

An empirical contribution is that the use of narratives and the subsequent creation of adhocracies may facilitate the articulation of opportunities when none may be otherwise present. For example, under the discovery perspective in entrepreneurial opportunity (Kirzner 1973, 1983, 1997), an entrepreneur may only discover an opportunity when he or she perceived a market imbalance. If the entrepreneur does not perceive the imbalance, or if the disequilibrium does not exist, then no entrepreneurship may occur. Alternatively, creation-based theories of entrepreneurship (Baker and Nelson 2005; Sarasvathy 2001, 2003, 2010) rely heavily on individual-based enactments, yet if an entrepreneur cannot visualize, or does not have the resources to make a dream a reality, then the opportunity cannot be realized.

The story-based approach avoids some of these problems associated with individual-based and teleological-oriented entrepreneurship and opportunity, respectively. In contrast to the discovery viewpoint of entrepreneurial opportunity, narratives thrive on potentiality, and so therefore, are not restricted to a gap in the market that may or may not exist at any given time. Narratives also rely on co-construction of ideas and resources. This suggests that through both intellectual and material contributions of stakeholders, opportunities that are unavailable under individual resource bases and enactments, as well as absent within a rigid bureaucratic structure, may be more easily reached through teamwork and its respective enhanced agency.

The use of autoethnography is particularly appropriate due to the nature of the study. Although bureaucratic behaviour is rigorously documented, much less information exists about adhocracies due to their intuitive and temporary nature (Autier 2001). By exploring the formation of an adhocracy from the first person perspective, this methodology and empirical setting support ideas from entrepreneurship literature advocating research that is influenced by practice and designed to influence the daily routines of individuals (Engstrom 2012; Fletcher 2011; Johannisson 2011), and to desires of qualitative scholars who attempt to render research more accessible (Ellis, Adams, and Bochner 2011). Furthermore, since this paper is about the telling of the entrepreneurial story, a method revolving around stories, such as autoethnography, is an appropriate way to explore and describe this novel vision of entrepreneurship.

A final contribution of this paper is to redefine the entrepreneur's role in storytelling. The use of narratives, while not specifically discussed in more mainstream literature, is supported by the ideas of a heroic of charismatic individual, who can tell a story full of potentiality designed to make others move (Hjorth and Gartner 2014) or to alter practices. However, this work presents a slightly different perspective of the entrepreneurial story. This work illustrates that the entrepreneur's story is not told in abstraction or ex nihilo. Unlike a bureaucratic narrative, the entrepreneur's narrative is dependent on stakeholder buy in and therefore participation. If an entrepreneur is isolated, difficult, or imposing, then surely they will fail, as I initially did. This failure can lead to the searching for solutions outside a bureaucracy, especially in the feedback from stakeholders. So perhaps entrepreneurship is about abandoning previous mentalities, co-constructing a narrative, integrating perspectives of others and working together in new ways to overcome problems posed in a traditional bureaucratic mindset.

There are a variety of limitations to this study. One such limitation relates to the underlying process theory utilized. Unfortunately, process theory represents a type of orientation, but basic beliefs or ontologies are not able to be disputed, only supposed. The same limitation applies to the individualist epistemology underlying autoethnography. If it is accepted that the power of the unique and co-constructed story is a robust sensemaking tool (Foss 2004; O'Connor 2002), then likewise must one accept a key limitations of such a story: a lack of generalizability, an inability to form greater level laws or theories based on individual experiences (Steyaert 2004), and a small sample size (i.e. $n = 1$, plus the voices of the other characters of the story). Yet I believe the value of this story may outweigh the strength of its limitations. Stories are, and remain a fundamental sensemaking device (Gioia and Chittipedi 1991), by which people understand their world (Buckler and Zien 1996) and we tend to think in narratives, and not in normal distributions. Furthermore, stories give voice to the voiceless including those of inner monologues and struggles. Perhaps this alternate orientation and its accompanying story may shed light on entrepreneurship and new organizational formation, in spite of its limitations.

Disclosure statement

No potential conflict of interest was reported by the author.

References

Anderson, L. 2006. "Analytic Autoethnography." *Journal of Contemporary Ethnography* 35 (4): 373–395.

Atkinson, P. 2006. "Rescuing Autoethnography." *Journal of Contemporary Ethnography* 35 (4): 400–404.

Autier, F. 2001. "Bureaucracy vs. Adhocracy: A Case of Overdramatisation? In 17th EGOS Colloquium, "The Odyssey of Organizing", Theme of "European Group for Organizational Studies". Lyon.

Aurelius, M. 2008. *Meditations*. Salt Lake City, UT: Project Gutenberg.

Baker, T., and R. Nelson. 2005. "Creating Something from Nothing: Resource Construction through Entrepreneurial Bricolage." *Administrative Science Quarterly.* 50 (3): 329–366.

Barnard, C. 1938. *The Functions of the Executive*. Cambridge, MA: Harvard University Press.

Barringer, B. R., and A. C. Bluedorn. 1999. "The Relationship between Corporate Entrepreneurship and Strategic Management." *Strategic Management Journal* 20 (5): 421–444.

Bartel, C. A., and R. Garud. 2003. "Narrative Knowledge in Action: Adaptive Abduction as a Mechanism for Knowledge Creation and Exchange in Organizations." In *The Blackwell Handbook of Organizational Learning and Knowledge Management*, edited by Mark Easterby-Smith, 324–342. New York: Wiley.

Bennis, W. 1966. "The Coming Death of Bureaucracy." *Think Magazine*.

Bickham, S. 2009. "The Metaphysics of Causality and Novelty." *The Pluralist* 4 (3): 64–68.

Borup, M., N. Brown, K. Konrad, and H. Van Lente. 2006. "The Sociology of Expectations in Science and Technology." *Technology Analysis & Strategic Management*. 18 (3–4): 285–298.

Boutaiba, S. 2004. "A Moment in Time." In *Narrative and Discursive Approaches in Entrepreneurship*, edited by Daniel Hjorth and Chris Steyaert, 22–56. Cheltenham: Edward Elgar.

Buckler, S., and K. Zien. 1996. "The Spirituality of Innovation: Learning from Stories." *Journal of Product Innovation Management* 13 (5): 391–405.

Burgelman, R. 1983a. "Corporate Entrepreneurship and Strategic Management: Insights from a Process Study." *Management Science* 29 (12): 1349–1364.

Burgelman, R. 1983b. "A Model of the Interaction of Strategic Behavior, Corporate Context, and the Concept of Strategy." *Academy of Management Review* 8 (1): 61–70.

Cornelissen, J., and J. Clarke. 2010. "Imagining and Rationalizing Opportunities: Inductive Reasoning and the Creation and Justification of New Ventures." *Academy of Management Review* 35 (4): 539–557.

Currie, G., M. Humphreys, and D. Ucbasaran, S. McManus. 2008. "Entrepreneurial Leadership in the English Public Sector: Paradox or Possibility?" *Public Administration* 86 (4): 987–1008.

Deleuze, G., and F. Guattari. 2004. *A Thousand Plateaus*. London: Continuum.

Deleuze, G. 1994. *Difference and Repetition*. New York: Columbia University Press.

Derrida, J. 1978. *Writing and Difference*. Chicago, IL: University of Chicago Press.

Dewitt, L. 1965. *Flowers on the Wall*. Columbia.

Doloriert, C., and S. Sambrook. 2012. "Organisational Autoethnography." *Journal of Organizational Ethnography* 1 (1): 83–95.

Dugger, W. 1980. "Corporate Bureaucracy: The Incidence of the Bureaucratic Process." *Journal of Economic Issues* 14 (2): 399–409.

Durkheim, E. 1915. *The Elementary Forms of Religious Life*. London: Allen &Erwin.

Eliade, M. 1958. *Patterns in Comparative Religion*. London: Sheed & Ward.

Ellis, C. 1999. "Heartful Autoethnography." *Qualitative Health Research* 9 (5): 669–683.

Ellis, C., T. Adams, and A. Bochner. 2011. "Autoethnography: An Overview." *Historical Social Research/ Historische Sozialforschung* 12 (1): 273–290.

Emerson, H. 2004. *Oral History of Henry E. Emerson*. Carlisle Barracks, PA: US Army Military History Institute.

Emirbayer, M., and A. Mische. 1998. "What is Agency?" *American Journal of Sociology* 103 (4): 962–1023.

Engstrom, C. 2012. "An Autoethnographic Account of Prosaic Entrepreneurship." *Journal for Critical Organization Inquiry* 10 (1): 41–54.

Fletcher, D. 2011. "A Curiosity for Contexts: Entrepreneurship, Enactive Research and Autoethnography." *Entrepreneurship and Regional Development* 23 (1–2): 65–76.

Follett, M. 1919. "Community is a Process." *The Philosophical Review* 28: 576–588.

Follett, M. 1924. *Creative Experience*. http://mpfollett.ning.com.

Follett, M. 1940. *Dynamic Administration*. http://mpfollett.ning.com.

Foss, L. 2004. "'Going against the Grain'… Construction of Entrepreneurial Identity through Narratives." In *Narrative and Discursive Approaches in Entrepreneurship*, edited by Daniel Hjorth and Chris Steyaert, 80–104. Cheltenham: Edward Elgar.

Gartner, W. 2007. "Entrepreneurial Narrative and a Science of the Imagination." *Journal of Business Venturing* 22 (5): 613–627.

Gartner, W., B. Bird, and J. Starr. 1992. "Acting as If: Differentiating Entrepreneurial from Organizational Behavior." *Entrepreneurship Theory and Practice* 16 (3): 13–31.

Garud, R., H. Schildt, and T. Lant. 2014. "Entrepreneurial Storytelling, Future Expectations, and the Paradox of Legitimacy." *Organization Science* 25 (5): 1479–1492.

George, M., and M. George. 2003. *Lean Six Sigma for Service*. New York: McGraw-Hill.

Gioia, D. A., and K. Chittipeddi. 1991. "Sensemaking and Sensegiving in Strategic Change Initiation." *Strategic Management Journal* 12 (6): 433–448.

Gore, A., Jr., 1994. "The New Job of the Federal Executive." *Public Administration Review* 54 (4): 317–321.

Griffin, D. 2006. "An Introduction to Process Cosmology." *Cosmology and Process Philosophy in Dialogue*. Claremont, CA: Claremont Graduate University.

Greenwood, R., and R. Suddaby. 2006. "Institutional Entrepreneurship in Mature Fields: The Big Five Accounting Firms." *Academy of Management Journal* 49 (1): 27–48.

Hales, C. 2002. "'Bureaucracy-Lite' and Continuities in Managerial Work." *British Journal of Management* 13 (1): 51–66.

Hayward, M., D. Shepherd, and D. Griffin. 2006. "A Hubris Theory of Entrepreneurship." *Management Science* 52 (2): 160–172.

Heidegger, M. 1927. *Being and Time*. Oxford: Blackwell.

Hernes, T. 2014. *A Process Theory of Organization*. Oxford: Oxford University Press.

Hjorth, D. 2003. *Rewriting Entrepreneurship: for a New Perspective on Organisational Creativity*. Stockholm: Liber.

Hjorth, D. 2004. "Creating Space for Play/Invention–Concepts of Space and Organizational Entrepreneurship." *Entrepreneurship & Regional Development* 16 (5): 413–432.

Hjorth, D. 2007. "Lessons from Iago: Narrating the Event of Entrepreneurship." *Journal of Business Venturing* 22: 712–732.

Hjorth, D. 2014. "Organizational Entrepreneruship: An Art of the Weak?" In *Handbook on Organizational Entrepreneurship*, edited by Daniel Hjorth, 169–192. Cheltenham: Edward Elgar.

Hjorth, D., and W. Gartner. 2014. "Moving and Being Moved: Ideas, Perspectives and 59 Theses on Entrepreneurial Leadership." In *Handbook on Organizational Entrepreneurship*, edited by Daniel Hjorth, 362–376. Cheltenham: Edward Elgar.

Humphreys, M. 2005. "Getting Personal: Reflexivity and Autoethnographic Vignettes." *Qualitative Inquiry* 11 (6): 840–860.

Janssens, M. and C. Steyaert. 1999. "The World in Two and a Third Way out? The Concept of Duality in Organization Theory and Practice." *Scandinavian Journal of Management* 15 (2): 121–139.

Johansson, A. W. 2004. "Narrating the Entrepreneur." *International Small Business Journal* 22 (3): 273–293.

Johannisson, B. 2011. "Towards a Practice Theory of Entrepreneuring." *Small Business Economics* 36: 135–150.

Johannisson, B., and L. Olaison. 2007. "The Moment of Truth—Reconstructing Entrepreneurship and Social Capital in the Eye of the Storm." *Review of Social Economy* 65 (1): 55–78.

Johannisson, B., M. Ramirez-Pasillas, and G. Karlsson. 2002. "The Institutional Embeddedness of Local Inter-firm Networks: A Leverage for Business Creation." *Entrepreneurship and Regional Development* 14: 297–315.

Kirzner, I. 1973. *Competition and Entrepreneurship*. Chicago, IL: University of Chicago Press.

Kirzner, I. 1983. *Perception, Opportunity, and Profit: Studies in the Theory of Entrepreneurship*. Chicago, IL: University of Chicago Press.

Kirzner, I. 1997. "Entrepreneurial Discovery and the Competitive Market Process: An Austrian Approach." *Journal of Economic Literature* 35 (1): 60–85.

Langley, A., and H. Tsoukas. 2010. "Introducing Perspectives on Process Organization Studies." *Process, Sense-Making and Organizing* 1 (9): 1–26.

Lampel, J. 2001. "Show and Tell: Product Demonstrations and Path Creation of Technological Change." In *Path Dependence and Path Creation*, edited by R. Garud and P. Karnoe, 303–328. Mahwah, NJ: Lawrence Erlbaum Associates.

Lindh de Montoya, M. 2004. "Driven Entrepreneurs: A Case Study of Taxi Owners in Caracas." In *Narrative and Discursive Approaches in Entrepreneurship*, edited by Daniel Hjorth and Chris Steyaert, 57–79. Cheltenham: Edward Elgar.

Lounsbury, M., and M. Glynn. 2001. "Cultural Entrepreneurship: Stories, Legitimacy, and the Acquisition of Resources." *Strategic Management Journal* 22 (6–7): 545–564.

Llewellyn, N., and G. Jones. 2003. "Controversies and Conceptual Development Examining Public Entrepreneurship." *Public Management Review* 5 (2): 245–266.

Lyotard, J. 1979. *The Post Modern Condition: A Report on Knowledge*. Translated by G. Bennington and B. Massumi. Manchester: Manchester University Press.

Mandell, M., and T. Steelman. 2003. "Understanding What Can Be Accomplished through Interorganizational Innovations: The Importance of Typologies, Context and Management Strategies." *Public Management Review* 5 (2): 197–224.

Massumi, B. 2002. *Parables for the Virtual: Movement, Affect, Sensation*. Durham, NC: Duke University Press.

Martin de Holan, P. 2014. "The Bitter Truth about Entrepreneurial Success." *Financial Times*, December 21.

Miller, D. 1983. "The Correlates of Entrepreneurship in Three Types of Firms." *Management Science.* 29 (7): 770–791.

Mintzberg, H. 1981. "The Adhocracy." In *Structure in Fives: Designing Effective Organizations*, edited by H. Mintzberg, 253–282. Englewood Cliffs, NJ: Prentice Hall.

Nayak, A., and R. Chia. 2011. "Thinking Becoming and Emergence: Process Philosophy and Organization Studies." *Research in the Sociology of Organizations* 32: 281–309.

O'Connor, E. 2000. "Plotting the Organization: The Embedded Narrative as a Construct for Studying Change." *The Journal of Applied Behavioral Science* 36 (2): 174–192.

O'Connor, E. 2002. "Storied Business: Typology, Intertextuality, and Traffic in Entrepreneurial Narrative." *Journal of Business Communication* 39 (1): 36–54.

Orlikowski, W. J., and J. Yates. 2002. "It's about Time: Temporal Structuring in Organizations." *Organization Science* 13 (6): 684–700.

Plato. 2012. *Republic*. Salt Lake City: Project Gutenberg.

Plato. 2013. *Meno*. Salt Lake City: Project Gutenberg.

Pierce, C. 1998. *The Essential Writings*. New York: Prometheus Books.

Rae, D., and M. Carswell. 2000. "Using a Life-story Approach in Researching Entrepreneurial Learning: The Development of a Conceptual Model and Its Implications in the Design of Learning Experiences." *Education and Training* 42 (4–5): 220–228.

Rambo, C. 2005. "Impressions of Grandmother an Autoethnographic Portrait." *Journal of Contemporary Ethnography* 34 (5): 560–585.

Sarasvathy, S. 2001. "Causation and Effectuation: Toward a Theoretical Shift from Economic Inevitability to Entrepreneurial Contingency." *Academy of Management Review* 26 (2): 243–263.

Sarasvathy, S. 2003. "Entrepreneurship as a Science of the Artificial." *Journal of Economic Psychology* 24 (2): 203–220.

Sarasvathy, S. 2010. "Entrepreneurship as Economics with Imagination." *The Ruffin Series of the Society for Business Ethics* 3: 95–112.

Schumpeter J. 1934. *The Theory of Economic Development: An Inquiry into Profits, Capital, Credit, Interest, and the Business Cycle*. Vol. 55. Piscataway: Transaction Publishers.

Sharma, P., and J. Chrisman. 1999. "Toward a Reconciliation of the Definitional Issues in the Field of Corporate Entrepreneurship." *Entrepreneurship Theory and Practice* 23 (3): 11–28.

Smith, R., and A. Anderson. 2004. "The Devil is in the E-Tale: Form and Structure in the Entrepreneurial Narrative." In *Narrative and Discursive Approaches in Entrepreneurship: A Second Movements in Entrepreneurship Book*, edited by Daniel Hjorth and Chris Steyaert, 125–143. Cheltenham: Edward Elgar.

Sørensen, J. 2007. "Bureaucracy and Entrepreneurship: Workplace Effects on Entrepreneurial Entry." *Administrative Science Quarterly.* 52 (3): 387–412.

Sparkes, A. 2000. "Autoethnography and Narratives of Self: Reflections on Criteria in Action." *Sociology of Sport Journal* 17 (1): 21–43.

Spinosa, C., F. Flores, and H. L. Dreyfus. 1999. *Disclosing New Worlds: Entrepreneurship, Democratic Action, and the Cultivation of Solidarity*. Cambridge: MIT Press.

Spry, T. 2001. "Performing Autoethnography: An Embodied Methodological Praxis." *Qualitative Inquiry* 7 (6): 706–732.

Steyaert, C. 2004. "The Prosaics of Entrepreneurship." In *Narrative and Discursive Approaches in Entrepreneurship*, edited by Daniel Hjorth and Chris Steyaert, 8–23. Cheltenham: Edward Elgar.

Steyaert, C. 2011. "Entrepreneurship as In(ter)Vention: Reconsidering the Conceptual Politics of Method in Entrepreneurship Studies." *Entrepreneurship and Regional Development* 23 (1–2): 77–88.

Stopford, J., and C. Baden-Fuller. 1994. "Creating Corporate Entrepreneurship." *Strategic Management Journal* 15 (7): 521–536.

Suchman, M. 1995. "Managing Legitimacy: Strategic and Institutional Approaches." *Academy of Management Review* 20 (3): 571–610.

Teske, P., and M. Schneider. 1994. "The Bureaucratic Entrepreneur: The Case of City Managers." *Public Administration Review* 54 (4): 331–340.

Thompson, V. 1969. *Bureaucracy and Innovation*. Tuscaloosa: University of Alabama Press.

Toffler, A. 1970. *Future Shock*. London: Bodley Head.

Tripsas, M., and G. Gavetti. 2000. "Capabilities, Cognition, and Inertia: Evidence from Digital Imaging." *Strategic Management Journal* 21 (10–11): 1147–1161.

Trope, Y., and N. Liberman. 2003. "Temporal Construal." *Psychological Review* 110 (3): 403–421.

Tsoukas, H., and M. Hatch. 2001. "Complex Thinking, Complex Practice: The Case for a Narrative Approach to Organizational Complexity." *Human Relations* 54 (8): 979–1013.

van Lente, H. 2012. "Navigating Foresight in a Sea of Expectations: Lessons from the Sociology of Expectations." *Technology Analysis & Strategic Management* 24 (8): 769–782.

von Burg, U., and M. Kenney. 2000. "Venture Capital and the Birth of the Local Area Networking Industry." *Research Policy* 29 (9): 1135–1155.

Warren, L. 2004. "A Systemic Approach to Entrepreneurial Learning: An Exploration Using Storytelling." *Systems Research and Behavioral Science* 21 (1): 3–16.

Weber, M. 1958. "The Three Types of Legitimate Rule." *Berkeley Publications in Society and Institutions* 4 (1): 1–11.

Whitehead, A. 1978. *An Essay in Cosmology*. Washington, DC: Free Press.

Zahra, S. 1991. "Predictors and Financial Outcomes of Corporate Entrepreneurship: An Exploratory Study." *Journal of Business Venturing* 6 (4): 259–285.

A CULTure of entrepreneurship education

Steffen Farny, Signe Hedeboe Frederiksen, Martin Hannibal and
Sally Jones

ABSTRACT
High hopes are invested in a rapid institutionalization of an enterprise
culture in Higher Education (HE). This has heightened the importance
of entrepreneurship education (EE) in most Western societies; however,
how values and beliefs about entrepreneurship are institutionalized
in EE remains relatively unchallenged. This study applies the lens of
the cult, in particular three elements *Rituals*, *Deities* and the *Promise
of Salvation*, to reflect on the production and reproduction of
entrepreneurship in EE. In doing so, the paper addresses uncontested
values and beliefs that form a hidden curriculum prevalent in EE. We
argue for greater appreciation of reflexive practices to challenge
normative promotions of beliefs and values that compare with forms
of evangelizing, detrimental to objectives of HE. Consequently, we
call for a more critical pedagogy to counteract a 'cultification' of
entrepreneurship in EE.

Introduction

In recent years, entrepreneurship education (EE) has become a topic of growing interest in
Higher Education Institutions (HEI). Policy has positioned EE as a key intervention in the
promotion and realization of an enterprise culture (Holmgren and From 2005; EC 2012).
Since, 'education is society's media of manifesting fundamental ideas' (Kyrö 2005, 75), the
policy objective is to embed EE across the curriculum at all levels of education (EC 2012),
and dramatically increase the number of university entrepreneurship courses (Blenker et al.
2012; Kuratko 2005) in order to support a cultural shift in Western economies. By advocating
this logic, policy has also fed a growing academic interest in supporting these aims through
research and education. As a result, entrepreneurship becomes a 'cultural movement', created
and reproduced as a cultural ideology through channels such as education (Rae 2010, 592).

In spite of a growing interest in exploring the institutionalization of entrepreneurship
and the entrepreneur in broader society, the institutionalization of entrepreneurship in education has not been through the same kind of deconstruction (Rehn et al. 2013). Still, it is
essential to subject EE to critical reflections by challenging its foundations and assumptions

if it is to progress as a discipline (Fayolle 2013). We therefore ask: How are values and beliefs about entrepreneurship institutionalized in EE?

To address this issue, we use a religious lens – the 'cult' – specifically, its components of deities, rituals and promises of salvation, to critically reflect on the role of EE in reproducing and legitimizing a belief system. This methodological choice is a consequence of the ideological content in entrepreneurship (Nicholson and Anderson 2005; Ogbor 2000) which defies reflexivity in the conventional sense of the term (Styhre 2005). An ideology is a belief system (Jost, Federico, and Napier 2008) and represents a comprehensive normative vision, in the sense that it describes a set of conscious and unconscious ideas that instruct goals, expectation, and motivations. Cascardi (1999, 200) argues that ideology consists of 'discursive forms through which a society tries to constitute itself as such on the basis of closure, of the fixation of meaning, of the non-recognition of the infinite play of differences'. Ideology is therefore always inherent in ways of thinking and speaking and not a detachable layer, which makes it difficult to isolate and analyse using standard procedures for reflexivity (Styhre 2005). It is important to stress, that we do not argue that entrepreneurship in education is a cult, or that beliefs in entrepreneurship are like religious beliefs. Rather, cult and the notion of religiosity is our way of 'fighting familiarity' (Delamont, Atkinson, and Pugsley 2010), gaining a research position outside normativity by employing a different analytic prism. In this sense, the cult lens acts as our tool to provide analytical distance and reflexivity.

Following a social constructionist ontology (Berger and Luckmann 1966), we position EE as the pedagogical concerns linked to educating about, for, and through entrepreneurship (Blenker et al. 2011; Hannon 2005). Through numerous educational programs, entrepreneurship is offered as a meaningful description of social reality whilst prescribing desirable actions and ways of engaging in this world. This promotion suggests a hidden curriculum that is driven by wider taken-for-granted assumptions of entrepreneurship. Conceptualized as 'what schooling does to people' (Martin 1976, 135), this particular hidden curriculum underpins mainstream practices in EE. In the concept lies a contrast between what the intent of teaching is and what, although not openly intended, students in fact learn (Martin 1976). It includes transmission of unspoken and unchallenged norms, values and beliefs linked to particular paradigms, and their socialization function (Gair and Mullins 2001).

In applying the lens of the cult, we contribute to existing research that addresses the institutionalization of entrepreneurship (e.g. Landström and Benner 2013; Landström, Harirchi, and Åström 2012; Watson 2013; Welter and Lasch 2008). Through classroom vignettes, and a discussion of deities, rituals, and ideas of salvation evident in EE, we discuss how the institutionalization of entrepreneurship involves a normative promotion of beliefs and values and therefore compares with forms of evangelizing (Du Gay 1996; Tedmanson et al. 2012). Looking at the specific case of EE, thus, enhances our understanding of the potential for embedded agents – educators in our case – to promote or potentially challenge uncritical reproduction of this belief system.

In the following, we present the political incentives constituting the development of EE. Then we explain in more detail how and why we employ the religious cult as an analytical lens. With a focus on three major elements of a cult (deities, rituals and salvation), we discuss the production and reproduction of entrepreneurship as a belief system in EE. Finally, we present the consequences of our analysis and how to possibly escape cult-like promotions through reflexivity into what we teach and what students potentially learn.

The rise of EE

It is impossible to isolate activities within EE from wider societal understandings of who and what the entrepreneur and entrepreneurship is (Ehrensal 2001; Holmgren and From 2005; Jones 2014). Entrepreneurship is posited as a remedy to some of the fundamental problems of today's economies, such as unemployment and stagnating economic growth (Rasmussen et al. 2011) and seems to offer a solution to problems associated with the increased pace and turbulence of social and economic change (Anderson and Jack 2008).

Government policy pinpoints the rationales for developing an enterprise culture (Lewis and Llewellyn 2004; OECD 2009). It suggests that EE is an important intervention, since it plays a role in developing and improving entrepreneurial aspirations and abilities, stimulating entrepreneurship and unleashing a 'spirit of enterprise', presented in terms of innovation, creativity, initiative and a tolerance of risk and uncertainty (e.g. EC 2004). These policy interventions frame EE as an entrepreneurial pipeline (Huggins 2008; Kyrö 2006), expected to unleash the transformational powers needed to create economic wealth. The development of EE programmes is therefore suggested as a way to increase the supply of entrepreneurial talent (Henry, Hill, and Leitch 2005). In short, the main rationale to expose students to EE is to contribute to more entrepreneurship and entrepreneurial activities.

Consequently, EE in higher education (HE) aims to transform students' attitudes, values, and self-understandings (Holmgren and From 2005), creating an imperative for *all* students to become enterprising (Pittaway and Cope 2007). This transformation manifests as an increased focus on the entrepreneur as a person, identified by certain abilities and practices, which should be stimulated and trained. Hence, the entrepreneur stands out as a driving identity in the new economy, which more individuals are encouraged to take up (Lewis and Llewellyn 2004). Although policy goals are not uniformly translated into EE practices, and educators are not necessarily 'victims' of policy discourses (Robinson and Blenker 2014) such glorification risks promoting a deified picture of entrepreneurs that students might feel obliged to aspire to. Therefore, we apply the lens of the cult to reflect on the production and reproduction of entrepreneurship in EE.

The cult as analytical lens

Scholars have emphasized the influence of religious ethics on economic action. For instance, religion has been considered a cultural background for capitalism and the shaping of economic institutions (Deutschmann 2001; Weber 2002). Durkheim (2001) regarded religion as the representation of society's moral rules and collective existence, with all religions involving a set of symbols and feelings of reverence linked to the rituals and deities of a community of believers (Giddens and Sutton 2009). Geertz (1973) defined religion as a cultural system which gains its strength through formulating correspondence between people's ethos i.e. 'the tone, character, and quality of their life, its moral and aesthetic style and mood', and their world view i.e. 'the picture they have of the way things in sheer actuality are' (Geertz 1973, 89). He argues that sacred symbols formulate this basic congruence between a specific metaphysic and a particular lifestyle, which are both sustained by 'the borrowed authority of the other' (Geertz 1973, 90). Consequently, there is an alignment and mutual confirmation between the 'subjective' qualities of life and what is considered the 'objective' realities of the world. Geertz famously stated that religion as a cultural system becomes both a model 'of' as well as a model 'for' reality (Geertz 1973, 93). As a framework that simultaneously provides descriptions of the world and prescriptions for how to act in it, such belief systems may thus form a 'totalising discourse' which presses for a single truth and extinguishes alternative understandings (Robbins 1988).

Religion has also been examined as a variable that influences entrepreneurship (Dodd and Seaman 1998). Recent studies in entrepreneurship have highlighted parallels with religious concepts such as the myth of creation (Sørensen 2008). Ogbor (2000) shows how entrepreneurship theory constructs and promotes mythical figures – the deities – such as 'the warrior' (Gomez and Korine 2008) and 'the hero' (Dodd and Anderson 2007). Ong (2006) suggests that the enterprise culture can be regarded as a 'style of living' that provides guidance through given values in line with a particular ethical goal. Hence, enterprise culture compares to religion as it empowers a specific 'scheme of virtue fostering particular forms of self-conduct and visions of the good life' (Ong 2006, 22).

In fact, the term 'cult' has previously been associated with enterprise culture, highlighting the existence of hegemony and ideology in entrepreneurship (Du Gay and Salaman 1992). A cult is a 'mystic collectivity' defined by a distinct system of beliefs (Campbell 1977). It is a group or movement that exhibits great devotion to a person, idea or thing often with a charismatic leader, who increasingly becomes the object of worship (Singer 2003). A cult can also be a secular group e.g. developing around specific brands, events or personalities (Belk and Tumbat 2005).

Gallagher (2007) argues that 'cult' is used as an indicator of 'otherness'. This implies a classification between what is to be considered conventional or unconventional. By choosing membership of a cult, one chooses not to be part of the mainstream. This choice involves stepping out of social conformity to enact alternatives or deviations from conventional behaviour (Campbell 1977). This 'us vs. them' segregation is often accompanied by specific guidance in the form of rituals (Geertz 1973), deities (de Nebesky-Wojkowitz 1956), and explicit descriptions of salvation (Belk and Tumbat 2005).

The cult explains why conventional life is not what it should be and offers utopias where the ills of human kind will be cured (Singer 2003). It provides an account of an alternative perfection and provides the means for salvation (Heelas 1996). Singer (2003) defines cults as thought reform groups, which aim at producing attitudinal changes in individuals and self-improvement. Yet, in academia, the term 'cult' is considered to be a pejorative term that stigmatizes certain groups and propagates fear. Cults are also defined by the unethical manipulative or coercive techniques of persuasion and control that they employ (Tobias and Lalich 1994). In cults, people are lured in by manipulative techniques, false promises, and bogus ideology; they are seduced, brainwashed, abused, and controlled in the thought reform process, robbed of their liberty and often their money (Singer 2003).

In research, cult is often replaced with the more neutral term New Religious Movement (Gallagher 2007). Robbins (1988, 5) argues that the growth of New Religious Movements is allied with a growth in the 'human potential movement' and therapeutic mystiques oriented towards growth and self-actualization. In capitalist, and utilitarian individualistic societies it is perhaps unsurprising that human potential should be closely linked to economic potential and the generation of wealth, power, freedom and status for individuals.

Watson (2012) argues that it is hazardous to 'contaminate' scholarly study of entrepreneurial activity with assumptions or ambiguities from popular and political culture. This makes EE a specifically interesting research field, since the boundaries between policy-driven research and scholarly research are not always obvious, even though there is a call for more theory-driven and critical research on EE (Fayolle 2013). This does not mean that the conceptualization of entrepreneurship in policy documents is directly translated into pedagogical practices (Robinson and Blenker 2014). However, there is a widespread understanding of the existence and necessary teaching of entrepreneurial mindsets, which transcends from research into policy or perhaps the other way around (Holmgren and From 2005). Berglund and Johansson (2007) argue that entrepreneurship is simply associated with goodness, which delimits the discursive domain in ways that make it difficult if not impossible to challenge. Yet, critical scholarship on entrepreneurship should be 'uncomfortable with complacency about or fixation on, any particular position idea, theory and method' (Tedmanson et al. 2012, 537). Consequently, in order to investigate how values and beliefs are institutionalized in education, we use the lens of the cult to establish an analysis of EE, which is not readily encapsulated within its own ideology.

Cult elements of EE

As promoted in education, entrepreneurship offers a credible description of the true workings of the world while simultaneously prescribing meaningful and desirable actions and ways of being in this world. Thus, the institutionalization of entrepreneurship in EE is described by social practices, routine-reproduced programmes or rules (Jepperson 1991). Through teaching practices, symbols and beliefs are produced and reproduced, institutionalizing myth and taken-for-granted assumptions (Hallett 2010). In light of this, EE – a societal institution where entrepreneurship is (re)constituted as a 'model of', as well as a 'model for' reality – potentially falls victim to being based on automated values and beliefs (Rehn et al. 2013).

By using the cult as a lens we are able to critically reflect on these taken-for-granted beliefs and values. We explore three elements identified in the literature on new religious movements: Deities, Ritual and the Promise of Salvation. Each subsection is introduced by auto-ethnographic vignettes that offer insights into concrete lecture episodes experienced by the authors. The vignettes are intertwined with a review of how each cult element has been used, discussed, employed, etc. in contemporary entrepreneurship research. This review is complemented by illustrations of how these theory developments have been institutionalized in EE.

We then discuss the consequences of this institutionalization of entrepreneurship in EE and how it represents a totalizing discourse that underpins a hidden curriculum. As the hidden curriculum cannot be uncovered directly, we examine what is learned as a result of the practices, procedures, rules, relationships, structures and physical characteristics employed (Martin 1976) that constitute deities, rituals and the promise of salvation. In doing so, we offer opportunities for a critical and reflective approach to EE.

Deities

In the classroom I challenge the stereotypes of successful entrepreneurs. One exercise involves drawing an entrepreneur and typically students will draw people such as Steve Jobs, Richard Branson and Mark Zuckerberg to illustrate who they see as successful entrepreneur. Indeed, they are eager to learn about such people in class. This creates a tension for me as an educator when I try and highlight other less well-known entrepreneurs, some of whom may be women or involved in more socially focused entrepreneurship. This seems to have little effect on student understanding and they continue to refer to Jobs, Branson, Zuckerberg, etc. as classes continue. (Educator in UK)

During an introduction lecture in entrepreneurship at graduate level a student eyes down the lecturer's CV and questions if the lecturer has ever started a new venture himself? The lecturer admits that the only venturing he has ever undertaken was some cleaning for old people during his many years of study. The student replies with ill-concealed contempt: "how can you then lecture on the topic?" And continues to argue that what is really needed is insight from for example [a well-known local entrepreneur]. (Educator in Denmark)

In line with formal definitions, we conceptualize a 'Deity' as a supreme being, one who is exalted as supremely good, or omnipotent and the embodiment of all that is desirable. Authors in the field have noted that societal stereotypical scripts have constrained the metaphor of 'the entrepreneur' (Down and Warren 2008). This metaphor sanctions an individual heroic figure that embodies a number of distinct characteristics (Nicholson and Anderson 2005) prescribing social norms for what is expected from the role 'entrepreneur'. This involves the deification of the individual entrepreneur (Kaufmann and Dant 1999). Consequently, and seemingly by default, this entrepreneur is closely linked to figures such as Richard Branson, Steve Jobs etc. implicitly establishing both the psychological traits of the entrepreneur and also of entrepreneurs as wealth creators and saviours of the economy (Sørensen 2008) and illustrating their commonality with the charismatic leaders or gurus of new religious movements (Robbins 1988). This establishes a figure or a deity that the student should aspire to become. Entrepreneurship events, connected to curriculum activities, fuel this conception and usually include elaborate marketing materials that, to an extent, glamourize entrepreneurship by providing keynote speeches from successful local, alumni and/or nationally recognized entrepreneurs (deities). The foundations of this deified character are inspired by, and evident in, the writings of for example Schumpeter (1934) and involve autonomy, uniqueness and super-human powers. In other words, the entrepreneur is constructed as a charismatic hero – the embodiment of superior agency (Giesen 2005, 276). The liturgical components (or public worship) are pushed to the forefront and, as programme managers include successful entrepreneurs as keynote speakers to tell great stories about their experiences, students are impelled towards re-enacting these stories. This deified entrepreneur fulfils a specific role in the EE classroom, with students being primed to put their own agency into action through imitation. In literature this path is often connected to the need for achievement or other psychological characteristics of the entrepreneur (McClelland 1961). This theoretical turn emphasizes the individual actor, resulting in a 'cult of the individual' (Stevenson and Jarillo 1990, 20) linked to specially endowed individuals and implying that not all individuals hold these traits (Shane and Venkataraman 2000). In acting on these thoughts EE often focuses on developing such traits in students, in order for them to become more closely aligned with the template of the supreme entrepreneur (Jones 2014).

Other authors in the entrepreneurship field argue that this image of the heroic entrepreneur actually undermines any attempts to present entrepreneurship as inclusive (Gibb 2002). Indeed, the stereotype of the charismatic – and often lone – hero has been brought into question both in seminal writings (Gartner 1988; Ogbor 2000) and in more recent publications on the subject (Ramoglou 2013). Gartner (1989) argues that there is nothing that distinguishes entrepreneurs from other individuals except their entrepreneurial behaviour;

what they do is more important than who they are (Gartner 1988). Hence, Gartner (1989) questions whether a focus on specific characteristics of specific individuals (deities) is a futile research agenda. Employing the same trait-centred conceptual basis in EE could be equally problematic. Indeed, this actively undermines the idea that anyone can learn to become an entrepreneur and that entrepreneurship can be taught. In line with Gartner's (1989) critique, more recent research questions this lone hero character by analysing how young Europeans understand entrepreneurship and the 'Entrepreneur' (Dodd, Jack, and Anderson 2013). This research suggests that 'Entrepreneurs' are value-laden social constructs, which carry substantial differences across Europe. In spite of evidence of a core, cross-national discourse that holds strong linkage to the economic contribution of enterprise (Dodd, Jack, and Anderson 2013) students may come to struggle to position themselves in relation to such representations of the deities that inform EE curricula. This highlights a fundamental tension in EE, which educators and students have to grapple with and yet this is rarely acknowledged in the classroom (Jones 2014).

Ritual

> In-class evaluations are held as part of a first semester course in entrepreneurship. Evaluating an embedded start-up camp, a young male student argues that the business start-up camp and the simple 'Osterwalder'-tools which were provided in a specific sequence during this, along with the final pitch competition has been very useful to him. He goes on to state that: "Now I know exactly how to start my own business" (Educator in Denmark)

> In each student cohort, some students challenge the value of writing a final dissertation to graduate with a Master's degree from a science university. During the discussion about the dissertation requirements, a student stands up arguing fiercely: "Hands up who thinks that writing a thesis is useless, and instead Business Plans are more important and should be accepted for graduating" (Educator in Finland)

A ritual is a formalistic type of behaviour (Goody 1977) and in entrepreneurship this relates to the activities, actions or behaviours regularly and invariably followed by successful entrepreneurs (the deities). In line with commonly held values and beliefs about entrepreneurship, these rituals also suggest societal templates for the accepted and acceptable process of starting up and developing a successful business (Gibb 2000). Such beliefs are further emphasized in popular culture with popularized television programmes such as Dragons' Den and The Apprentice emphasizing the path to successful entrepreneurship as being linked to presenting a successful business plan to be judged as worthy of investment (Swail, Down, and Kautonen 2013).

The accompanying liturgy creates and supports the belief that business planning is a necessary ritual, which the would-be entrepreneur needs to perform to become successful, with a viable and attractive business plan suggested as a necessity for attracting external investment (Kaplan, Sensoy, and Strömberg 2009). A further strengthening of this tendency to draw on broader business trends is found when educators are pressured to incorporate the latest popularized literature into their teaching. However, these canons such as the Business Model Canvas (Osterwalder and Pigneur 2010), The Lean Startup (Ries 2011) and The Startup Manual (Blank and Dorf 2012) are often conveyed as the (divine) solutions to success by back office managers in the start-up support system. Accordingly, at the managerial and political level, entrepreneurship educators are expected to adopt them and promote their rites to meet the responsibility of delivering results. This legitimizes submitting students to rituals such as business plan competitions, leaving room for the Dragons' Den thumbs up or down notions.

One of the most prominent elements in the cult concept is the ritual that manifests and re-enforces the values and beliefs embedded in that cult (Geertz 1973). Critical researchers have long documented the role of education generally as a cultural system involving ritual performances and rites of passage, constructing frameworks that extend specific situational meanings further than the context of the classroom (Bernstein, Elvin, and Peters 1966).

Ritual is also strongly linked to the act of teaching itself and to classroom activities and pedagogies (McLaren 1999, 27) and EE is based upon commonly accepted and legitimatized approaches in this respect. In reviewing 108 articles, Mwasalwiba (2012) found that the most common subjects embedded in entrepreneurship courses were resource management and finance, marketing and sales, idea generation and opportunity discovery, as well as business planning. These practices are indeed recognized as core elements in venture creation.

Gibb (2000) points to these as mythical concepts and rituals that are perpetuated through entrepreneurship research, which arguably underpin and provide rationales for EE. These concepts become ritualized through their embodiment in: '[…] ways of doing things; ways of seeing things; ways of communicating things and ways of learning things' (Gibb 2000). This in turn, drives the teaching and learning practices (rituals) – enacted and reproduced in the EE curriculum and classroom.

EE does indeed attempt to change the way that students do things, how they view the world, how they learn to do this, with an emphasis on experiential and action learning (Rae 2012). These outcomes ultimately crystallize around the present consensus on the goals of EE: 'to make changes in society via changes in individual behaviour' (Pittaway and Cope 2007, 479). In this way EE can be conceptualized as an 'Identity Transformation Organisation', something that Robbins (1988, 83) argues is also true of cults, which '[…] endeavour to create "social cocoons" through patterns of physical and/or social and/or ideological encapsulation'. In this way, EE is positioned as, not only student-transforming, but also world-transforming. EE can therefore be seen as having a purpose that reaches beyond itself – ultimately seeking to have a broader, measurable societal impact through the resulting actions of EE students, which are based upon their acceptance and adherence to the rituals of EE.

Bernstein, Elvin, and Peters (1966) make a distinction between consensual and differentiating rituals in education, with consensual rituals seeking to bind together all individuals within a particular educational institution and differentiating rituals seeking to mark groups from each other within an educational setting. In this context we can argue that EE employs differentiating rituals. This is evident in the ways that entrepreneurship educators are encouraged to use 'novel', 'new', or 'creative' approaches to teaching such as live case studies (Hynes 2007), computer simulations (Bellotti et al. 2012) and business plan pitches and competitions (Honig and Karlsson 2004). EE arguably also seeks to move students away from traditional academic or career models towards activities that will help them to think differently and behave differently from those who do not pursue EE (Krueger Jr. 2003). Educators further emphasize this different way of thinking and being by bringing in 'real' entrepreneurs (deities) into the classroom to tell their stories and invoke the 'myths […] of the community and its gods' (Friedlander 2010, 125).

Indeed, entrepreneurship training has previously been defined as a 'ritual context' (Hägg 2012) in which students transition from one status (student) to another (nascent entrepreneur). In this way EE has been likened to a 'rite of passage' (Turner 1996; Van Gennep 1960). EE thus works instrumentally in overturning the status quo to create new identities and relations. In doing so it supports the enculturation of students into an enterprise culture through displays of, and engagement with, ritual and (sacred) symbols and signifiers.

Although there is a value in offering inspiring educational programmes that give insights into a given field – in this case entrepreneurship – there seems to be a distinction to be made between this and liturgical 'entre-tainment'. Thus, educators (cultists), prepare students to enter the cult through grooming them via rituals in recognized ways of 'behaving' (Anderson and Warren 2011) or playing the role (Cornelissen 2004) of an entrepreneur. Such practices bear the scarlet letter of entrepreneurship, branding anyone who successfully performs these rituals and puts these methods into practice as closer to what HEIs and policy-makers want students to become – the successful (deified) entrepreneur.

A promise of salvation

> In the UK students pay £9000 per year for their degree and over the past decade many more people attend university (up from 10% of the population in the 1980s to nearly 50% today). This means that many more graduates are chasing fewer graduate level jobs. Entrepreneurship is increasingly seen as a way of addressing the gap in graduate, entry-level jobs by encouraging students to create their own jobs. Indeed, in 2013 self-employment/entrepreneurship was recognized as a valid form of graduate level employment. Graduate entrepreneurship is therefore seen as addressing the potential lack of graduate employment opportunities, ensuring that universities are still seen as providing successful and rewarding graduate careers. (Educator in UK)

In general, religions address themselves to the problems of individuals and the path to salvation (Campbell 1977, 380). Therefore, the beliefs and practices of a cult involve the hope of redemption and provide moral sanction and insurance of achieving it (Rey 2004). Employing the cult as a lens demonstrates EE's connection to notions of transformation and liberation at both an individual and societal level. It has been argued that entrepreneurship is important to humanity, not only as an important source of economic growth – itself a highly contested notion (Johanisova, Crabtree, and Fraňková 2013) – but also as a wellspring of personal development (Hindle 2007). As a consequence, high hopes are invested in EE as an instrument that delivers outcomes that transcend the teaching and learning situation. It is positioned as a pathway to ensure survival and success in an uncertain world. In order to face the challenges of accelerated globalization, it is considered imperative to improve economies by encouraging the start-up of new businesses as a source of innovation and new job creation (EC 2004). A high level of entrepreneurship is the suggested cure for economic stagnation (Acs and Armington 2006).

Following this established consensus, the goal of EE is to raise awareness of entrepreneurship and self-employment as a career option as well as providing skills and knowledge of how to start and run a company successfully (EC 2012). Still, the benefits of EE are not limited to boosting start-ups, innovative ventures and new jobs. Beyond their application to business activity, entrepreneurial skills and attitudes such as 'creativity and a spirit of initiative' are regarded as useful to all in their working activity and daily lives (EC 2012). In fact, European policy recognizes 'initiative' and 'entrepreneurship' as one of eight 'key competences' that *all* individuals need for personal fulfilment and development, active citizenship, social inclusion, and employment (EU 2006). Entrepreneurship thus becomes a non-negotiable, basic skill and competence for every citizen (Komulainen, Räty, and Korhonen 2009).

Consequently, EE not only supports the macro-level strive for economic growth and world-transformation; at a micro-level, it supports individual self-fulfilment and the possibility of breaking down barriers of class, race or gender (Henry, Hill, and Leitch 2003). A recent policy report argues that '[e]ntrepreneurship education seeks to prepare people to be responsible, enterprising individuals who have the attitudes, skills and knowledge necessary to achieve the goals they set for themselves to live a fulfilled life' (EC 2012). In this way, it is clear that the 'key competence' that EE cultivates is vital to a range of human endeavours.

In response EE has broadened its scope, with the understanding that an entrepreneurial mindset and its related attitudes and behaviours are life skills and thus beneficial for all students in a variety of situations, including but not limited to business start-ups (Blenker et al. 2011; Hynes and Richardson 2007). It is considered essential for all to develop an entrepreneurial mindset, because of the reality of portfolio careers, demanded flexibility in jobs, more responsibilities at work, fast advancements in technologies, and a globalized market (Gibb 2002; Henry, Hill, and Leitch 2003). EE is therefore closely linked to issues of employability (Berglund 2013) and career self-management (Bengtsson 2014). It prepares individuals for a world where they will increasingly need to manage their own careers and lives in an entrepreneurial way (Hytti and O'Gorman 2004). It enables students to settle with, or possibly even enjoy, living in a world of increased uncertainty and complexity (Gibb 2002). Consequently, entrepreneurship becomes a vision of empowerment and emancipation, transcending the conformity of waged labour, leading to a way of life where you are in control of your own destiny, reminiscent of the general 'human potential movement' identified in the literature as a generative milieu for cults (Robbins 1988). EE does not only offer descriptions of a world in which entrepreneurial skills and mindsets are important. It also offers prescriptions for action within this world and may deliver the means to acquire the ability to act. Hence, EE is constituted as a model of as well as a model for reality and behaviour, which Geertz (1973) emphasized as the basic structures of religion as a cultural system. This can also be seen as a totalizing discourse, as being entrepreneurial and enterprising is not confined to the action of setting up a business but encapsulates a way of being in the world for both organizations and individuals to which there is no alternative, given the demands of globalization.

In entrepreneurship research, scholars highlight how entrepreneurship is an ideological construct concerned with salient attitudes, values, and forms of self-understandings (Keat 1991; Peters 2001; Styhre 2005) and discuss how enterprise as a belief system ascribes positive value and provides a moral imperative to being enterprising (Du Gay 1996; Tedmanson et al. 2012). Individuals must reform themselves and become entrepreneurs of 'the self' (Rose 1999). Consequently, EE has become an instrument of transformation and emancipation that facilitates and prepares pathways to satisfaction and self-fulfilment. Following the deification of the entrepreneur, the enterprising self is cast as a character in opposition to modes of self-understandings where the self is assumed to be dependent on others and 'weak' (Heelas 1991). Hence, entrepreneurship and EE closely relate to moral virtues, imperatives and qualities of (self) responsible and respectable citizens (Berglund 2013). An important idea in Western culture is that everybody lives at his or her best when we realize and actualize what each of us are (Brinkmann 2005). In this way, EE is strongly related to a discourse and demand of self-realization. Through learning entrepreneurship and attaining an enterprising self, EE offers a road towards becoming who we 'really' are. Therefore, when the entrepreneur is portrayed as a 'saviour with no less God-like qualities than earlier saviours' (Sørensen 2008, 86), EE provides first of all the possibility for everybody to become saviours, but also the promise that everyone can save themselves.

EE and the totalizing discourse of the enterprise culture

In this paper we use the cult as a lens to explore how the institutionalization of entrepreneurship in EE involves the conveyance and reproduction of supposedly uncontested values, and beliefs. Such values and beliefs construct a monistic worldview, which prescribes not only who the entrepreneur is or can be, but also the world in which the entrepreneur operates, and what it requires to be an economically successful individual. Our consideration of the deities, rituals and salvation of entrepreneurship depicts this dominant institutionalization in EE. First, EE involves the identification and reverence of certain personalities and role models (deities) that students should aspire to become. Second, in EE students are taught to replicate behaviour through the educator's application of distinct pedagogies and practices (rituals). Third, EE promotes a professional skill set for entrepreneurship, but is also considered a life skill, which is necessary for survival and self-fulfilment (salvation). In this way we argue that EE is a context where entrepreneurship is institutionalized as an uncontested and incontestable belief system or ideological worldview, equalling Geertz's (1973) model of and model for reality. At the same time, education presumes and simultaneously constructs the world in which the entrepreneur acts. Taken together, we suggest that this forms a monistic totalizing discourse evident in a 'set of descriptions, explanations, principles, criteria of acceptability, directives or metatheories that delimit the discursive domain or systematically reduce the array of voices that can speak to any issue or state of affairs' (Gergen 2001, 52). In analysing the impact of belief systems (or ideologies) Cascardi (1999, 200) argues that the ideological is 'the will to 'totality' of any totalizing discourse'. We argue that this dominant and dominating discourse in turn creates a hidden curriculum of lessons learnt, although educators may not consciously intend this. In the following paragraphs, we discuss this hidden curriculum, and then critically reflect upon the possibilities to counteract it through pedagogical interventions.

As such, EE endorses and reproduces values and beliefs about entrepreneurship, where the deities, rituals and promise of salvation inherent in EE forming the symbolic dimensions of a hidden curriculum (Margolis et al. 2001). This hidden curriculum builds a framework of meaning that extends beyond the classroom or curriculum but is not explicitly articulated (Bernstein, Elvin, and Peters 1966). Thus, the hidden curriculum, underpinning mainstream EE, involves more than (just) lessons learnt in the classroom. It comprises lessons learnt from students' engagement with wider society or, in other words, off stage (Miller 1998). Following this, the hidden curriculum deals with the 'forces by which students are induced to comply with dominant ideologies and social practices related to authority, behaviour and morality' (McLaren 2003, 86). Accordingly, the hidden curriculum reflects the 'deeply held beliefs' of a society (Bain 1990, 29).

Importantly there are different levels of 'hiddenness' and degrees of intentionality within the hidden curriculum (Margolis 2008; Paechter 1999). By applying the cult as a lens, we highlighted the more explicit elements of the hidden curriculum in EE. Indeed, one might argue that the emphasis on becoming entrepreneurial and how this might lead to career success in responding to the uncertainties of modern, market driven societies is a very explicit aspect of the EE curriculum. Thus we have illustrated that the hidden curriculum in EE is manifested through predefined deities, carefully orchestrated rituals, and promises of salvation that are reproduced in the classroom. This 'cultification' is supported by the curriculum and the encouragement of collaboration with off-stage actors such as business networks, business angels, and the individual entrepreneurs that educators bring into the classroom. Thus, this hidden curriculum stifles consideration of the unspoken values and beliefs that underpin contemporary rationales for entrepreneurship. Such values and beliefs also extend into the public sector, social enterprise and other new areas (Nicholls 2010) to become a totalizing discourse.

Accordingly, little scope is provided for imagining how entrepreneurship can be enacted towards alternative futures or non-economic outcomes. Therefore, at a deeper level of hiddenness, or simply less explicit, the hidden curriculum crystallizes around a totalizing discourse of entrepreneurship. As a totalizing discourse, the hidden curriculum of EE instils taken-for-granted notions about entrepreneurship as a universal and intrinsic good, which will lead to salvation and the promised land of individual and national success, wealth and status for the chosen. This makes it difficult, if not impossible, to question why entrepreneurship is to be promoted. Consequently, there is a risk that educators respond to the accepted and acceptable 'rules of the game' (Bourdieu 1977). Hanks (2005, 78) suggests that 'what is valued is what fits the demands of the field, and the effective producer is the one best attuned to the field'. This increases the likelihood of success and reward for educators who perpetuate established notions and discourses linked to entrepreneurship, particularly when judged against changes in student aspirations for entrepreneurship and the effects on enterprising activities. However, we suggest that such aspirations are not built upon a balanced exposure to entrepreneurship. Instead they are the result of the cult-like pronouncements and framings as suggested above.

The monistic worldview inherent in such a totalizing discourse undermines the importance and values of HE, as it provides a form of moral education, transmitting a set of expectations and obligations of being in an ever-changing world. Indeed, one of the suggested roles of the hidden curriculum is to send 'a silent, but powerful message to students with regard to their intellectual ability, personal traits, and the appropriate occupational choice' (Margolis 2008, 440). Warnock (1984) suggests all moral education must be by means of the hidden curriculum, and it is further suggested that moral education can only be taught by example (Portelli 1993). This approach is highly prevalent in EE teaching, which uses case studies, draws upon entrepreneur biographies, characteristics and behaviours (for example those of Richard Branson and Steve Jobs) and brings entrepreneurs into the classroom, all the while encouraging students to learn from, and imitate, their example. Wilson (1985) argues that when we link learning by example with certain disciplines we risk losing the cognitive or intellectual element in more practically orientated disciplines, such as EE, suggesting that critical intellectual engagement is not necessary for entrepreneurial success. This suggests students in EE are studying a discipline that values the practical and experiential over the critical and intellectual, undermining the importance and value of a HE.

Thus, EE should have an interest in addressing and challenging the hidden curriculum, instilling reflexive practices that increase educators' and students' ability and readiness to critically reflect on the very same frameworks of meaning, and the totalizing discourse, they are constrained by. Through this, students could become more active and critical agents, engaging with the underpinning beliefs and values of entrepreneurship. This could also develop future entrepreneurs who are in the position to locally challenge a belief system that they themselves have become a part of (Martin 1976).

Escaping a cult: encouraging critical and reflective approaches in EE

Some criticize the concept of a hidden curriculum as underplaying the agency of both educators and students (Margolis 2008). While the concept of the hidden curriculum can highlight and describe some of the unintended consequences of teaching and learning, scholars could do more to explore means of resistance and challenge that do not position people as passive recipients of such hidden learning. Despite being constrained by institutional expectations to reproduce unspoken values and beliefs, educators occupy a unique position to develop challenging, diverse, accessible, and critical approaches to entrepreneurship in both the classroom and through curricula. Through their practices in a local context, educators can (and sometimes already do) highlight and challenge the hidden curriculum and make way for alternative framings of entrepreneurship (Steyaert and Katz 2004). Considerations of how the student lifeworld might be supported, undermined or ignored by the current cult-like framings of entrepreneurship could support a critical and reflective approach to entrepreneurship and strengthen educators' agency in confronting the hidden curriculum. However, this requires an approach to teaching and learning as reflexive practice to 'examin[e] critically the assumptions underlying our actions, [and] the impact of those actions' (Cunliffe 2004, 407). Summarized in Table 1, reflexive practices could assist in counteracting the effects of the hidden curriculum. The columns describe the unfolding of the hidden curriculum (column 1 and 2) and how it could be counteracted by educational interventions (column 3 and 4); the rows describe the cult elements previously outlined.

The dominant belief system that currently drives the institutionalization process could be addressed by strengthening the agency of both educators and the students. At the moment the entrepreneur is privileged in the classroom, even above the teacher and the student. This hierarchy emphasizes the god-like status of the entrepreneur and trumps both student and educator. By inverting this hierarchy and starting with the student, rather than the entrepreneur, we may subvert this tendency to privilege the entrepreneur in the classroom. In encouraging students to consider different types of entrepreneurship, especially those that challenge normative templates of the lone, heroic, profit-focused entrepreneur we also offer an environment where different approaches can be compared. To move beyond such profit-led and individualistic accounts we might introduce contexts and examples where entrepreneurship is positioned as consensus-based decision-making and the exploitation of opportunities for society. Such alternative constructions and contexts could include collective entrepreneurship, for instance location-based entrepreneurial activities initiated between community members (Somerville and McElwee 2011) or self-managed, politically-motivated workers' co-ops (Kokkinidis 2015), or contexts such as social entrepreneurship, where wealth creation is a means to an end and not an end in itself. Such approaches could support the development of 'more inclusive models of participation and the construction of rule-creating rather than rule-following individuals' (Kokkinidis 2015, 847). We therefore do not simply exchange one cult for another but open up possibilities for our students to critically reflect, rather than closing down such opportunities. Students may well choose to

Table 1. The unfolding of the hidden curriculum and critically reflective responses.

Hidden curriculum: Belief system underlying the cult in EE suggest that …	Unfolding of hidden curriculum in EE: Institutionalization of the entrepreneur as a …	A call for reflexive practices: To counteract the hidden curriculum, educators must develop environments where …	Examples of teaching and learning interventions
Entrepreneurs are the most important actors in the business world (deities)	Societal hero (Omnipotent, Value-Providers for Society)	Contextual relevance, and facets of entrepreneurial practices are introduced (the dark side, productive and unproductive, even mundane forms)	Suspending hierarchy between student/teacher and 'the entrepreneur'; Starting with the student lifeworld, not the entrepreneur, in designing learning interventions; Bring in collective and non-profit forms of enterprising.
Successful entrepreneurs show us the behaviour to follow (rituals)	Archetype of behaviour	Individual differences in behaviour and personality are appreciated and understood as a value/starting point for entrepreneurship education	Active falsification of normative ideas; create a safe learning environment; encourage students to find cases that differ from the mainstream; being allowed to fail – emphasize learning rather than ways to reach a specific outcome (e.g. the business plan and idea can be a 'failure' without students failing the class)
Individuals can reach emancipation, self-realization and find true happiness through enterprise (salvation)	Possessor of the right mindset	Students are empowered to accept the role of critical agents, questioning beliefs and practices in and about entrepreneurship	Bring student lifeworlds into the classroom; honour multiple perspectives and alternate ideologies

pursue and aspire to follow the traditional belief system of entrepreneurship but at least this agency is informed by, and enacted from, a point of critical reflection.

We recognize that we cannot easily escape mainstream values and beliefs and the totalizing discourse of entrepreneurship, as they so firmly underpin teaching in HE. However, we suggest that it is not a case of 'either/or' but 'both/and' and that educators could offer alternatives and challenges to this dominant belief system. In this way, EE would fulfil the aims of HE to encourage critical thinking and intellectual agency, which subverts the students' taken-for-granted world and helps them to see that 'things could always be other than they are' (Barnett 1990, 155).

Such critical and reflective approaches demand critical and reflective teaching practices. Critical pedagogy provides a vehicle to instil reflective practices as it actively seeks to highlight and address the hidden curriculum (Giroux and Giroux 2006). Critical pedagogy therefore offers a useful point of departure for educators who wish to critically engage – and encourage their students to critically engage – with the political, social, and societal norms that underpin the current drive for EE. It offers the potential to move away from a pedagogy that emphasizes deities, rituals and the promise of salvation of entrepreneurship to one that acknowledges historical and sociopolitical developments and how these have combined to create a vision of the 'true entrepreneur' and the 'right' way of being. Critical pedagogy could, therefore, provide opportunities for students and educators to work together, to co-produce knowledge, which highlights and contextualizes the diversity and possibilities of EE and takes account of the student lifeworld. However, as educators we must do this in a way that takes account of the power dynamics of the educator–student relationship and also the potential for us to merely exchange one cult for another.

Critical pedagogy can help educators and students to focus on the possibilities of education to challenge inequality and investigate dominant fictions (Keesing-Styles 2003) rather than encouraging students' oblivious acceptance of an extant hidden curriculum (Shor and Freire 1987). Critical pedagogy emphasizes that values, beliefs and unspoken social norms are not ahistorical or politically neutral entities and through contesting these further insight may be reached. This can be achieved by bringing the student lifeworld into the classroom and by reflective educators engaging with modes of knowledge production that question whose knowledge is privileged in the classroom.

In calling for reflexive approaches we argue that the current educational environment in which we find ourselves, lends little scope for staff or students to reflect on their own attitudes and positioning. In the apparent rush to produce more entrepreneurs, and entrepreneurial citizens, the acknowledgement of how entrepreneurship is framed, who is suggested as being successful, how this success is manifested and encouraged – indeed worshipped – is rarely discussed. Consequently, there is an important gap in our knowledge, given the suggested imperative to embed EE in all education at all levels (Herrmann 2008). Using the cult as a lens ultimately helps us to articulate and respond reflexively to a fundamental discussion embedded in any given teaching setting: what kind of engagement do we, as teachers want to stimulate? (Kyrö 2006) This encompasses the spoken and unspoken values and beliefs of educators, students and wider society.

Concluding thoughts

This study provides a critical perspective on the institutionalization of entrepreneurship in EE as a belief system. We make the candid claim, that by using the cult as an analytical lens, we are able to position ourselves outside normativity and expose the unfolding of a hidden curriculum in EE. However, we recognize that this paper offers one approach to viewing EE through a different lens that could be used to support alternative analyses. Hence, even though notions of enlightenment inform our critique, it should be noted that we neither position educators nor students as unthinking perpetrators or passive victims in this context. Having discussed unchallenged assumptions institutionalized as a belief system in and through education, we encourage future critical engagement with the institutionalization of entrepreneurship within and beyond education. We hope that our paper animates educators, researchers and policy-makers to continued critical examination of the role of EE in perpetuating or challenging the taken-for-granted beliefs that underpin entrepreneurship as a societal phenomenon. The novel method employed in this paper also offers a point of resistance to a 'cultification' of entrepreneurship in EE.

Recognizing the risk of being arbiters (and evangelists) and thereby complicit in the enculturation of our students into such uncontested values and beliefs of wider society (Giroux 2011), entrepreneurship educators could locally enact reflective practices to counteract a hidden curriculum. However, we do not intend to replace one approach to EE with another and develop our own cult. Instead we call for developing a number of alternative approaches to 'doing' entrepreneurship, through critical reflection on the underpinning system of values and beliefs. Future research could for instance investigate, beyond providing anecdotal evidence through vignettes, whether mainstream EE risks the creation of a conceptual metaphor (Lakoff and Johnson 1980a, 1980b), by promoting a belief system rather than a field of science. Quantitative metaphor analysis (Lachaud 2013) could further our understanding of what students understand by 'entrepreneurial' and 'entrepreneurship' as in (Dodd, Jack, and Anderson 2013). Likewise, researchers could highlight and explore the values underpinning, for example, social, sustainable, and community entrepreneurship, and in doing so emphasize the diversity of political, social and economic possibilities and their intertwined nature. 'In this sense, the act of escaping does not refer to quietism and passivity or a retreat from the economic sphere, but to exploring workable alternatives within capitalism' (Kokkinidis 2015, 867).

We recognize the proposed approaches would be implemented locally through individual educators, and there are dangers that it could result in EE not being recognized as such by the larger audience of policy-makers, education administrators, industry leaders and community collaborators. In turn this could lead to a crisis of legitimacy, as adopting this eclectic approach means that EE no longer provides a unified answer to the fundamental societal problems of unemployment and continuous economic growth. Entrepreneurship educators that adopt a critical reflective approach may even run the risk of being penalized, as the curriculum would not conform to the current institutionalization of entrepreneurship. However, what is hidden can rarely be challenged. In exposing and questioning the hidden beliefs and values of EE we propose a starting point for a broader debate about what it is that we are *actually* teaching when we teach EE. This is an important consideration, not only for educators, but also for policy-makers, researchers and related communities. To ignore this is to be complicit in the reproduction of a hidden curriculum that produces conflict and tension for more reflective and critical educators and could ultimately prove counterproductive in developing and promoting the diversity and accessibility of entrepreneurship.

Acknowledgements

We thank Codrin Kruijne who contributed to the early development of this paper. We received valuable feedback on earlier versions of the paper from Peter L. Jennings and Paula Kyrö. We would also like to thank the editors and the two anonymous reviewers for their insightful commentary and constructive revisions work. Signe Hedeboe Frederiksen and Martin Hannibal were generously sponsored by the Innovation Fund Denmark and carried out within the PACE project (http://www.mgmt.au.dk/pace).

Disclosure statement

No potential conflict of interest was reported by the authors.

References

Acs, Zoltan J., and Catherine Armington. 2006. *Entrepreneurship, Geography, and American Economic Growth*. Cambridge: Cambridge University Press.
Anderson, Alistair R., and Lorraine Warren. 2011. "The Entrepreneur as Hero and Jester: Enacting the Entrepreneurial Discourse." *International Small Business Journal* 29 (6): 589–609. doi:10.1177/0266242611416417.
Anderson, Alistair R., and Sarah L. Jack. 2008. "Role Typologies for Enterprising Education: The Professional Artisan?" *Journal of Small Business and Enterprise Development* 15 (2): 259–273.

Bain, Linda L. 1990. "A Critical Analysis of the Hidden Curriculum in Physical Education." In *Physical Education, Curriculum and Culture: Critical Issues in the Contemporary Crisis*, edited by D. Kirk and R. Tinning, 23–42. Basingstoke: Falmer Press.

Barnett, Ronald. 1990. *The Idea of Higher Education*. Buckingham: Society for Research into Higher Education and Open University Press.

Belk, Russell, and Gülnur Tumbat. 2005. "The Cult of Macintosh." *Consumption Markets & Culture* 8 (3): 205–217. doi:10.1080/10253860500160403.

Bellotti, F., R. Berta, A. De Gloria, E. Lavagnino, F. Dagnino, M. Ott, M. Romero, et al. 2012. "Designing a Course for Stimulating Entrepreneurship in Higher Education through Serious Games." *Procedia Computer Science* 15: 174–186. doi:10.1016/j.procs.2012.10.069.

Bengtsson, Anki. 2014. "Enterprising Career Education: The Power of Self-Management." *International Journal of Lifelong Education* 33 (3): 362–375. doi:10.1080/02601370.2014.896085.

Berger, Peter L., and Thomas Luckmann. 1966. *The Social Construction of Reality: A Treatise in the Sociology of Knowledge*. London: Penguin Books.

Berglund, Karin. 2013. "Fighting against All Odds: Entrepreneurship Education as Employability Training." *Ephemera* 13 (4): 717–735.

Berglund, Karin, and Anders W. Johansson. 2007. "Constructions of Entrepreneurship: A Discourse Analysis of Academic Publications." *Journal of Enterprising Communities: People and Places in the Global Economy* 1 (1): 77–102.

Bernstein, B., H. L. Elvin, and R. S. Peters. 1966. "Ritual in Education." *Philosophical Transactions of the Royal Society B: Biological Sciences* 251 (772): 429–436.

Blank, Steven Gary, and Bob Dorf. 2012. *The Startup Owner's Manual: The Step-by-Step Guide for Building a Great Company*. Pescadero, CA: K&S Ranch, Incorporated.

Blenker, Per, Signe Hedeboe Frederiksen, Steffen Korsgaard, Sabine Muller, Helle Neergaard, and Claus Thrane. 2012. "Entrepreneurship as Everyday Practice: Towards a Personalized Pedagogy of Enterprise Education." *Industry and Higher Education* 26 (6): 417–430.

Blenker, Per, Steffen Korsgaard, Helle Neergaard, and Claus Thrane. 2011. "The Questions We Care about: Paradigms and Progression in Entrepreneurship Education." *Industry and Higher Education* 25 (6): 417–427. doi:10.5367/ihe.2011.0065.

Bourdieu, Pierre. 1977. *Outline of a Theory of Practice*. Vol. 16. Cambridge: Cambridge University Press.

Brinkmann, Svend. 2005. "Selvrealiserings Etik." Ethics of Self-Realisation. In *Selvrealisering: Kritiske Diskussioner Af En Grænseløs Udviklingskultur* [Self-Realisation: Critical Discussions of a Boundless Culture of Development], edited by S. Brinkmann and C. Eriksen, 41–64. Aarhus: Klim.

Campbell, Colin. 1977. "Clarifying the Cult." *The British Journal of Sociology* 28 (3): 375–388.

Cascardi, Anthony J. 1999. *Consequences of Enlightenment*. Vol. 30. Cambridge: Cambridge University Press.

Cornelissen, Joep P. 2004. "What Are We Playing at? Theatre, Organization, and the Use of Metaphor." *Organization Studies* 25 (5): 705–726. doi:10.1177/0170840604042411.

Cunliffe, Ann L. 2004. "On Becoming a Critically Reflexive Practitioner." *Journal of Management Education* 28 (4): 407–426.

Delamont, Sara, Paul Atkinson, and Lesley Pugsley. 2010. "The Concept Smacks of Magic: Fighting Familiarity Today." *Teaching and Teacher Education* 26 (1): 3–10.

Deutschmann, Christoph. 2001. "Capitalism as a Religion? An Unorthodox Analysis of Entrepreneurship." *European Journal of Social Theory* 4 (4): 387–403.

Dodd, Sarah D., Alistair R. Anderson. 2007. "Mumpsimus and the Mything of the Individualistic Entrepreneur." *International Small Business Journal* 25 (4): 341–360. doi:10.1177/0266242607072561.

Dodd, Sarah D., and Paul T. Seaman. 1998. "Religion and Enterprise: An Introductory Exploration." *Entrepreneurship* 23 (1): 71–86.

Dodd, Sarah D., Sarah Jack, and Alistair R. Anderson. 2013. "From Admiration to Abhorrence: The Contentious Appeal of Entrepreneurship across Europe." *Entrepreneurship & Regional Development* 25 (1–2): 69–89.

Down, Simon, and Lorraine Warren. 2008. "Constructing Narratives of Enterprise: Clichés and Entrepreneurial Self-Identity." *International Journal of Entrepreneurial Behaviour & Research* 14 (1): 4–23.

Du Gay, Paul. 1996. *Consumption and Identity at Work*. London: Sage.

Du Gay, Paul, and Graeme Salaman. 1992. "The Cult[Ure] of the Customer." *Journal of Management Studies* 29 (5): 615–633. doi:10.1111/j.1467-6486.1992.tb00681.x.

Durkheim, Emile. 2001. *The Elementary Forms of Religious Life*. Oxford: Oxford University Press.

EC (Commission of the European Communities). 2004. *Action Plan: The European Agenda for Entrepreneurship*. Brussels: European Commission. http://cordis.europa.eu/pub/incubators/docs/action_plan_on_entrepreneurship.pdf.

EC (European Commission). 2012. *Effects and Impact of Entrepreneurship Programmes in Higher Education*. Brussels: Directorate-General for Enterprise and Industry.

Ehrensal, Kenneth N. 2001. "Training Capitalism's Foot Soldiers: The Hidden Curriculum of Undergraduate Business Education." In *The Hidden Curriculum in Higher Education*, edited by E. Margolis, 97–114. New York: Routledge.

EU (European Union). 2006. "Recommendation of the European Parliament and of the Council of 18 December 2006 on Key Competences for Lifelong Learning." *Official Journal of the European Union* 49 (L394): 10–18.

Fayolle, Alain. 2013. "Personal Views on the Future of Entrepreneurship Education." *Entrepreneurship & Regional Development* 25 (7–8): 692–701.

Friedlander, Larry. 2010. "Sacred Geographies: Myth and Ritual in Serious Games." In *Interdisciplinary Models and Tools for Serious Games: Emerging Concepts and Future Directions*, edited by R. Van Eck, 125–146. Hershey, PA: Information Science Reference.

Gair, M., and G. Mullins. 2001. *Hiding in Plain Sight*. New York: Routledge.

Gallagher, Eugene V. 2007. "'Cults' and 'New Religious Movements.'" *History of Religions* 47 (2): 205–220. doi:10.1086/524210.

Gartner, William B. 1988. "Who is an Entrepreneur? Is the Wrong Question." *American Journal of Small Business* 12 (4): 11–32.

Gartner, William B. 1989. "Some Suggestions for Research on Entrepreneurial Traits and Characteristics." *Entrepreneurship Theory and Practice* 14 (1): 27–38.

Geertz, Clifford. 1973. *The Interpretation of Cultures: Selected Essays*. New York: Basic Books.

Gergen, Kenneth J. 2001. *Social Construction in Context*. London: Sage.

Gibb, Allan A. 2000. "SME Policy, Academic Research and the Growth of Ignorance, Mythical Concepts, Myths, Assumptions, Rituals and Confusions." *International Small Business Journal* 18 (3): 13–35. doi:10.1177/0266242600183001.

Gibb, Allan. 2002. "In Pursuit of a New 'enterprise' and 'entrepreneurship' Paradigm for Learning: Creative Destruction, New Values, New Ways of Doing Things and New Combinations of Knowledge." *International Journal of Management Reviews* 4 (3): 233–269. doi:10.1111/1468-2370.00086.

Giddens, Anthony, and Philip W. Sutton. 2009. *Sociology*. Cambridge: Cambridge Polity Press.

Giesen, Bernhard. 2005. "Performing Transcendence in Politics: Sovereignty, Deviance, and the Void of Meaning." *Sociological Theory* 23 (3): 275–285.

Giroux, Henry A. 2011. *On Critical Pedagogy*. Vol. 1. New York: Continuum.

Giroux, Henry A., and Susan S. Giroux. 2006. "Challenging Neoliberalism's New World Order: The Promise of Critical Pedagogy." *Cultural Studies ↔ Critical Methodologies* 6 (1): 21-32.

Gomez, Pierre-Yves, and Harry Korine. 2008. *Entrepreneurs and Democracy: A Political Theory of Corporate Governance*. Cambridge: Cambridge University Press.

Goody, Jack. 1977. "Against "Ritual": Loosely Structured Thoughts on a Loosely Defined Topic." In *Secular Ritual*, edited by S. F. Moore and B. G. Myerhoff, 25–35. Amsterdam: van Gorkum.

Hägg, Outi. 2012. "Ritual Pedagogy in Entrepreneurial Identity Development." Paper presented at the EURAM, Rotterdam, The Netherlands, June 6–8.

Hallett, Tim. 2010. "The Myth Incarnate: Recoupling Processes, Turmoil, and Inhabited Institutions in an Urban Elementary School." *American Sociological Review* 75 (1): 52–74. doi:10.1177/0003122409357044.

Hanks, William F. 2005. "Pierre Bourdieu and the Practices of Language." *Annual Review of Anthropology* 34: 67–83. doi:10.1146/annurev.anthro.33.070203.143907.

Hannon, Paul D. 2005. "Philosophies of Enterprise and Entrepreneurship Education and Challenges for Higher Education in the UK." *The International Journal of Entrepreneurship and Innovation* 6 (2): 105–114. doi:10.5367/0000000053966876.

Heelas, Paul. 1991. "Reforming the Self: Enterprise and the Characters of Thatcherism." In *Enterprise Culture*, edited by R. Keat and N. Abercrombie, 72–90. London: Routledge.

Heelas, Paul. 1996. *The New Age Movement: The Celebration of the Self and the Sacralization of Modernity*. Cambridge, MA: Blackwell.

Henry, Colette, Frances Hill, and Claire Leitch. 2003. *Entrepreneurship Education and Training*. Aldershot: Ashgate.

Henry, Colette, Frances Hill, and Claire Leitch. 2005. "Entrepreneurship Education and Training: Can Entrepreneurship Be Taught? Part I." *Education + Training* 47 (2): 98-111. doi:10.1108/00400910510586524.

Herrmann, Keith. 2008. *Developing Entrepreneurial Graduates: Putting Entrepreneurship at the Centre of Higher Education*. London: NESTA.

Hindle, Kevin. 2007. "Teaching Entrepreneurship at University: From the Wrong Building to the Right Philosophy." In *Handbook of Research in Entrepreneurship Education: A General Perspective*, edited by A. Fayolle, 104–126. Cheltenham: Edward Elgar.

Holmgren, Carina, and Jorgen From. 2005. "Taylorism of the Mind: Entrepreneurship Education from a Perspective of Educational Research." *European Educational Research Journal* 4 (4): 382–390. doi:10.2304/eerj.2005.4.4.4.

Honig, Benson, and Tomas Karlsson. 2004. "Institutional Forces and the Written Business Plan." *Journal of Management* 30 (1): 29–48. doi:10.1016/j.jm.2002.11.002.

Huggins, Robert. 2008. "Universities and Knowledge-Based Venturing: Finance, Management and Networks in London." *Entrepreneurship & Regional Development* 20 (2): 185–206. doi:10.1080/08985620701748342.

Hynes, Briga. 2007. "Creating an Entrepreneurial Mindset: Getting the Process Right for Information and Communication Technology Students." In *Information Systems and Technology Education: From the University to the Workplace*, edited by G. R. Lowry and R. L. Turner, 105–127. Hershey, PA: Information Science Reference.

Hynes, Briga, and Ita Richardson. 2007. "Entrepreneurship Education: A Mechanism for Engaging and Exchanging with the Small Business Sector." *Education + Training* 49 (8–9): 732–744. doi:10.1108/00400910710834120.

Hytti, Ulla, and Colm O'Gorman. 2004. "What is "Enterprise Education"? an Analysis of the Objectives and Methods of Enterprise Education Programmes in Four European Countries." *Education + Training* 46 (1): 11–23. doi:10.1108/00400910410518188.

Jepperson, Ronald L. 1991. "Institutions, Institutional Effects, and Institutionalism." In *The New Institutionalism in Organizational Analysis*, edited by Walter W. Powell and Paul J. DeMaggio, 143–163. Chicago, IL: University of Chicago Press.

Johanisova, Nadia, Tim Crabtree, and Eva Fraňková. 2013. "Social Enterprises and Non-Market Capitals: A Path to Degrowth?" *Journal of Cleaner Production* 38: 7–16.

Jones, Sally. 2014. "Gendered Discourses of Entrepreneurship in UK Higher Education: The Fictive Entrepreneur and the Fictive Student." *International Small Business Journal* 32 (3): 237–258. doi:10.1177/0266242612453933.

Jost, John T., Christopher M. Federico, and Jaime L. Napier. 2008. "Political Ideology: Its Structure, Functions, and Elective Affinities." *Annual Review of Psychology* 60 (1): 307–337. doi:10.1146/annurev.psych.60.110707.163600.

Kaplan, Steven N., Berk A. Sensoy, and P. E. R. Strömberg. 2009. "Should Investors Bet on the Jockey or the Horse? Evidence from the Evolution of Firms from Early Business Plans to Public Companies." *The Journal of Finance* 64 (1): 75–115. doi:10.1111/j.1540-6261.2008.01429.x.

Kaufmann, Patrick J., and Rajiv P. Dant. 1999. "Franchising and the Domain of Entrepreneurship Research." *Journal of Business Venturing* 14 (1): 5–16. doi:10.1016/S0883-9026(97)00095-5.

Keat, Russell. 1991. "Introduction: Starship Britain or Universal Enterprise?" In *Enterprise Culture*, edited by Russell Keat and Nicholas Abercrombie, 1–17. London: Routledge.

Keesing-Styles, Linda. 2003. "The Relationship between Critical Pedagogy and Assessment in Teacher Education." *Radical Pedagogy* 5 (1): 1–20.

Kokkinidis, George. 2015. "Spaces of Possibilities: Workers' Self-Management in Greece." *Organization* 22 (6): 847–871.

Komulainen, Katri, Hannu Räty, and Maija Korhonen. 2009. "Risk-Taking Abilities for Everyone? Finnish Entrepreneurship Education and the Enterprising Selves Imagined by Pupils." *Gender and Education* 21 (6): 631–649. doi:10.1080/09540250802680032.

Krueger Jr., Norris F. 2003. "The Cognitive Psychology of Entrepreneurship." In *Handbook of Entrepreneurship Research: An Interdisciplinary Survey and Introduction*, edited by Z. J. Acs and D. B. Audretsch, 105–140. Boston, MA: Kluwer Academic.

Kuratko, Donald F. 2005. "The Emergence of Entrepreneurship Education: Development, Trends, and Challenges." *Entrepreneurship Theory and Practice* 29 (5): 577–598. doi:10.1111/j.1540-6520.2005.00099.x.

Kyrö, Paula. 2005. "Entrepreneurial Learning in a Cross-Cultural Context Challenges Previous Learning Paradigms." *The Dynamics of Learning Entrepreneurship in a Cross-Cultural University Context. Entrepreneurship Education Series* 2: 68-102.

Kyrö, Paula. 2006. "The Continental and Anglo-American Approaches to Entrepreneurship Education—Differences and Bridges." In *International Entrepreneurship Education - Issues and Newness*, edited by A. Fayolle, 93–111. Cheltenham: Edward Elgar.

Lachaud, Christian Michel. 2013. "Conceptual Metaphors and Embodied Cognition: EEG Coherence Reveals Brain Activity Differences between Primary and Complex Conceptual Metaphors during Comprehension." *Cognitive Systems Research* 22: 12–26.

Lakoff, George, and Mark Johnson. 1980a. "Conceptual Metaphor in Everyday Language." *The Journal of Philosophy* 77 (8): 453–486.

Lakoff, George, and Mark Johnson. 1980b. "The Metaphorical Structure of the Human Conceptual System." *Cognitive Science* 4 (2): 195–208.

Landström, Hans, Gouya Harirchi, and Fredrik Åström. 2012. "Entrepreneurship: Exploring the Knowledge Base." *Research Policy* 41 (7): 1154–1181. doi:10.1016/j.respol.2012.03.009.

Landström, Hans, and Mats Benner. 2013. "Entrepreneurship Research: A History of Scholarly Migration." In *Historical Foundations of Entrepreneurship Research*, edited by Hans Landström and Franz Lohrke, 15–45. Cheltenham: Edward Elgar.

Lewis, Patricia, and Nick Llewellyn. 2004. "Enterprise and Entrepreneurial Identity." *International Journal of Entrepreneurship and Innovation* 5 (1): 5–8. doi:10.5367/000000004772913737.

Margolis, E. 2008. "Hidden Curriculum." In *Encyclopedia of Social Problems*, edited by V. N. Parrillo, 440–441. Thousand Oaks, CA: Sage.

Margolis, E., M. Soldatenko, S. Acker, and M. Gair. 2001. "Peekaboo: Hiding and Outlining the Curriculum." In *Teh Hidden Curriculum in Higher Education*, edited by E. Margolis, 1–20. New York: Routledge.

Martin, Jane R. 1976. "What Should We Do with a Hidden Curriculum When We Find One?" *Curriculum Inquiry* 6 (2): 135–151.

McClelland, David C. 1961. *The Achieving Society*. New York: The Free Press.

McLaren, Peter. 1999. *Schooling as a Ritual Performance: Towards a Political Economy of Educational Symbols and Gestures*. New York: Rowman & Littlefield.

McLaren, Peter. 2003. "Critical Pedagogy: A Look at the Major Concepts." In *The Critical Pedagogy Reader*, edited by A. Darder, M. P. Baltodano and R. D. Torres, 61–83. London: Routledge.

Miller, Richard E. 1998. "The Arts of Complicity: Pragmatism and the Culture of Schooling." *College English* 61 (1): 10–28.

Mwasalwiba, Ernest S. 2012. "Entrepreneurship Education: A Review of Its Objectives, Teaching Methods, and Impact Indicators." *IEEE Engineering Management Review* 40 (2): 72–94. doi:10.1109/EMR.2012.6210519.

de Nebesky-Wojkowitz, René. 1956. *Oracles and Demons of Tibet. The Cult and Iconography of the Tibetan Protective Deities*. The Hague: Mouton.

Nicholls, Alex. 2010. "The Legitimacy of Social Entrepreneurship: Reflexive Isomorphism in a Pre-Paradigmatic Field." *Entrepreneurship: Theory and Practice* 34 (4): 611-633. doi: 10.1111/j.1540-6520.2010.00397.x.

Nicholson, Louise, and Alistair R. Anderson. 2005. "News and Nuances of the Entrepreneurial Myth and Metaphor: Linguistic Games in Entrepreneurial Sense-Making and Sense-Giving." *Entrepreneurship Theory and Practice* 29 (2): 153–172.

OECD. 2009. *Evaluation of Programmes concerning Education for Entrepreneurship. OECD Working Party on SMEs and Entrepreneurship.* OECD. https://www.oecd.org/cfe/42890085.pdf.

Ogbor, John O. 2000. "Mythicizing and Reification in Entrepreneurial Discourse: Ideology-Critique of Entrepreneurial Studies." *Journal of Management Studies* 37 (5): 605–635. doi:10.1111/1467-6486.00196.

Ong, Aihwa. 2006. *Neoliberalism as Exception: Mutations in Citizenship and Sovereignty.* Durham, NC: Duke University Press.

Osterwalder, Alexander, and Yves Pigneur. 2010. *Business Model Generation: A Handbook for Visionaries, Game Changers, and Challengers.* Hoboken, NJ: John Wiley & Sons.

Paechter, Carrie. 1999. "Issues in the Study of Curriculum in the Context of Lifelong Learning." Paper presented at the annual meeting of the British Educational Research Association, Brighton, England, September 2–5.

Peters, M. 2001. "Education, Enterprise Culture and the Entrepreneurial Self: A Foucauldian Perspective." *Journal of Educational Enquiry* 2 (2): 58–71.

Pittaway, Luke, and Jason Cope. 2007. "Entrepreneurship Education: A Systematic Review of the Evidence." *International Small Business Journal* 25 (5): 479–510. doi:10.1177/0266242607080656.

Portelli, John P. 1993. "Exposing the Hidden Curriculum." *Journal of Curriculum Studies* 25 (4): 343–358.

Rae, David. 2010. "Universities and Enterprise Education: Responding to the Challenges of the New Era." *Journal of Small Business and Enterprise Development* 17 (4): 591–606.

Rae, David. 2012. "Action Learning in New Creative Ventures." *International Journal of Entrepreneurial Behaviour & Research* 18 (5): 603–623.

Ramoglou, Stratos. 2013. "Who is a 'non-Entrepreneur'?: Taking the 'others' of Entrepreneurship Seriously." *International Small Business Journal* 31 (4): 432–453. doi:10.1177/0266242611425838.

Rasmussen, Erik S., Martin Hannibal, Rene Lydiksen, and Per Servais. 2011. "Sub-Suppliers in the Life Science Industry: The Case of Two Danish University Spin-Offs." In *Life Science New Ventures: Local Players on a Global Stage*, edited by M. Jones and C. Wheeler, 159–174. Cheltenham: Edward Elgar.

Rehn, A., M. Brannback, A. Carsrud, and M. Lindahl. 2013. "Challenging the Myths of Entrepreneurship?" *Entrepreneurship & Regional Development* 25 (7–8): 543–551. doi:10.1080/08985626.2013.818846.

Rey, Terry. 2004. "Marketing the Goods of Salvation: Bourdieu on Religion." *Religion* 34 (4): 331–343.

Ries, Eric. 2011. *The Lean Startup: How Today's Entrepreneurs Use Continuous Innovation to Create Radically Successful Businesses.* New York: Crown Pub.

Robbins, Thomas. 1988. *Cults, Converts and Charisma: The Sociology of New Religious Movements.* Thousand Oaks, CA: Sage Publications.

Robinson, Sarah, and Per Blenker. 2014. "Tensions between Rhetoric and Practice in Entrepreneurship Education; an Ethnography from Danish Higher Education." *European Journal of Higher Education* 4 (1): 80–93.

Rose, Nikolas. 1999. *Governing the Soul: The Shaping of the Private Self.* London: Free Association Books.

Schumpeter, Joseph A. 1934. *The Œtheory of Economic Development: An Inquiry into Profits, Capital, Credit, Interest, and the Business Cycle.* Oxford: Oxford University Press.

Shane, Scott, and Sankaran Venkataraman. 2000. "The Promise of Entrepreneurship as a Field of Research." *Academy of Management Review* 25 (1): 217–226. doi:10.2307/259271.

Shor, Ira, and Paulo Freire. 1987. *A Pedagogy for Liberation: Dialogues on Transforming Education.* Westport, CT: Greenwood Publishing Group.

Singer, Margaret Thaler. 2003. *Cults in Our midst: The Continuing Fight against Their Hidden Menace.* San Francisco, CA: Jossey-Bass.

Somerville, Peter, and Gerard McElwee. 2011. "Situating Community Enterprise: A Theoretical Exploration." *Entrepreneurship & Regional Development* 23 (5–6): 317–330.

Sørensen, Bent Meier. 2008. "'Behold, I Am Making All Things New': The Entrepreneur as Savior in the Age of Creativity." *Scandinavian Journal of Management* 24 (2): 85–93. doi:10.1016/j.scaman.2008.03.002.

Stevenson, Howard H., and J. Carlos Jarillo. 1990. "A Paradigm of Entrepreneurship: Entrepreneurial Management." *Strategic Management Journal* 11 (5): 17–27.

Steyaert, Chris, and Jerome Katz. 2004. "Reclaiming the Space of Entrepreneurship in Society: Geographical, Discursive and Social Dimensions." *Entrepreneurship & Regional Development* 16 (3): 179–196. doi:10.1080/0898562042000197135.

Styhre, Alexander. 2005. "Ideology and the Subjectification of the Entrepreneurial Self." *International Journal of Management Concepts and Philosophy* 1 (2): 168–173.

Swail, Janine, Simon Down, and Teemu Kautonen. 2013. "Examining the Effect of 'Entre-Tainment' as a Cultural Influence on Entrepreneurial Intentions." *International Small Business Journal* 32 (8): 869–875. doi:10.1177/0266242613480193.

Tedmanson, Deirdre, Karen Verduyn, Caroline Essers, and William B. Gartner. 2012. "Critical Perspectives in Entrepreneurship Research." *Organization* 19 (5): 531–541.

Tobias, Madeleine Landau, and Janja Lalich. 1994. *Captive Hearts, Captive Minds: Freedom and Recovery from Cults and Abusive Relationships*. Alameda, CA: Hunter House.

Turner, Victor. 1996. *From Ritual to Theatre: The Human Seriousness of Play*. Vol. 1. New York: PAJ.

Van Gennep, Arnold. 1960. *The Rites of Passage*. London: Routledge & Kegan Paul.

Warnock, Mary. 1984. "Broadcasting Ethics: Some Neglected Issues." *Journal of Moral Education* 13 (3): 168–172.

Watson, Tony J. 2012. "Entrepreneurship - a Suitable Case for Sociological Treatment." *Sociology Compass* 6 (4): 306–315.

Watson, Tony J. 2013. "Entrepreneurial Action and the Euro-American Social Science Tradition: Pragmatism, Realism and Looking beyond 'the Entrepreneur.'" *Entrepreneurship & Regional Development* 25 (1–2): 16–33. doi:10.1080/08985626.2012.754267.

Weber, M. 2002. *The Protestant Ethic and the "Spirit" of Capitalism and Other Writings*. London: Penguin Classics.

Welter, Friederike, and Frank Lasch. 2008. "Entrepreneurship Research in Europe: Taking Stock and Looking Forward." *Entrepreneurship Theory and Practice* 32 (2): 241–248. doi:10.1111/j.1540-6520.2007.00224.x.

Wilson, John. 1985. "Example or Timetable? A Note on the Warnock Fallacy." *Journal of Moral Education* 14 (3): 173–176.

A theoretical and methodological approach to social entrepreneurship as world-making and emancipation: social change as a projection in space and time

Nicolina Montesano Montessori

ABSTRACT

This article presents and analyses three cases, which integrate features of both social movements and social entrepreneurship (SE). It is the result of a longitudinal study (January 2012 to September 2015). The study contributes new insights to the theoretical and methodological discussions on SE, focusing on 'the social' in SE literature. The three selected movements, active in the Netherlands, are: 'The Dutch Chapter of Zeitgeist' henceforth Zeitgeist (TZM), (2010–present), 'Giving is All we Have' (henceforth GIAWH, (2011–2014) and 'MasterPeace' (MP) (2010–present). Each movement shows a strong inclination towards social transformation, while being rooted in organizational structures, therefore considered 'social entrepreneurial movements'. Specific contributions entail: the presentation of these innovative cases, the design of a methodology based on critical discourse analysis, state theory, narrative analysis, political theory and discourse theory and a thorough analysis and interpretation of these cases in the national and global contexts in which they emerged. More specifically, it contributes to SE literature on emancipation, defined as 'breaking free' when further developing the method in the direction of world-making, defined as 'creating new worlds'. This study suggests that transition theory can be useful for the study of the impact of social entrepreneurial movements.

Introduction

This study contributes to research on social entrepreneurship (SE) in various ways. SE has been broadly defined by Mair and Martí (2006, 36) as:

> a process that catalyzes social change and addresses important social needs in a way that is not dominated by direct financial benefits for the entrepreneurs. SE is seen as differing from other forms of entrepreneurship in the relatively higher priority given to promoting social value and development versus capturing economic value.

This study aims at inserting the 'social' more firmly in available SE literature, emphasizing the potential for social transformation while also presenting relevant theories and a methodology to analyse SE (Steyaert and Hjorth 2006). It draws on and further develops literature on SE in combination with social movement theory (Mair and Martí 2006), SE as emancipation (Rindova, Barry, and Ketchen 2009) and SE as world-making (Sarasvathy 2012) and attempts to be a contribution to help resolve Hjorth's critique that within SE literature, 'the social is too weak, and the entrepreneurship […] too managerialized' (Hjorth 2013, 35).

The three selected cases, Zeitgeist, Giving is All we Have and MasterPeace, combine features of social movements and social enterprises, through their strong focus on social transformation, while maintaining formal organization structures. It therefore broadens and amplifies existing definitions of SE, by adding the element of 'social movements', a suggestion previously made by Mair and Martí (2006, 41–42). I analyse these movements in the national and global contexts in which they emerged.

I designed a theoretical–methodological–analytical framework based on discourse theory (Laclau and Mouffe 1985), critical discourse analysis (CDA) (Reisigl and Wodak 2002; Fairclough 2003), state theory (Jessop 2002), political theory (Chilton 2004) and post-structural perspectives on space (Harvey 1996) and time (Adam and Groves 2007) in order to analyse these movements and to interpret them in the light of recent strands of literature on SE. My model pays strong attention to the aspect of ontology and ontological narratives, making use of Somers (1994)[1] a point which was made by Steyaert and Bachmann (2012). In addition, I recommend using transition theory to look at the impact and processes of constructive power of social entrepreneurial movements (Avelino and Rotmans 2009). My research design and methodology expand Rindova's theory on SE as emancipation in the direction of a model for world-making. In the process, it further develops research methodology of CDA, especially by adding the post-structural notions of 'space' and 'time' to an existing model (Chilton 2004). The need for a methodology to analyse SE has been addressed by various authors. Short, Moss, and Lumpkin (2009) make this point for SE studies in general, while Sarasvathy (2012) and Calas, Smircich, and Bourne (2009) make this point for studies related to world-making.

Selection of the cases, methodological considerations and research questions

The selected cases, the Dutch Chapter of the global Zeitgeist movement, a private corporation entitled 'Giving is All we Have' and a global movement, MasterPeace, either started or are active in the Netherlands. I selected them because they integrate features of both social movements and of social enterprises. In terms of social movements, each of them presents a critical analysis of the status quo of the current world and its underlying power relations and mechanisms; each of them shows a strong focus on social and/or economic transformation, they hold innovative views on leadership and power and they have developed and brought into being innovative mechanisms that help create the more sustainable world that they envision. However, they show features of SE in that each movement invests their efforts under different legal bases: Zeitgeist Netherlands and MasterPeace are foundations, while GIAWH constituted a one-person corporation (Ltd). These organizational bases make them stronger than mere activist groups (Mair and Martí 2006); therefore, I identified them as *social entrepreneurial movements*. A final reason to select them entails their holistic worldviews. Rather than catering to one particular cause, such as the provision of free meals and the construction of homes for the handicapped, (as presented in existing case studies, see Alter 2002; Bornstein 2004) these movements share the intention of changing the general orientation of humankind, or rather, to create radically new worldviews and engage in world-making to create new 'spaces' for living, thinking and interacting.

These movements have been analysed in the light of 'social entrepreneuring', defined as 'efforts to bring about new economic, social, institutional, and cultural environments through the actions of an individual or groups of individuals'. These innovations can entail new possibilities, new institutions or new ideas (Rindova, Barry, and Ketchen 2009, 477–478). While Sarasvathy (2012) suggests that the entrepreneurial methodology is needed to study processes of world-making, I follow the line of thought presented in the *Handbook of Research Methods on Social Entrepreneurship* (Seymour 2012, xiii) that no new theories or methodologies are needed. I demonstrate that the abductive approach used in CDA offers both enough flexibility to study dynamic processes and worlds in the making, and enough structure to reach scientific conclusions. I provide and apply an example of such a method, thus producing a thorough analysis of these three movements. I situate these movements in the social context of the entrepreneurization of Dutch society, the need for a moral economy to address the current financial and ecological crises (Sayer 2014), and the urge for rethinking humanity in terms of a dialectic 'web of life' (Harvey 2000). Within this context, I strongly suggest that these movements have the potential to play an important role in the emancipation of democratic citizenship and the emancipation and survival of humans and nature, thus representing what Harvey (2000) called 'spaces of hope'. It is for these reasons that I claim that these movements deserve academic attention. In performing this study, I addressed the following research questions:

How can a new methodology be developed that allows for the analysis of social movements in the light of SE as emancipation and world-making?

What are, in these cases, particular moments in the transition from formulating world views to engaging in world-making?

Social entrepreneurship as a potential for social change and emancipation: a review of literature

SE was broadly defined by Mair and Martí (2006, 37) as 'a process involving the innovative use and combination of resources to pursue opportunities to catalyze social change and/or address social needs'. Much work has been done on describing and rethinking SE in terms of processes of social entrepreneurship, on the individual entrepreneurs or about social enterprises – the outcome of specific initiatives (see Mair and Martí 2006 and Short, Moss, and Lumpkin 2009 for overviews). However, much of the existing mainstream literature was criticized because 'the social in SE is too weak, and the entrepreneurship (…) too managerialized' (Hjorth 2013, 35). The potential for social change through entrepreneurship is being addressed in at least three different but related directions. In general terms, there is a (fast) growing bulk of literature that mostly sets itself apart from the mainstream entrepreneurship literature and claims the need for a stronger knowledge base to study SE (e.g. Austin, Stevenson, and Wei-Skillern 2006; Mair and Martí 2006; Steyaert and Hjorth 2006; Short, Moss, and Lumpkin 2009). Others consider 'world-making capacity' as the very heart of the entrepreneurship phenomenon, and view it as 'fundamentally a process of social change' (Calas, Smircich, and Bourne 2009, 553; Sarasvathy 2012). Rindova, Barry, and Ketchen (2009) were influential in sketching an initial research agenda under the header of 'entrepreneuring as emancipation', which involves creating and amplifying cracks in otherwise stable (and potentially rigidified) social and economic relationships that impose constraints on agents, thus opening the way for emancipation (479). These authors suggest that there are three core elements in entrepreneurial change efforts, namely: 'Seeking autonomy', 'Authoring' and 'Making declarations'. 'Seeking autonomy' refers to 'breaking free from authority and breaking up conceived constraints' (idem, 479).

Breaking up draws attention to 'striving to imagine and create a better world' (Arasvathy, Dew, Velamuri and Venkataraman, 2003, 155, quoted in Rindova, Barry, and Ketchen 2009). 'Authoring' refers to 'taking ownership over oneself and one's actions'. Having broken free from a given authority, one must become one's own author. 'With this, the entrepreneur must necessarily attend to the variety of relationships, structures, norms, and rules within which an entrepreneurial project is undertaken' (idem, 483). 'Making declarations' refers to 'unambiguous discursive and rhetorical acts regarding the actor's intentions to create change – as an important part of the change creation process' (idem, 485).

While these new directions in SE literature are certainly interesting, they present the problem that no methodology has been developed to analyse or compare them. I therefore design, present and apply a method that allows analysis of these movements in terms of their spatial and temporal orientations, their world views and their attempts at world-making. The model has also been designed to analyse processes of emancipation and world-making. Therefore, the outcome of each stage of the research will be related to the three concepts outlined above: authoring, making declarations and autonomy, and I take the concept of 'breaking up' as a crucial concept to relate their theory to the concept of world-making.

Social relevance of the identified movements

Before describing the theoretical and methodological frameworks, I will now place these movements in their national and socio-political contexts.

The national context: neoliberal rule and entrepreneurialization in the Netherlands

Entrepreneurship is 'hot' in the Netherlands, for several reasons. Dominant neoliberal discourse promotes entrepreneurship in the context of the free market economy and the envisioned participatory society. This perspective implies a shift from citizen rights to individual, entrepreneurial responsibilities and freedoms. While the Netherlands traditionally managed to mix capitalism with socialism through a well-developed welfare state and tripartite counselling between representatives of employers, employees and the government, the hegemony of the neoliberal discourse within the EU has caused the government to radically cut down on public budgets, decrease the welfare state and recently (1 January 2015) to hand over the responsibility for health care and the care of vulnerable citizens to the municipalities while simultaneously cutting their budgets. Secondly, we are seeing a transition in Dutch democracy with interplay between the traditional representative democracy and the emerging participatory democracy recently coined as the 'Montessori-Democracy' (Tonkens et al. 2015). The emphasis is on resolving problems through direct action rather than political discussion and deliberation. In addition, there is a tendency for citizens to organize themselves in new bottom-up initiatives that often take the shape of a social entrepreneurship in order to escape the top-down, instrumental control and restrictions of their formal workplace. Critics of current capitalism indicate that a return to entrepreneurship, where the responsibility for enterprise lies with the entrepreneurs rather than an abstract layer of management, would help integrate multiple – including environmental – values, in the politics and strategies of corporations (Tellegen 2014). Within Dutch society, these movements are relevant in the current political climate of neoliberal austerity policies, its cutbacks on the public sector and the so-called 'Participatory Society'. The Dutch king officially declared the end of the 'welfare state' during his annual speech to the Dutch people in 2013. A pragmacracy (Boutellier 2015) has emerged that introduces neoliberal technocratic rule, while it lacks a moral dimension and ignores the concerns and voice of the people. As Joke Hermsen, a Dutch philosopher states: the current government sees its role as a financial gatekeeper, whereby the realm of politics has been reduced to a budgetary discipline. Initiatives to create new spaces of solidarity are set up in bottom-up initiatives, small-scale neighbourhood initiatives or, indeed, forms of social entrepreneurship, all outside the government's sphere of influence (Hermsen 2014). She refers mostly to groups that distribute food, grow biological food, etc. In this light, the three movements discussed here stand out, in that they create and disseminate new 'myths' as defined as an alternative to the status quo (Laclau and Mouffe 1985). In my view, the three selected movements operate from the desire to create alternative world views, practices and podia that escape the narrow, individualized, economy-oriented frames of the neoliberal era, while creating new podia which can be used by this array of emerging social agents. As opposed to the neoliberal emphasis on entrepreneurialization of the *individual* citizen, they create podia for new forms of *collective* organization through cooperation and co-creation.

The global context: the financial and ecological crises and the volitional period of evolution

The current era of globalization is marked by a financial and ecological crisis that cannot be resolved within capitalism as we know it, since increased growth will further deteriorate the environment. Sayer (2014) suggests a future led by a moral economy, which serves society rather than dominates it. Furthermore, he addresses the need for the majority (99%) of people to reclaim their social, political and economic rights in the light of the current free market economy that shifts too much capital and social and political power to the 1%. Harvey (2000) states that humans, through our accumulated technological and scientific powers, have reached a volitional stage of evolution that provides us with the means either to deliberately destroy the world or to reshape it. He states that humans have become the architects of our future. As such, the question ahead of us is, who do we want to become as a human species and how do we care for other species? Harvey claims that there exists a 'witches' brew' of distinct visions and political arguments with competitive solutions to avoid the end of 'life as we know it' in the light of the ecological crisis. As an alternative to this perspective, Harvey supports the metaphor of human agents being caught in 'a web of life' to reconstruct our life world, which requires a translation of different languages (legal, scientific, managerial, popular, etc.) so that a common language can be construed to imagine and implement new practices away from the current neoliberal hegemony and other forms of authoritarianism. Based on this metaphor, he advocates a solution in which humans take into account their dialectic relations with other species for whom we are also responsible. This vision provides us with agency since humans are in a position to choose new balances and more productive forms of competition in improved harmony with the environment.

The movements presented in this article present a holistic approach to social change as well as innovative podia for creating innovative social relations. It is in this light, and without attributing perfection, that they are worth studying both for their emancipatory potential as well as their potential to represent 'spaces of hope'.

Theoretical and methodological frameworks

In order to fulfil the task ahead, I employ post-structural perspectives on social change as a theoretical and methodological framework (Harvey 1996, 2000). Specifically, I draw on State Theory (Jessop 2002), which claims that capitalism develops in a sequence of various spatio-temporal 'fixes' which are models that are fixed in time and space, such as Fordism, the Keynesian welfare state and the Neoliberal era. Each fix tends to end in a crisis. When a crisis occurs, typically new narratives emerge throughout society, which present (competing) accounts of 'what went wrong in the past' as well as envisioned improvements for the future. My research methodology relies on post-structural approaches to social research, specifically CDA (Fairclough 2003; Reisigl and Wodak 2002, 2009), Discourse Theory (Laclau and Mouffe 1985) and Narrative Analysis (Somers 1994), which are described in greater detail below. Laclau and Mouffe (1985), following Gramsci (1971), developed a theory of hegemony, in which the concepts of 'myth' and 'social imaginaries' play a significant role. They define 'myth' as an alternative to the status quo. A social imaginary exists when a majority of social groups support this myth and/or when it is implemented in social reality (Montesano Montessori 2009, 2011).

The analytical framework

The analysis is performed in five consecutive stages. The first stage consisted of a thematic analysis of the interviews with the three leaders; the second stage consisted on the analysis of the websites of the movements; the third and fourth stages were more interpretive as they analysed the outcome of the first stages through theoretical approaches on narratives (Somers 1994) and on deixis (Chilton 2004). The fifth stage entailed written interviews with participants who had been active during the period of research (2012–2015). I will now explain in more detail the interpretive part of the analysis – the second layer – and the theories it relies on. A detailed account on the collection of data and the first two stages of research will follow below. The narrative analysis used a model developed by Somers (1994), which I have previously applied in my research on the Zapatistas in Mexico (Montesano Montessori 2009, 2011; Montesano Montessori and Morales López 2015) and the Indignados in Spain (Montesano Montessori and Morales López 2015). Somers has designed this model as a new approach to analyse narratives in the social sciences. It is an approach that no longer sees narratives as representing social life, but as powerful instruments to shape social reality (in SE terminology: to shape new world views or to engage in world-making). Somers' model distinguishes between a meta-narrative, an ontological narrative and a public narrative. Meta-narratives refer to the 'master-narratives in which we are embedded' as contemporary actors – 'the epic dramas of our time: Capitalism vs. Communism; The Individual vs. Society' (Somers 1994, 619). Ontological narratives provide 'narrative location', endowing social actors with identities (Idem, 618), and form the basis for action. 'Ontological narratives affect activities, consciousness and beliefs and are in turn, affected by them' (Somers 1994, 618). They contain the basic presuppositions and the vision of the movements related to the status quo in the present world, and its problems. Ontological narratives are embedded in, and related to public narratives. These are, according to Somers (1994, 619), 'those narratives attached to cultural and institutional formations larger than the single individual'. Public narratives refer to, and consist of, the process of community building and how it is to be achieved (i.e. the main project of each initiative).

The subsequent deictic analysis is based on political theory (Chilton 2004). Deixis refers to the analysis of relational, spatial and temporal references outside the text. A text has a deictic centre – the agent from whose perspective the text is written – and a contextual deixis in terms of social relations, time and space. The analysis of deixis reveals how from the centre, space represents a line from what is considered 'here' to 'there', (for example, the line from 'us' in the West to 'them' in the East). Temporal deixis typically shows a continuum that runs from the past to the present and extends to the future, while the deixis of social relations situates subjects in terms of 'I', 'You' and 'Them' (Chilton 2004). I enriched this model with the post-structural notion of space (Harvey 1996) and time (Adam and Groves 2007). The latter envision social change as a matter of space–time distance. In particular, they move away from a linear approach to time that regards the future as a continuation of the present. They present a perspective on the future as a rupture with the present, visualizing the future as a space in which new knowledge, new ethics and new actions are being projected. Harvey 1996, 2000 sees the concept of 'space' as a less physical form of place, upon which change and hopes can be projected. I inserted these categories in the model for deictic analysis (See Table 4). The outcome of each analytical stage will be related to the theoretical concepts of Rindova, Barry, and Ketchen (2009) and to the concepts of 'worldviews' and 'world-making'.

The research procedure

In this section, I will describe the three cases and data collection methods, and present the analytical procedure in detail.

Description of the cases

This section describes the three social entrepreneurial movements in terms of their history, structures and goals, motivation of the leaders and the public attention they received. Their world view will become apparent throughout the analysis.

Zeitgeist (http://thezeitgeistmovement.com) is a global social movement that started in Canada and the U.S.A in 2008. For this study, I interviewed the coordinator of the Dutch chapter (https://www.zeitgeistbeweging.nl). The legal structure of Zeitgeist Netherlands is a foundation, initiated in 2010. The mission statement of Zeitgeist is to move the world away from a scarcity-based economy to a resource-based economy (RBEM) of abundance. Zeitgeist conducts community-based activism and awareness projects. Their envisioned model for the future is the RBEM in interdependence with the resulting moral behaviour via having the individual's needs met (as understood p.e. via Maslow's pyramid). This goal is made visible in a fragment of the movie: Zeitgeist Moving Forward[2] and fully described in a recent book: The Zeitgeist movement defined and the scientific method.[3]

The interviewee was Seth Lievense; at the time of the interview, he was a bachelor student in his third year. He was the national coordinator (until late 2013) and considered it an honour to perform that function. He shared the ideals of Zeitgeist and wished to contribute as a volunteer. Zeitgeist international is active in 51 countries around the world.

The main goal of GIAWH (http://www.givingisallwehave.com) is to change the world from 'having' as its central value towards one that revolves around 'giving'. Its mission is to 'mobilize the experience of unconditional giving & receiving to reframe our Economy towards the heart' (website, about us). GIAWH was a private company (Ltd) initiated by the director, Jeroen Timmers, in 2011. He quit his job as a strategy consultant for corporations since he did not feel comfortable with the general focus on capital and interest and was discomfited with his own salary. He travelled to Latin America and found that the true nature of life is 'giving' rather than 'having'. This epiphany started GIAWH. On his return, he gave away an expensive ticket to Lowlands, an annual music festival in the Netherlands.[4] This particular event caused so much public enthusiasm, that it became a trigger to set up his one-person corporation centred on giving. Timmers considers 'interest' as one of the constraints since it automatically creates debt and a perpetual need for economic growth and accumulation. A summary of his philosophy can be seen on the website[5] and his blog.[6] During the first review cycle of this article, I found that the movement is on hold and its director has moved to Austria. In personal correspondence, he clarified this was due to a quest for further personal development (see endnote 12 for details). GIAWH has widely spread his ideas in the (inter)national arena. Films of his presentations are collected on his website. In the Netherlands, he entered the media through the main quality newspaper, NRC, Volzin (a magazine of the church) and presentations on television for national public channels. He has presented the giveshop, a shop where you could only give and accept items and services for free (see endnote 14) various times at Lowlands music festival and elsewhere.

MasterPeace, (www.masterpeace.org), presents its goal as 'to win the hearts of millions of people for the cause of peace'. Its mission is to inspire citizens to contribute to a more sustainable world with less armed conflict. Its legal structure is a foundation. A nickname for MasterPeace is the 'Just Do It Campaign For Peace'. MasterPeace officially started in 2011 in 14 countries and is now active in 47 countries. Its main slogans are: 'Big changes start with small things', 'The opposite of love is not hate: it is indifference' and 'Creating peace together' (website). It is a bottom-up movement that wishes to unleash human talent and energy. MasterPeace seeks to activate and to mobilize people around the world to undertake peace initiatives in their neighbourhood through art and concerts or through conflict mediation. The director, Ilco van der Linde, had previously initiated Dance4life, a campaign for a world without AIDS, which started in 2004 and is still active. His aim to set up social movements started with a request from his father, who gave him a hundred guilders to make liberation day locally attractive for youngsters. Van der Linde organized a pop concert that attracted many young people. He now has over 30 years' experience of organizing concerts and events for peace and human rights. An online video summarizes his philosophy.[7] MasterPeace now has 65 clubs in 47 countries, with 610 initiatives (website, 15 December 2015). The movement received a certificate by Ban Ki-Moon on 18 December 2013, in recognition of its contributions to peace through art and music. The Rockefeller Foundation added both leaders to the list of 'The Top 100 of Next Century's Innovators'. Very recently (2 October 2015), the two founding members won the Luxemburg Peace Prize.

Collection of the data

Research started in early 2012 when the three movements were identified for the reasons explained above. I then invited the leaders of each movement for a face-to-face interview. I interviewed Seth Lievense (then coordinator of the Dutch Chapter of Zeitgeist) at VU Amsterdam (3 February 2012). It lasted one hour. I interviewed Jeroen Timmers (initiator and director of GIAWH at VU Amsterdam (15 March 2012, 46 min). I then interviewed Ilco van der Linde, the founder of MasterPeace, in the Lloyd hotel in Amsterdam (7 June 2012, 50 min). The interviews were semi-structured in that I sent the same set of topics and questions to each of the participants prior to the interview and invited them to address these topics during the interview, while I used the format as a checklist. These topics included: (1) the goals and orientation of the movement; (2) internal and external leadership; (3) communication and decision-making; and (4) integration of new members and how to stimulate activism. These categories were based on the literature on structures of social movements, McAdam, McCarthy, and Zald (1996) and Touraine (1985). I fully transcribed each interview, annotating the recorded times. Between January 2012 and December 2015, I followed the blogs and newsletters of these movements, as well as their websites. In the summer of 2015, I performed three written interviews per movement with people who had been active in these movements since at least January 2012.[8] The purpose was to check if these activists shared the same notions as the leaders and what their experiences were. Therefore, I asked them the exact same questions as the initial interviewees in terms of both their knowledge about and their experience with these very topics. In the case of GIAWH – which had ceased to exist in late 2014 – I asked participants for their opinion about the decision of the founder to stop with the initiative. I performed the same analysis as for the initial interviews. The results are inserted in this article through vignettes and endnotes.

Performance of the data analysis

Following the abductive[9] approach of CDA, I engaged in a layered research process, in which I combined the analysis of empirical data with theoretical perspectives and social context.

The first layer of analysis was a basic content analysis, in which I used the transcribed interviews to schematically write down the answers that each of the leaders provided for each topic (see Table 1). The second step included an analysis of the three websites in terms of goals and orientation and the temporal and spatial and social relational frames of the worldviews (Table 2). The next layer was more interpretive in that I used theoretical frameworks to perform a narrative analysis based on a model developed by Somers (1994, see Table 3), while a deictic analysis focused on the spatial, temporal and relational orientations of the movements based on Chilton (2004, see Table 4), as will be further explained below.

In this section, I provide the main results of the initial interviews, especially the topics of: (1) the goals and orientation of the movement; (2) internal and external leadership; and (3) integration of new members and how to stimulate activism. For reasons of space, I eliminate communication – the third topic of the interviews – since it was generally centred around the Internet, emergent processes of communication, decision-taking and trust.

Goals and orientations of the movements

For Zeitgeist, the goal is to create consciousness and awareness, so that new actions emerge, out of which a new mentality will emerge. The desired change is to move away from outdated paradigms that maintain an unjust financial economy that creates scarcity towards an economy based on abundance facilitated by modern technology and science, the so-called natural law/resource-based economy or RBE.

> Our current society is based on outdated technology and outdated paradigms. It is good to see electric cars, but this was possible already 30 years ago. People in power attempt to withhold change, because they gain by an economy based on scarcity. (…) We can create abundance through the use of solar energy. We can create hydrogardens in offices, which makes food locally available to everybody. Money is a symbol of scarcity. It will become redundant in the resource based economy. (Lievense, 5:45–7:45)

The Internet allows decentralization of power: 'modern technology allows decentralization. You are no longer dependent on power structures that resist change. Many of these ideas and possibilities bring us to our goal: the shift towards a RBE of abundance' (4:44–5:38).

GIAWH wishes to change the world from one that is centred on 'possession' to one that is centred on 'giving'. Timmers states that

> all our systems are based on the consciousness of a particular time. Systems are material, consciousness is non-material. This implies that all systems are slower than our consciousness. So if we look at current structures, we look into the past. While our consciousness jumps ahead. Our consciousness now tells us: property does not bring us a happier future. In fact, all crises of today are crises of property. (Timmers, 1:30–2:45)

We need to change from an old paradigm that is centred around reason, control and property to one that is centred around the heart and giving and letting go.

> We need to step out of the traditional frame of rationality that is based on ratio, control, security and having, towards a new frame of freedom, the heart, or 'giving', as our natural drive. (…) We need to articulate, emphasize and disseminate a new vision on growth: immaterial growth of consciousness is always possible. Material growth is reduced, scarce, and relies on an old consciousness based on the Descartian dualism. It blocks growth of consciousness (39:00–41:10).

The goal of MasterPeace is to mobilize millions of people so that they want to become active for the sake of peace.

> We asked a research office to investigate in ten countries how well-known the UN peace week was. It turned out that less than 6% of the population knew about it. Then you can do two things: either you abolish it, or you make it loved. And that is what we want: to make that day an incentive for many beautiful initiatives (Van der Linde, 18:33–18:58).

The wrongs they want to address are the erroneous priorities of our current society where more money is invested in weapons and conflict than in human development:

> Actually, it is too absurd to be true that each year, again, all governments in the world together spend more on buying new weapons. Last year the expenses were 411 billion dollars. And that is enough to feed and educate people and to resolve the problems in Greece. So there is no financial crisis at all – there is a problem to do with priorities. (3:40–4:20)

Internal and external leadership

The interviewee of Zeitgeist stated that he is a coordinator rather than a leader. He will hold his position as long as he wants to do it and others trust him to do it.

During this research we should let go of the term "leader". I am a coordinator. That is not just a difference in words. I facilitate the work of volunteers. I have no formal power. (…) We are now going to improve the website so that people in the regions can find each other. If I have all the information, I have more knowledge than others. That will give me power. But this new website will make the role of coordinator redundant. (19:58–22:00)

> Resp. 1 TZM: TZM is a leaderless movement. There are coordinators and members. The reason is that the general plan needs to be achieved. This philosophy is central to TZM: not to any person.
>
> Resp. 3 TZM: We arrange among ourselves who does what: the person with most experience and skills will take the lead. People learn from each other and rotate roles.

When asked about the strategy, Lievense said: 'We do not really have a strategy: it is what everybody does. We bring initiatives together' (19:58–20:15). He explained that activists work in teams, for instance, the translation team which translates material from the global movement or the education team which teaches about the philosophy of Zeitgeist. Specific instruments to create change are hydrogardens in offices, which make global transport redundant: people can become self-sufficient. But Lievense also mentioned a person who rented out his garage and used the money to buy an iPad for a young boy who was paralysed. Using the iPad, the boy could express himself and be in touch with the world again (22:57–24:00).

In the case of GIAWH, the founder was on his own. From this position, he organized various initiatives and in the process, he gathered ambassadors around him who shared his ideals. In this context, he sees leadership as a matter of staying close to himself:

> To me, leadership means that I remain close to myself and distant to the expectations of today's paradigm. Because that implies that I need a mortgage and I must earn money. This is what I need to let go of. That, to me is leadership: keeping close to myself and letting go of expectations based on old paradigms. (Timmers, 29:20–30:50)

His main strategy is 'to start initiatives and people organically sense the same and have the same intuition and they also spread the message and bring the mechanism of giving into life' (Timmers: 28:36–29:10). The main envisioned mechanism is 'to make traditional companies give goods and services to social enterprises. And it is not to do with money. It can be space, knowledge, or providing a professional from HR who wishes to use her talents in a different company'. Timmers, (12:00–12:40). 'And in Lowlands 2012 I hope to make sure that 55,000 people start to give. This fits in with the general trend towards a share-economy: look at Wikipedia and Couch surfing' (35:05–35:50).

> Resp.1 GIAWH: Jeroen trusted me and let me be free. I did the same, so people enjoyed autonomy. People were intrinsically motivated.

The founder of MasterPeace, Van der Linde, made his friend Mohammed Helmy in Cairo the director of MasterPeace, and asked him to start an office there. Van der Linde did not want to create another Western concept and spread it around the world; he wanted to create a bridge between the East and the West. Also, he wanted to make the masses and grassroots the leaders of MasterPeace: 'Power is in the streets. Every moment of social transformation is the result of the mobilization of civil society' (24:52–24:56). His own role is that of inspiring, communicating, messaging and finance (23:22–23:52).

As a leader, I want to let go of control. I want to let myself be surprised by the grassroots. I allow others to unleash their talents and creativity and that way I get 10x more than if I would control their contributions. People can start clubs and once we trust them, they become owners of MasterPeace. We expect from them that they 'walk their talk'. (34:11–34:27)

The main strategy is to invite people around the world to start clubs. The main mechanisms are massive concerts, the envisioned concert in Cairo during the Peace Week of 2014. He also maintains contact with people from business and the cultural industry:

After each presentation I say: 'I don't need an applause. Just give me your business card and we set up a product'. Now I have 70 founding partners, who agreed to pay me 75,000 euros per year until 2015, which covers my basic expenses. (32:08–33:00)

Resp. 1 MP: MP asks everybody to be a leader in their own area, by creating a club. MP wants to stimulate leadership among young people who have the potential to make a difference.

Resp. 3: MP is more a social enterprise. It aims to create shareholders for peace with existing companies

---

From slactivism to activism

The terminology comes from MasterPeace, but the issue is: How do you activate the grassroots?

Zeitgeist has yearly meetings – Z-day – the next one was to be held a week after the interview, 10 February 2012. On that day, they would launch a new version of their website, which promised to be more interactive so that people could find each other and join groups in their own area. In terms of the accommodation of new members, Zeitgeist organizes introduction days. People can join existing teams or start new ones. Zeitgeist maintains one principle: activists should be proactive and generate their own activity and fundraising if necessary.

Resp. 2 ZG: ZG wants us to become active agents, that we learn about the philosophy of ZG and then make our own, personal decisions as to how to contribute to the general idea.

GIAWH did not have a system at the time of the interview. People would follow him on the Internet or join him after activities that he organized.

An organization is growing around me with people who share the same intention. I create a lot of ambassadors around me who help me and who spread their own personal messages. It is a very organic, emerging process. (28:36–29:15)

Last week, I was invited by Princess Irene (the sister of former Dutch Queen Beatrix, NMM) to participate in a round table discussion on the future of our society. Somehow something resonates: people are aligned and then I recognize that we have the same drive. (34:22–35:00)

Resp.1 GIAWH: The main mechanism was the giveshop: There we invited people to give their talents or goods and people became involved. Resp 2 GIAWH: media and blogging, Lowlands, giveshops, events around Europe.

MasterPeace aims at creating a 'tunnel of engagement: from slactivism to activism. This implies going from "being liked" to activism' (19:38–20:00). He describes Kenya as an example where Kofi Annan operated as mediator in 2007, got global support from the media and public opinion, which in turn helped end violence.

To me, this was a turning point. I understood what collective action – the sum of many individuals – can reach. Therefore we need to create a movement that can jump into conflict areas to attempt to stimulate dialogue and to avoid escalations. (30:10–31:00)

MasterPeace has a manual[10] which explains the main principles for a club to function. In addition, people can get assistance from a specialized team in Cairo and are invited to start clubs for grass-roots activities around the world. At the time of the interview, there were 19 clubs in 22 countries. For Van der Linde, it is a matter of redefining the question:

You need to create interesting perspectives, a good brand, to become active, organize good campaigns, (…) develop a lot of local leadership and entrepreneurship and integrate that in the concepts you develop. (…) Internet is normally used for friendships. But the medium has a huge potential to connect people around the world across religious and other boundaries, to connect people in a different way. (5:40–6:49)

Resp1 MP: activism is encouraged in three stages: (1) To support and empower new leaders; (2) to encourage companies to invest in social initiatives and organizations through a business matchmaking program; and (3) by starting more clubs around the world.

Table 1. Summary analysis: original interviews with the leaders of the movement.

	Zeitgeist NL	GIAWH	MasterPeace
Goals and orientations	From consciousness raising to a new awareness and new actions	Turning the world from one that is centred on 'possession' to one that is centred around giving	To become the most heart-warming peace movement To create the 'just do it' campaign for peace To make the annual UN Peace Day more widely known
Desired change	From an outdated paradigm of a scarcity-based financial economy towards an economy of abundance based on technology and science.	From a world that is based around ratio to a world that is centred around the heart	From priorities that emphasize arms and conflict to an open atmosphere of peace From indifference to engagement
Strategies	Chapters, teams	Public performance at universities, on television and in magazines	Clubs
Mechanisms	Education; creating consciousness and awareness; technological initiatives, such as creating hydrofarms in empty offices	Getting traditional companies to give to social enterprises	Concerts
Leadership and power	Coordinator rather than leader Decentralization of power Absence of formal power Power positions based on mutual trust Leadership as a matter of organic growth	Remaining true to oneself To remain close to personal beliefs and distant to the expectations of the current paradigm	Shared leadership Headquarters in Cairo Relationship with advisory board based on confidence The leader wants to be surprised by the grassroots To unleash talents of young leaders Power has to come from the masses Contacts with business and cultural industry
Integration of new members	Introduction Days The yearly Z Day Invitation to participate in a team or to start a new one Activists should be pro-active and generate (and finance) their own initiatives	Resonance: people start to help in their own way Organizing activities	Manual for new Clubs Grassroots organize their own clubs and become the owners of their initiatives The creation of a tunnel of engagement

This thematic content analysis brings to light that the three leaders coincide in their diagnoses that current society hinges on outdated models and priorities, which artificially block potential solutions to the many crises and injustices we face today. Their suggested solutions, an economy of abundance, and an emphasis on giving and peace, respectively represent the change they want to make. This seems to be the nucleus of their 'declarations' in Rindova's sense. It is to be noted that to them the 'constraint' is not one particular blockage, but an outdated worldview and outdated power relations. Their proposed solutions, then, represent their dreams, and also form the basis for 'breaking up' these constraints, or for making change. In terms of leadership – authoring – Zeitgeist and MasterPeace aim at transferring leadership to grassroots, while Timmers (GIAWH) sees leadership as a matter of remaining close to his own values. All three state that solutions will have to be created beyond existing structures. This, by itself, is a statement made by academics such as Harvey (1996) and Sayer (2014), as stated above.

Analysis of the websites

The analysis of the websites was performed throughout the whole period of research[11], but all links were uploaded or checked on 5 October 2015. The movements present themselves and their goals as follows:

Zeitgeist Netherlands (www.zeitgeistbeweging.nl) is a foundation. In its slider (homepage), it represents itself as a non-profit organization which introduces a new economic model that focuses on efficiency and sustainability for the well-being of the world community. All natural resources are considered unconditional gifts to the world community. The desired RBE will give the entire world population access to health, and it will bring war and poverty to an end. It calls on people to 'be the change that you wish to see in the world'.

GIAWH (www.givingisallwehave.com) was a one-person corporation. It 'mobilizes the experience of unconditional giving & receiving to reframe our Economy towards the heart'. It formally stopped in December 2014, but is dormant.[12]

MasterPeace (www.masterpeace.org) is a foundation, and presents itself as 'the most heartwarming peace campaign'. Its passion statements are: Music above Fighting, Dialogue above Judgement, Bread above Bombs and Creation above Destruction. It helps lead the way to a more sustainable world with fewer conflicts. Its target is to mobilize at least 400,000 new peace builders by 2020. Peace building is considered a *verb*. Therefore, it launches the 'just *do* it campaign' (my italics) for peace. It aims at togetherness across identity, colour, religion or walk of life.

In terms of space, Zeitgeist considers the Earth as a planet of resources that need to be distributed more efficiently. It is not that people do not have access to the resources per se, but they lack access to the means of getting it (capital). Zeitgeist started in the U.S. and Canada and has chapters in 51 countries. This video[13] contains an overview of the RBEM. The spatial orientation of GIAWH is a world centred on giving, made possible through the giveshop[14] (initiated at Lowlands 2012). As for MasterPeace, they consider their website a peace platform 2.0, which links members who created an account to grassroots around the world. There are clubs in 47 countries. Since 2014, some countries have private sites, such as Mexico, Netherlands and Nepal. The website shows how concerts were held by people belonging to communities in conflict, such as from North and South Sudan, Israel and Palestine.[15]

In terms of time, the website of Zeitgeist has a Google calendar with announcements of all its meetings. There was no specific timepath.[16] In its worldview, wrongs are situated in outdated structures from the past and the future is dominated by the RBEM of abundance. GIAWH functioned from 2011 to late 2014. It also did not have an exact timeline: it proclaimed 'change as we are speaking'. It situates wrongs in outdated structures based on rational thinking and envisions a future centred on giving, inspired by the heart. MasterPeace lists a series of key performance indicators in its strategic plan for 2014–2020.[17]

Zeitgeists social relations are arranged through (annual) meetings, Google hangouts and through teams: currently, the media team, the translation team, the IT team, the aquaponics team and the education team in which people work together. For GIAWH, it was through the giveshop and the many ambassadors who supported the movement. For MasterPeace, social relations are maintained through clubs, the recent campaign 'Be a Nelson' and international concerts. Additionally, it maintains social relations with its grassroots through boot

Table 2. Summary of the analysis of the websites.[a]

	Zeitgeist Netherlands (2008–present) www.zeitgeistbeweging.nlwww.thezeitgeistmovement.com	GIAWH (2011–2014) www.givingisallwe-have.com	MasterPeace (2010–present) www.masterpeace.org
Goals and orientation	The promotion of the natural law/resource-based economy (NL/RBE) to resolve current ecological, social and economic problems. (home; slides)	Mobilization of the experience of unconditional giving and receiving to reframe our Economy towards the Heart (our mission)	To reduce conflict around the world and to construct peace To become the world's most heart-warming peace movement (home)
Mission and vision	The movement recognizes that issues such as poverty, corruption, pollution, homelessness, war and starvation appear to be 'symptoms' born out of an outdated social structure. The proposed scientific method should help finding optimized solutions	To move from a rational world to a world that follows the heart :	MasterPeace aims to inspire everyone to use their talent and energy for building peace and togetherness towards a more sustainable world with less armed conflict MasterPeace is the fastest growing grass-roots peace movement in the world, with the ambition to reach out to millions and mobilize at least 400,000 new peace builders by 2020
Place	Zeitgeist sees the Earth as a global planet of resources that need to be distributed more efficiently	A world centred around giving; Lowlands Festival	The website is a peace platform 2.0 which connects grassroots around the world
Time	No specific time path	No specific time path	Strategic plan 2014– 2020 with key performance indicators (endnote xviii)
Social Relations	Teams: translation team, aquaponics team for windowfarms, media team, IT team and education eam	Ambassadors	Clubs, trust, unleash talents and potential of the seven billion inhabitants of this world
		The art of giving and receiving unconditionally	MasterPeaces' main currency is talent
		The giveshop	Partners and Friends (about.masterpeace.org)

[a]I last checked all the links in the table and the article 15 December 2015. See also note 11. In a final review prior to publication, I again checked all links and changed those that had changed on 24 May 2016.

camps and training activities. It also maintains relations with business, sponsors and the UN. It has founding partners (NGOs, a social bank and the peace fund) and business and collaborative partners (among others, the Dutch Ministry of Foreign Affairs, International Radio Festival, Movies that Matter and the Lloyd Hotel).[18]

The analysis of the websites makes visible the mission and vision of the movements, their main organizational mechanisms, such as teams (Zeitgeist), the giveshop (GIAWH) and clubs and 'Be a Nelson' (MasterPeace), which correspond to 'authoring' in Rindova's terminology. All websites have additional information through (digital) books, blogs, films and links (considered the realm of 'making declarations'). In the case of MasterPeace, there is also a strategic plan. The spatial scope shows that all movements hold a global worldview. However, GIAWH restricted its activity mostly to the Netherlands, whereas Zeitgeist Netherlands is the Dutch chapter of a global movement. MasterPeace, on the contrary, started in the Netherlands and then went global. A temporal worldview in terms of clear targets is present for MasterPeace, but seemed to be absent for the other two movements.

Findings: radical modification of worldviews as a condition for emancipation

This section presents the results of the interpretive stage of the analysis, which is based on the first two stages of the analysis, and relates the outcome of each stage to the concepts of Rindova, Barry, and Ketchen (2009): making declarations and authoring.

Narrative dimensions

Zeitgeist depicts, in its goals and orientation (Table 1), a *meta-narrative* that analyses the world as situated in an economy of scarcity of resources. The ontological narrative depicts present-day society as the result of old power structures that can now be modified due to the role of technology and science. Powerful groups, considered a symptom of the dominant social–economic system, keep scarcity in place while resisting potential changes towards a sustainable, abundant economy. However, Zeitgeist envisions the world as a place of abundant resources to which all people should have equal access via local, decentralized use of technology providing abundance, which allows the community to shape itself around its personal/communital needs rather than the needs of the elite of the global economy.

These narrative dimensions relate to Rindova, Barry, and Ketchen's (2009) concept of 'making declarations', through which they formulate their worldviews. Zeitgeist's public narrative purports that it is necessary to engage in a process of consciousness-raising so that a new mentality will emerge, which in turn will lead to new actions in the direction of the desired resource-based world order. It corresponds to Rindova's concept of 'authoring' and lays the basis for world-making.

GIAWH presents a meta-narrative of a world that is stuck in old rationalist paradigms, (e.g. dichotomous divisions, such as mind vs. body), and oriented towards possession, accumulation and control. The ontological narrative purports that 'the present-day world' is hindered by this materialist paradigm. It is the mind that wishes to control. Consciousness is immaterial and changes more slowly, but it is in movement now. Again, the meta-narrative and the ontological narrative represent 'presenting a worldview through making declarations'. The public narrative is to reach corporations and to get them to give money, knowledge and other means to encourage social enterprise. Timmers advocates a world centred around the

Table 3. Summary results: narrative analysis (Somers 1994).

Analytical categories, their definitions and data sources	Zeitgeist	GIAWH	MasterPeace
Meta-narrative *Source:* Goals and orientations found in analyses of initial interviews and websites Mission and vision of websites	The current world is trapped in a financial economy of scarcity, artificially sustained by outdated power structures	The current world is stuck in rationalism that emphasizes accumulation and control of possessions. All current crises are to do with possession	The current world is characterized by conflicts that endanger the potential for peace and predominantly open up the possibility of war
Ontological narrative	Scarcity is maintained by outdated power structures that can now be changed through the decentralizing power of the Internet and modern technology	The world is hindered by this paradigm: the mind wants to control and to accumulate but the essence of life is actually about giving	Conflicts are the result of erroneous priorities and current solutions are overly concentrated in the hands of experts
Source: Goals and orientation initial interviews and mission and vision of websites	The problem of the current world is not that there is a lack of goods, but the means to have access to these resources: capital		
Public narrative	Consciousness-raising and activation of millions of people around the world to take action to enhance the desired resource-based economy	To reach corporations seen as a role model in modern society and to get them to give to social corporations	Create a tunnel of engagement: to break indifference and create involvement
Source: answer to the question in initial interviews: What are your main goals?	Establishment of the RBE economy	An economy without interest, where the purchaser defines the value of the product obtained	Create a movement where many individuals come together so that it can interrupt conflicts, enhance dialogue and avoid escalation of conflicts

heart rather than the mind and an economy focused on sharing, which abandons the concept of 'interest'. This corresponds to 'authoring' and lays the basis for world-making.

MasterPeace depicts a meta-narrative that describes the current world as characterized by conflicts that endanger the potential for peace and open up the possibility of war. The ontological narrative is that conflicts are the result of erroneous priorities which need to be modified. These two dimensions represent the 'declarations'. The public narrative involves the aim of the movement, which is to make the Peace Week of the UN more generally known, as well as the organization of major projects such as global peace concerts, the 'Be a Nelson' campaign and supportive activities by, for instance, corporations. During the UN International Day of Peace in 2014, the movement organized a global wave of MasterPeace concerts in around 50 countries in Asia, the Middle East, U.S. and Europe[19] (www.masterpeace.org, consulted on 29 May 2015). It again corresponds to Rindova's concept of 'authoring' and lays the basis for world-making.

This part of the analysis demonstrates that each narrative entails an account of what went wrong in the past and what is wrong in the present, which reminds us of the narratives as described by Jessop (2002). The problems are stated in both the meta-narrative and in the ontological narrative. The meta-narrative presents the constraints of the current world system, while the ontological narrative in all cases – albeit presented in different terms – presents the need for a paradigm shift, for a radical new vision of the dominant worldviews: from scarcity to abundance, from rationality to the heart and from conflict and war to peace. This analysis allows us to relate the meta-narrative and the ontological narratives to the concept of 'making declarations' in SE literature on emancipation and 'worldviews', while the public narratives relate to 'authoring' (Rindova, Barry, and Ketchen 2009) and to the concept of world-making (Sarasvathy 2012). Interestingly, it shows that in these cases, the ontological narrative is the key condition to social change. A radically different ontology – or perception of this world – is required for social change to happen. Their movements aim at breaking up outdated visions of the world and create the mechanisms and new relationships necessary to start a process of world-making: the domain of their public narratives.

Temporal, spatial and relational deixis

Zeitgeist presents a timeframe that contains models from the past that are outdated but resilient in the present. It depicts a future dominated by the positive sides of knowledge, the arts, science and technology, which make both money and labour redundant. This envisioned world will be run through arguments and action. Its main ethics is to do with sustainability and making resources publicly available. The past, this 'economy of scarcity', is situated in places, in countries such as Canada and Japan. It is directed by hierarchical power in a top-down structure. The future or the RBE of abundance is global, facilitated through the Internet and characterized by the decentralization of power. Social relations will be horizontal rather than vertical and are shaped through chapters. This new space is, in part, made possible through the technical re-contextualization of traditional places such as offices, that will become gardens and hot-houses for products that no longer need to be imported. In the case of GIAWH, the temporal frame runs from the past as the realm of systems to the present that remains fixed in this old paradigm and is hindered by it. It is heading towards a future that will be centred around the heart and focuses on 'giving'. Physical space is focused on the world at large, but the giveshops are the places where the new ideas are put into practice. The future represents a rupture with the present. Its knowledge base is this new consciousness, and it is essential to listen to our true self. The desired action is giving and embracing positivity. These actions will be ethically inspired and engaged. The past is situated in traditional places that embrace systems, while the future includes space as the realm of a new consciousness in an immaterial world. Social relations are set around the principle of giving and receiving unconditionally.

In terms of social relations, MasterPeace encourages bottom-up initiatives and seeks to empower people to unleash their talents and creativity in processes of co-creation, 'authoring' in Rindova's sense. The present is dominated by erroneous priorities. The future is envisioned as a time in which millions of people will actively contribute to peace. The knowledge base is intuition and truth-finding, along with the work of authors such as Paolo Coelho. Actions entail music, arts and dialogue as part of peace building. Ethics will be 'walk your talk', trust and living up to peace. MasterPeace is certainly rooted in traditional places and cities. Their headquarters are in Cairo, which is meant to create a bridge between the East and the West. Projections in space consist of building a tunnel of engagement, based on connections of the hearts. See Table 4.

Conclusion: the deictic analysis reveals a regular pattern in that these movements see that wrongs in the past and present are due to outdated power structures and worldviews, earlier analysed as public narratives and see the future in terms of knowledge base, ethics

Table 4. Overview of results of relational, spatial and temporal deixis (Chilton 2004).

	Zeitgeist	GIAWH	MasterPeace
Social Relations *Source*: Initial interviews (communication and integration of new members) Website: Social relations	With grassroots, coordinators and people from all ranks of society Empowerment of volunteers and transfer responsibilities	Ambassadors, talking to many people, convincing traditional enterprise to donate to social enterprise	Co-leaders Volunteers Businesspeople and friends from cultural industry UN Co-creation, unleashing energy
Place *Sources*: Initial interviews: (goals and orientation) Websites: place	A global planet Economy of scarcity	Material world (systems) Companies	Pyramids in Egypt Hiroshima
	Hierarchical power (Lack of) office space for TZM	Broadcasting Universities Lowlands The website GIAWH; the giveshop	Kenya, conflict areas and Lloyd hotel Offices in Amsterdam, Cairo and Istanbul. Peace platform 2.0
Space	The RB economy that distributes resources, considered a gift to humanity	The realm of a new consciousness directed by the heart and focused on giving	A world with more peace and less conflict
Sources: Initial interviews: Goals and orientations Leadership Website: Goals, mission and vision; place	Decentralized power relations	A share economy	Human involvement rather than indifference
Past Interviews: Goals and orientation	Take a step back in history; and see how change (electric cars) was boycotted	The realm of systems	Using Kenya (2007) as an example for mediation.
Strategy **Present** Interviews: Goals and orientations Website: mission and vision	Current society hinges on old paradigms and power structures.	Old paradigm based on possession and control and the mind above the heart, theory above practice; the realm of a birth of a new consciousness.	Erroneous priorities: too much money is spent on the arms industry.
Future Interviews: Goals and orientation Websites: mission and vision.	Resource-based economy	A world that makes 'giving' a central feature Social enterprises, (in the future, no difference between profit and non-profit)	Millions of people are actively contributing to Peace Points at the horizon Strategic plan 2014–2020

(continued)

Table 4. (*Continued*).

	Zeitgeist	GIAWH	MasterPeace
Knowledge	Consciousness through a critical attitude Innovation through in-depth awareness	Consciousness Listening to the (true) self, it is in the genes Increased awareness	Paolo Coelho, the alchemist Knowledge of numbers (how much capital is spent on arms trade) and history (the example of Kenya)
Based on initial interviews (various moments)	Technology Social science		
Mission and vision and related documents	Empirical, scientific method Arguments		
Action *Sources:* Interviews (leadership, strategy)	Arguments and action	Embracing positivity, giving things to others	A pilgrimage to Cairo Activities in 22 (initial interview)/now 45 countries (website)
Ethics	Sustainability: abundance rather than scarcity	Giving and receiving unconditionally Being true to yourself	Values, peace, music and dance rather than war and conflict, trust, involvement and perseverance Walk your talk Confidence and trust (rather than control)
Sources: Initial interviews Goals and orientation Leadership Websites: Goals and orientation			

and actions. In terms of space, they make use of formal places as we know them, such as offices, but project their ideas in future spaces that still have to come about: a RBEM, a share economy and a peaceful world. Each of them has introduced mechanisms in our present world in their various attempts of world-making. The post-structural take on the future demonstrates that their worldviews, indeed, imply rupture with the present. In relation to Rindova's theory, it now becomes visible that the aspect of 'making declarations' has a time-line that runs from past to present to future. Their ways of 'authoring' play out at the level of social relations. They hinge between concrete places and spaces on which they project their dreams. So far, the analysis indicates that 'public narratives', 'future' and 'space' mark significant dimensions in the process of world-making.

Autonomy, world-making and emancipation

The three movements described in this study, each have a legal structure through which they are given power to legally act and interfere with society. It gives them both autonomy and a place for making declarations and authoring their mission in terms of Rindova, Barry, and Ketchen (2009). These movements formulated new worldviews and made statements about the inefficiency of the current hegemonic worldviews. In this sense, they formulated narratives as described by Jessop (2002), giving accounts as to what went wrong and calling for social change in times of crisis. But they did more: apart from formulating alternatives for the current society (myth in the sense of Laclau and Mouffe 1985), they brought into being innovative social practices, created innovative social relations and mobilized activists and supporters. In SE terms, they did not just present innovative world views; they initiated processes of world-making. If we look at this through the lens of transition theory, it can be argued that these movements enjoy innovative power (Avelino and Rotmans 2009). These authors distinguish between *regimes*, the most dominant configuration of actors, structures and practices which defend the status quo; *landscapes,* which refer to the surroundings of a particular societal social system; and *niches,* which are part of the societal system, but are able to create autonomous space in which non-conformism and innovation can develop. In this article, I argued that global capitalism and neoliberalism represent the *landscape* (implic-itly present in the meta-narratives of the movements), which surrounds a *regime* made of a budget-oriented Dutch Government that stimulates individual entrepreneurship as part of an attempt to break down the public sector. I believe that these movements represent *niches* in that they created autonomous space, mobilized people and initiated global action.

I suggest that 'niches' hinge between the discourse theoretical concepts of myth (formu-lating an alternative) and 'social imaginaries', which implies broad support from other move-ments and sections of society or implementation in a new system – Montesano Montessori 2009, 2011). I suggest that these movements definitely show the characteristics of a niche, but are still in the pre-development stage; they do not (yet) have an impact on the current system. The analysis has indicated that their innovative world views for the future are situated in the domains of 'public narratives', 'future', 'space' and 'myth'. I strongly suggest that these domains represent essential moments in the process of moving from worldview to world-making. These are the domains where imaginations can formulate, share and exper-iment. After all, their worldviews represent (radical) rupture with the current status quo: transition space is needed to start imagining and shaping new worldviews. I furthermore suggest that it is productive to take into account transition theory. The concept of 'niche' seems to me to be a highly significant concept in relation to a process of 'breaking up'. In fact, Rindova, Barry, and Ketchen (2009) make this point where they argue that 'entrepreneuring involves creating and amplifying cracks in otherwise stable (and potentially rigidified) social and economic relationships' (481). The advantage of relating this idea to transition theory is that it allows for research about the dynamics between niches, structures and landscapes. In other words, it allows for an analysis on structure and agency and how these mutually influence each other in times of social transition. The need for a model which involves studying structuration has been raised in SE literature (Mair and Martí 2006).

Results of the analysis

The purpose of this paper was to emphasize the 'social' in existing approaches to SE, by broadening the existing perspective on SE from organizations in the direction of social entrepreneurial movements, with a focus on emancipation and world-making. A research design was created, explained and executed to analyse three social entrepreneurial movements and to trace their processes from formulating world views to world-making. In terms of SE as emancipation, it has demonstrated that the aspect of 'making declarations' can be fruitfully enriched with a timeline and the narrative distinctions of 'public narratives', 'meta-narratives' and 'ontological narratives'. In these cases, authoring was mostly present in the 'public narratives', while making declarations belonged to the realms of the meta-narratives and the ontological narratives. In fact, the ontological narratives turned out to be crucial since for each of these movements, a radical change of existing, dominant worldviews is a precondition for social change. As for world-making, the analysis has shown that 'public narratives', 'space', 'future' and 'myth' are dimensions in the process of world-making. I suggested taking on board transition theory, with its dynamic concepts of niches, landscapes and regimes.

The designed methodology indicated that these three social entrepreneurial movements are hybrid in form, but represent regular patterns in their ontological narratives, the creation of innovative mechanisms and social relations as an initial attempt at world-making. Each of them problematized power and sought ways of distributing power and relating their new practices to ethics. This methodology was based on existing research paradigms, the abductive approach in CDA. It allowed to fully answer the two research questions – the creation of a new methodology to analyse social entrepreneurial movements in the light of both emancipation and world-making, and the identification of particular moments in the transition from formulating world views to engaging in world-making.

Revisiting the movements

What did the analysis reveal about these movements? We have seen that they correspond in formulating the need for radically new world views, a shift in power relations and a preference for personal approaches initiated by the grassroots and inspired by the heart and personal inspiration. The interviews with the activists in 2015 revealed that the participants in the movements had the same knowledge about features such as goals, leadership and integration of members as the leaders. In providing an account on their experiences, they elaborated examples and insights related to recent history. They provided an overview of these years. They indicated that some intended mechanisms had changed. For instance, the intended concert in Cairo was replaced by a global wave of concerts in the case of MasterPeace (Resp. 3). GIAWH had not succeeded in getting traditional entrepreneurs to give to social entrepreneurs. Instead, the giveshop had emerged.

When looking at the question on how to create broad support, it is evident that MasterPeace is the most successful in this field. This movement is extremely skilful in packaging its message and making it both attractive and relatively easy for grassroots and business to engage. The participants of both Zeitgeist and GIAWH indicated that the movements had a strong and active nucleus, many interested people around them, but only a few became really engaged. I believe that Zeitgeist needs to find ways to reformulate – perhaps in pictures rather than in text – their sophisticated intellectual message. In this sense, they can learn from the other two movements. GIAWH was the least mature – the youngest movement and the initiative of one person. The question is why this movement did not succeed getting entrepreneurs to give, whereas MasterPeace manages to receive support from corporations.[20] A final observation is to do with the autonomy of the three movements, which is both their strength and their weakness. I would suggest that they seek ways to cooperate with existing political parties and institutions such as the UN and NGOs to create platforms for positive policies and actions formulated by these entities. Co-creating with formal institutions may give hands and feet to intended – but often stagnated – policies within existing institutions, and it might add to the strength and effectiveness of the movements presented above.

Suggestions for future research

Throughout the article, I argued that these movements deserve academic attention. I make the following suggestions for further research.

In the theoretical field, I suggest that further research is done to check whether transition theory can indeed be fruitfully combined with SE theory.

Methodologically, it would be useful to apply this model to other cases, to test it and to further develop it.

As for the movements, it seems helpful to generate knowledge – or make available existing knowledge – as to how to attract and mobilize a substantive group of supporters and participants.

A final suggestion would be to engage in forms of participatory action research to involve the grassroots and coordinators in the research performed, to investigate ways in which these movements can be more closely connected to existing political and institutional forces, so as to create global forms of co-creation in times of financial and ecological crises.

Conclusions

This research offers a methodology to analyse social entrepreneurial movements in the light of both emancipation and world-making, thus filling a gap in existing literature. I designed a methodology that expands the Rindova, Barry, and Ketchen (2009) approach to SE as emancipation in the direction of world-making. I have been able to do this within existing scientific paradigms as suggested by Seymour (2012). It has introduced three radically new case studies to SE literature: Zeitgeist, GIAWH and MasterPeace, which all started within the last seven years. The analysis was placed in the context of the neoliberal Dutch Government, the entrepreneuriaization of the Netherlands and the need for new social alternatives to envision a way out of the current financial and ecological crises. I created a post-structural theoretical and methodological framework that reveals common patterns in the structure of the three narratives and differences in their worldviews. By combining the narrative framework of Somers (1994) and the deictic analysis of Chilton (2004), and a post-structural notion of space (Harvey 1996) and time (Adam and Groves 2007), it reveals the key mechanisms of 'Entrepreneuring as emancipation' and key dimensions in the process of world-making. As for emancipation, it indicates that 'making declarations' entails meta-narratives, ontological narratives and temporal categories in which the past and present indicate what is wrong, while the desired change is situated in the future. 'Authoring' mostly takes place in the dimension of social relations. In terms of entrepreneuring as world-making, the analysis has pinpointed 'public relations', 'space', 'future' and 'myth' as dimensions within the realm of world-making. Drawing on transition theory, I have suggested that these movements represent 'niches' and are in pre-developmental stages of making social change. I suggest that 'niches' can be considered as a stage between the discourse theoretical concepts of 'myth' and 'social imaginary'.

Without claiming that these movements are perfect, I do claim that they are acutely relevant in a world of increased dehumanization and technological advances since they hold the promise of creating spaces for hope and human agency in a time when democratic governments are failing to do so. They offer space for citizens around the world to contribute to the kind of civic emancipation that Sayer (2014) calls for and the dialectical utopianism that Harvey (2000) advocates.

Notes

1. I used the work by Somers (1994) in earlier research on the Zapatista movement in Mexico. (Montesano Montessori 2009) and on the *Indignados* in Spain (Montesano Montessori and Morales López 2015).
2. https://www.youtube.com/watch?v=hKqCq_Knnbo&feature=youtu, uploaded on 14 December 2015.
3. https://www.zeitgeistbeweging.nl/media/boeken/, uploaded on 14 December 2015.
4. http://www.givingisallwehave.com/giving-away-my-ticket-lowlands/, 14 December 2015.
5. https://www.youtube.com/watch?v=k1XAF9zFEtl, 14 December 2015.
6. http://www.givingisallwehave.com/economic-economy-crisis-consciousness-part-1/.
7. https://www.youtube.com/watch?v=-07AmGcnAgA, 14 December 2015.
8. For Zeitgeist, RP1 is the current coordinator of the Dutch Chapter (active since 2009, he initiated the Dutch chapter by organizing the international Z day in Amsterdam in 2010); RP2 is the regional coordinator Amsterdam, active since March 2011. RP3 is the regional coordinator of the Dutch province Limburg, and active in Zeitgeist international since 2008. For GIAWH, RP1 was project and team leader, active since November 2011. He ran and managed the giveshop throughout 2012–2014; Rsp 2 met Timmers in Costa Rica and is from Denver, Colorado. He was actively involved since August 2011 and assisted the facilitation of the organizations presence at Lowlands Festival 2011 and 2012 in Holland. R3 did the design and was active since February 2012. For MP, R1 is talent banker and part of the Board of Inspiration (active since November 2011); RP2 is the current CEO; RP3 works at the Dutch national office for communication and IT (active since January 2012).
9. CDA considers abduction as a constant movement between theory, social context, methodology and empirical data (Reisigl and Wodak 2009; Montesano Montessori, 2011).

10. http://api.ning.com/files/0TyPLysMYmYf2Vas60cIIIMf9ILQafmnCEuj8*xVMPN4d7XKqJ7 ryww9TVCHqbEV0pDdvNPmuC9Y9y1BaKeppyBPJMyTcFzr/MasterPeaceClubManual3. 0reduced.pdf consulted 15 December 2015. It was available in 2012.
11. Since January 2012, I have followed these three websites. They are in continuous development. Early 2012, the website of Zeitgeist moved from a Dutch translation of the international website to a simplified site prepared for (potential) activists. GIAWH updated itself as it was going and the exact dates of all the uploads are visible today. Remarkable changes were the movie, available since November 2013 http://www.givingisallwehave.com/blog/ and the interactive giveshop. The final blog that announced the end of the movement dates 2 December 2014. With Masterpeace, new developments were the increase of clubs, moving up from 19 clubs in 22 countries during the initial interview to 65 clubs in 47 countries in September 2015. In 2014, the sponsors started to appear on the website. In 2013, a Dutch website was made (masterpeace.nl) (maintained by Respondent 1). In 2014, the Be a Nelson campaign was started.
12. Jeroen Timmers explained that he finished the movement after they had experimented various times with the giveshop. In general, he felt that the giveshop was the end of a stage in his personal development, rather than a beginning. A leading banker of Goldman Sachs had offered to help him grow the movement. Though Timmers went to London to discuss this, he did not want to follow this path (email 29 July 2015). He is now in the personal transition stage towards GIAWH 2.0, still gives presentations and is open for communication about his developing worldview (jeroentimmers.com). The concept of the giveshop is available for others to be taken over. He features on the documentary Normal is Over (normalisoverthemovie.com) by an award-winning film-maker, which was launched on 23 November 2015, one week before the UN environment talks in Paris.
13. https://www.youtube.com/watch?v=hKqCq_Knnbo, 14 December. 2015.
14. In 2012, however, the giveshop was created, www.givingisallwehave.com/category/give-shop/, a shop which looked like an ordinary shop but it was a place where you could only give something. In the open space at the end of the interview, this respondent who had been one of the main developers of the concept of the giveshop provided a link to a video https://www.youtube.com/watch?v=LabMZ1NyGdA. While certainly magic moments happened in the giveshop, the organizers also noticed that people are more eager to give than to receive unconditionally. Often they do not trust it or they find that they should do something in return (interview with Resp.1, received 29 August 2015).
15. https://www.youtube.com/watch?v=h6uP_y_LZuk, 24 May 2016.
16. However, ZG respondent 2 stated that the movement had passed through three stages since 2008. The formulation of the message, now completed in the Zeitgeist defined book; the birth of small projects such as the window farms and the future when big projects will happen
17. http://masterpeace2014.nl/bouwpakket/masterPeace-vision-paper.pdf, 24 May 2016.
18. http://masterpeace2014.nl/business-partners/, 24 May 2016.
19. A respondent of the last round of written interviews stated that the political situation in Egypt was too dangerous. They then attempted Istanbul; this is another magnificent bridge between East and West, but it was politically unsustainable. Then they remembered they were grassroots and facilitated a wave. In every country where an MP Club was active, there was a concert, while Amsterdam served as a 'beating heart where artists from conflict countries created new connections' (email Respondent 3, 28 August 2015). See https://www.youtube.com/watch?v=h6uP_y_LZuk for the official movie (downloaded on September 16, 2015 and link adapted on 24 May 2016).
20. R3MP said that raising support from business is not easy. But often managers understand that they need a sustainable world to do business. Mostly, they want to contribute by providing services rather than money. MP operates as the matching party.

Acknowledgements

I wish to thank the anonymous reviewers and the editor of this journal for their insightful comments and suggestions. I owe much to Karen Verduyn (VU Amsterdam) with whom I worked on this research for almost two years. She introduced me to the literature on SE. I thank the Amsterdam Gesture Centre and the Amsterdam Critical Discourse Community for the opportunity to present earlier stages of the research, which provided helpful comments, especially from Ida Sabelis, for further development. I furthermore am deeply grateful to Iain Munro (Newcastle Business School), Tom Bartlett (Cardiff University), Neil Thompson and David Barberá-Tomás (VU Amsterdam) for their detailed proofreading and valuable and supportive suggestions. I gratefully thank the VU Amsterdam faculty of humanities for providing me visiting scholar status (2011–2014) on invitation by Alan Cienki.

Disclosure statement

No potential conflict of interest was reported by the author.

References

Adam, B., and C. Groves. 2007. *Future Matters. Action, Knowledge, Ethics*. Leiden: Brill.

Alter, K. 2002. *Case Studies in Social Enterprise: Counterpart International's Experience*. Washington, DC: Counterpart International.

Austin, J., H. Stevenson, and J. Wei-Skillern. 2006. "Social and Commercial Entrepreneurship: Same, Different, or Both?" *Entrepreneurship Theory and Practice* 30 (1): 1–22.

Avelino, F., and J. Rotmans. 2009. "Power in Transition: An Interdisciplinary Framework to Study Power in Relation to Structural Change". *European Journal of Social Theory* 12 (4): 543–569.

Bornstein, D. 2004. *How to Change the World. Social Entrepreneurs and the Power of New Ideas*. New York: Oxford University Press.

Boutellier, H. 2015. *Het seculiere experiment. Hoe we van God los gingen samenleven* [The Secular Experiment. How We Separated Our Communal Life from God]. Amsterdam: Boom.

Calas, M., L. Smircich, and K. Bourne. 2009. "Extending the Boundaries: Reframing 'Entrepreneurship as Social Change' through Feminist Perspectives." *Academy of Management Review* 34 (3): 552–569.

Chilton, P. 2004. *Analyzing Political Discourse. Theory and Practice*. London: Routledge.

Fairclough, N. 2003. *Analyzing Discourse. Textual Analysis for Social Research*. London: Routledge.

Gramsci, A. 1971. *Selections from the Prison Notebooks*. New York: International Publishers.

Harvey, D. 1996. *Justice, Nature & the Geography of Difference*. Oxford: Blackwell.

Harvey, D. 2000. *Spaces of Hope*. Berkeley: University of California Press.

Hermsen, J. 2014. *Kairos. Een nieuwe bevlogenheid* [Kairos: A New Passion]. Amsterdam: De Arbeiderspers.

Hjorth, D. 2013. "Public Entrepreneurship: Desiring Social Change, Creating Sociality." *Entrepreneurship and Regional Development* 25 (1–2): 34–51.

Jessop, B. 2002. *The Future of the Capitalist State*. Cambridge: Polity Press.

Laclau, E., and C. Mouffe. 1985. *Hegemony and Socialist Strategy. Towards a Radical Democratic Politics*. London: Verso.

Mair, J., and I. Martí. 2006. "Social Entrepreneurship Research: A Source of Explanation, Prediction and Delight." *Journal of World Business* 41: 36–44.

McAdam, D., J. D. McCarthy, and M. N. Zald. (1996). *Comparative Perspectives on Social Movements. Political Opportunities, Mobilizing Structures, and Cultural Framings*. Cambridge: University Press.

Montesano Montessori, N. 2009. *An Analysis of a Struggle for Hegemony in Mexico: The Zapatista Movement versus President Salinas de Gortari*. Saarbrücken: VDM.

Montesano Montessori, N. 2011. "The Design of a Theoretical, Methodological, Analytical Framework to Analyse Hegemony in Discourse." *Critical Discourse Studies* 8: 169–181.

Montesano Montessori, N., and E. Morales López. 2015. "The Study of Innovative Discourses of Change. Reinventing Democracy in Spain: The Case of 15 M." *CADAAD (Critical Approaches to Discourse Analysis across Disciplines)*, 7 (2): 200–221.

Reisigl, M., and R. Wodak. 2002. *Discourse and Discrimination. Rhetorics of Racism and Antisemitism*. London: Routledge.

Reisigl, M., and R. Wodak. 2009. "The Discourse-historical Approach (DHA)." In *Methods of Critical Discourse Analysis*, edited by R. Wodak and M. Meyer, 87–121. 2nd ed London: Sage.

Rindova, V., D. Barry, and D. J. Ketchen. 2009. "Entrepreneuring as Emancipation." *Academy of Management Review* 34 (3): 477–491

Sarasvathy, S. 2012. "Worldmaking." In *Entrepreneurial Action. Advances in Entrepreneurship, Firm Emergence and Growth*, edited by Emerald Group, Vol. 14, 1–24. Bingley: Emerald Group.

Sayer, A. 2014. *Why We Can't Afford the Rich*. Bristol: Policy Press.

Short, J., T. Moss, and G. Lumpkin. 2009. "Research in Social Entrepreneurship: Past Contributions and Future Opportunities." *Strategic Entrepreneurship Journal* 3 (2): 161–194.

Somers, M. R. 1994. "The Narrative Constitution of Identity: A Relational and Network Approach." *Theory and Society* 23: 605–649.

Seymour, R. G., ed. 2012. *Handbook of Research Methods on Social Entrepreneurship*. Cheltenham: Edward Elgar.

Steyaert, C. and M. Bachmann. 2012. "Listening to Narratives." In *Handbook of Research Methods on Social Entrepreneurship*, edited by R. G. Seymour, 51–78. Cheltenham: Edward Elgar.

Steyaert, C., and D. Hjorth, eds. 2006. *Entrepreneurship as Social Change. A Third Movements in Entrepreneurship Book*. Cheltenham: Edward Elgar.

Tellegen, E. 2014. *Afscheid van het kapitalisme. Over de aarde en onze economische orde* [Farewell to Capitalism. About the Earth and Our Economic Order]. Amsterdam: Amsterdam University Press.

Tonkens, E., M. Trappenburg, M. Hurenkamp, and J. Schmidt. 2015. *De Montessori-Democratie. Spanningen tussen burgerparticipatie en de lokale politiek* [The Montessori Democracy. Tensions Between Citizen Participation and Local Politics]. Amsterdam: Amsterdam University Press.

Touraine, A. 1985. "An Introduction to the Study of Social Movements." *Studies in Comparative International Development* 35 (4): 30–58.

Destituent entrepreneurship: disobeying sovereign rule, prefiguring post-capitalist reality

Pascal Dey

ABSTRACT

This article introduces 'destituent entrepreneurship' as a way of imagining the political thrust of entrepreneurship under conditions of crisis. Taking its cues from Giorgio Agamben's work on destituent power, and from theories of prefigurative praxis by other thinkers, this analysis uses the occupied-enterprise movement in Argentina as an illustrative case to cultivate sensitivity for the more radical possibilities of entrepreneurship as they emanate from the free-floating conflictual energy at the heart of society. Specifically, refracting destituent entrepreneurship into its essential components, we highlight, first, how laid-off workers redefined themselves as resistant entrepreneurs who counter-acted the fraudulent close-down of their enterprises by reclaiming their right to work. Second, we point out how the reclaimed enterprises created new opportunities not only for creating income, but for prefiguring post-capitalist realities rooted in self-organized and dignified work, democratic decision-making and the creation of a common people. The key contribution this article makes is to alert us to how entrepreneurship under conditions of crisis is less a matter of necessity alone, i.e. making a living in hard times, but an opportunity to redefine the realm of economic practice by one's own rules.

Introduction

The recent economic crisis has witnessed a myriad of cases of disobedience and civil unrest in the face of perceived injustices and economic hardship. Examples include protests, direct action, the rise of (new) social movements, court mediations against powerful institutions such as banks, hunger strikes or people who chain themselves to their houses in order to prevent being evicted (Barbero 2015). Some commentators have argued that entrepreneurship too represents a response to the widespread suffering which the recent economic crisis has engendered, and a particularly effective one at that. We are talking here not about entrepreneurship as a strategy for employment generation, innovation, productivity and growth (cf. van Praag and Versloot 2007), but about entrepreneurship as a way of advancing, first and foremost, justice (Santos 2013), decommodification (Vail 2010), community building (Savaya et al. 2008), social innovation (Nicholls and Murdock 2011), or emancipation (Rindova,

Barry, and Ketchen 2009). Not surprisingly, entrepreneurship scholars have been keen to embrace 'crisis' as a topical area of research (Zikou, Gatzioufa, and Sarri 2011), understanding that it presents an opportunity to create fresh insights into how entrepreneurship generates value for society by nudging 'bottom-up social transformations that are neither rigid nor bureaucratic, that are neither formal nor fixed' (Daskalaki, Hjorth, and Mair 2015, 420).

Today, we find a growing and increasingly detailed literature on how entrepreneurship works to enliven communities and entire societies. Some of the clearest examples of this strand of research can be found in accounts of social entrepreneurship (Mauksch and Rowe 2016) or community-based entrepreneurship (Peredo and Chrisman 2006), which supposedly create social and financial value in situations where the state failed to do so.[1] It is unarguably one of the main merits of this literature, which is still in a nascent stage, to have created sensitivity for how entrepreneurship in the context of crisis functions as an 'engine' not only for economic recovery and growth, but for increasing the resilience and viability of neighbourhoods, communities or entire societies (Parra and Ruiz 2014).

However valuable these contributions are, they tend to delineate a rather sanitized image of entrepreneurship. Focusing largely on how entrepreneurship solves existing problems, replaces ossified structures through more efficient ones (Zahra et al. 2009), or incrementally makes conventional business more socially responsible (Driver 2012), existing research fails to grasp the inherent violence and brutality of neoliberal capitalism as the very root cause of recurring crises (Harvey 2010, 2014; Sassen 2014). The effect of this omission is an overly optimistic belief in the power of entrepreneurship as a vehicle of positive change in society. In a similar vein, existing research typically fails to consider that radical change, i.e. change which engages the capitalist edifice head-on, might presuppose subverting, disrupting, or even destroying existing relations of force.

These shortcomings have enticed commentators to suggest that the term entrepreneurship – including cognates such as social or ethical entrepreneurship – is inadequate for explaining (radical) social change (Hjorth 2013; Jones and Murtola 2012). We agree with this qualification, and suggest the neologism 'desituent entrepreneurship' to highlight a form of entrepreneurship which does not only operate in the context of crisis engendered by neoliberal capitalism, but actively challenges and disrupts neoliberal capitalism by suspending some of its foundational values and practices. Using the worker-occupied enterprises in Argentina as an illustrative example, our conceptualization harks back to two important works: first, Agamben's work on destituent power which conveys the key insight that the realization of new historical possibilities necessarily involves struggle, resistance and disobedience, and second, theories of prefigurative praxis advanced by other authors which chiefly explore possibilities of establishing alternative modes of individual and collective life from within existing conditions of possibility. Conjoining these bodies of literature offers a conceptual repertoire which permits a thoroughgoing reappraisal of neoliberal capitalism by providing insights on how radical forms of entrepreneurship emanate from the conflictual energy at the heart of society.

This article suggests that it would be naïve to believe that entrepreneurship under conditions of crisis is merely about fixing existing problems, whilst leaving the larger economic system untouched. Thus, the overarching contribution of this article is to demonstrate how destituent entrepreneurship disrupts and transcends neoliberal capitalism by way of building basic values of co-ownership, co-creation and the commons into the everyday life of entrepreneurship. In this way, our conceptualization contributes to extant research on entrepreneurship by drawing attention to the important, but largely overlooked, political dimension of entrepreneurship.

The remainder of the article is structured as follows. First, we problematize existing research on entrepreneurship in the context of crisis. This is followed, second, by a tentative overview of the economic crisis in Argentina and the worker-occupied enterprise movement. Third, a conceptual case description of the worker-occupied enterprise movement is presented. Moving back and forth between the historical facts of the occupations in Argentina and Agamben's work on destituent power and theories of prefigurative praxis developed by others, we incrementally advance the concept of destituent entrepreneurship. Fourth, we adumbrate the main elements of destituent entrepreneurship. A few short concluding observations draw the article to a close.

Entrepreneurship under conditions of crisis: a problematization

Recent years have witnessed a renewed interest in questions of how entrepreneurship can create value for society under conditions of crisis (van Putten II and Green 2011). This literature reflects broader attempts to (once again) render entrepreneurship socially meaningful by re-aligning the subject matter with the interests and desires of society (Cornwall 1998; Steyaert and Hjorth 2006; Steyaert and Katz 2004). At the risk of oversimplifying, the general thinking is that in moments of crisis entrepreneurship can contribute to rebuilding communities and even entire societies under strain by stimulating cooperation between private sector actors and community groups (Johannisson 1990), thereby strengthening the cultural, natural and social capital upon which societies are based (Peredo and Chrisman 2006). A conspicuous aspect of this perspective is that it associates entrepreneurship not so much with the capabilities of a rare breed of individuals, but with the kind of embedded and hybrid agency that typifies neighbourhoods or communities (Steyaert and Katz 2004). Entrepreneurship qua distributed agency is not limited to a particular sector or type of organization, but defined more by its effects, i.e. how entrepreneurship develops communities, creates social capital, and implements bottom-up revitalization strategies with no or minimal government funding (Bailey 2012).

Even if this literature is anything but homogeneous, it is united by an emphasis on entrepreneurship's redemptive and enabling qualities. For instance, stressing bottom-up innovation in the context of austerity and welfare state retrenchment (Mauksch and Rowe 2016), entrepreneurship is seen as an effective means for solving problems associated with the enormous budget cuts in public spending, and the deficiencies in public services more generally. Construing entrepreneurship as local, community-led regeneration and reforms in public service provision opens up new possibilities for thinking about how entrepreneurship can address increasing levels of pauperization by exploiting new opportunities which become available under conditions of crisis.

Although we are largely in agreement with many of the claims advanced by this literature, we also believe that it presents a one-sided view which does not lead to an adequate understanding of the crisis of neoliberal capitalism, nor the political role entrepreneurship can play therein. As briefly intimated before, the literature on entrepreneurship in the context of crisis is marked by considerable shortcomings. For instance, zooming in on the transformative potential of entrepreneurship in solving existing problems, available research tends to turn a blind eye to the larger politico-economic circumstances that have engendered the various problems in the first place (Dey, Schneider, and Maier 2016; Dey and Steyaert 2012). Thus, glossing over intricate issues pertaining to, for instance, power, values, or class which some commentators deem essential components of radical change (Jameson 1999), existing research on entrepreneurship obfuscates the broader political, economic, and legal under-pinnings of the crisis, and the systematic violence and brutality of neoliberal capitalism at large (Harvey 2010, 2014).

Arguably, these omissions are at least as much ideologically motivated as they are theo-retically informed, since they essentially work to consolidate a positive image of entrepre-neurship premised on the idea of harmonious and frictionless change. What we are most concerned about here is that the existing literature (re)assesses, if inadvertently, complex social, political and economic situations adopting a logic that promotes value-free problem solving. And second, this literature advances an understanding of social change that fails to take into account the broader conditions of the neoliberal capitalist economy. Hence, unlike those who saw the recent economic crisis as signalling the need for fundamental changes in the economic order to prevent similar meltdowns in the future (e.g. Harvey 2014; Roy 2014; Sassen 2014), the literature on entrepreneurship remains silent on this issue.

Thus, suggestive as the current literature on entrepreneurship in times of crisis is, it is ultimately inadequate to explain how neoliberal capitalism works and how it can be changed (Harvey 2010, 2014). As argued below, entrepreneurship can be more than just a prob-lem-solving device, but a form of political intervention geared towards the creation of real-ities that transcend the desiderata of neoliberal capitalism by contesting and re-negotiating its core values and practices. We thereby seek to overcome the theoretical rigidities discussed above by advancing the concept of 'destituent entrepreneurship'. Before doing so, we first provide some background information on our case study: the worker-occupied enterprises in Argentina.

Background: the Argentinean crisis in 2001

The recent economic crisis, and its ensuing fiscal crisis (Clarke and Newman 2012), has resulted in the curtailment of essential social services, and in many countries created frac-tured societies which left people excluded from basic human rights. Citizens who used to participate in public and commercial life were transformed into what Agamben (2000) calls the 'fragmentary multiplicity of needy and excluded bodies' (31), or more bluntly, the 'wretched, the oppressed, and the vanquished' (ibid.). Turning the time back to the year 2001, we can see that the people in Argentina experienced similar levels of disenchantment and social suffering. While the Argentine economy had been touted as a poster child of the IMF's structural adjustment policies throughout most of the 1990s, in 1998, the economy went into recession and in 2001, Argentina had to declare a default on some part of its external debt. Though this is not the space to explore in any detail the full complexity of the Argentine crisis, it is pertinent to point out that it was preceded by an era of emerging finance capitalism where Argentina tried to establish itself, with the support of transnational organ-izations such as the World Bank and the IMF, as part of the international financial architecture (Soederberg 2004). To achieve this end, the government during Carlos Menem's presidency (1989–1999) chiefly opened up the local economy to global capital, expanding the extensive borrowing practices which had already started in the 1970s (Teubal 2004). The overarching aim of Menem's government was to bring Argentina in line with a logic that envisioned free markets, trade and large corporations as the basic pillars of a thriving economy. This was to be accomplished by making access to capital a major priority.

The policy of attracting overseas investment to boost national productivity resulted in what Harvey (2005) called a 'neoliberal state', i.e. a state which elevates the interests of global capital to the position of a political imperative (Grugel and Riggirozzi 2007). Large companies were the main beneficiaries of official policies and programmes, which were geared towards privatizing and deregulating public services and utilities. During its neoliberal era, the state in Argentina was mainly catering to the interests of big businesses by increasing their share of the market in both the industry and the services (Teubal 2004). Furthermore, the state raised taxes for low and middle-income households and suspended all promotion regimes for small-size manufacturers in the context of public procurement. Further measures involved the reduction of public expenditure in the realm of education and welfare provision.

Menem's neoliberal strategy stimulated legal reforms designed to render labour laws more flexible, allowing owners to enhance the productivity of their enterprises by employing workers outside of collective bargaining agreements (Ranis 1999). Officially called a 'crisis prevention procedure', these legal reforms reduced wages and increased the precariousness of working conditions for employees. Although Menem's flexibilization of labour formed an important motif of the subsequent enterprise occupations, probably even more relevant was the realization that the economic crisis was 'often fraudulently used by the owners to decapitalize their firms, attain governmental credits for non-production-related financial speculation and, ultimately, to deprive the workers of their earned salaries' (Ranis 2005, 10, 11).

Together, these different interventions had the effect that many citizens felt that official norms and laws, although nominally binding, were not compelling since they had fallen out of step with the needs of society (Peñalver and Katyal 2010). The dwindling confidence in the integrity of the neoliberal state as the arbitrator of welfare and wealth, and the general distrust in its ability (and willingness) to ensure justice, eventually triggered an uprising in December 2001 when Menem's successor Fernando de la Rúa limited people's bank withdrawals to $1000 per month, thus effectively denying people access to their own savings (Cole 2007). Confronted with a situation in which 25% of the Argentine population was unemployed and 60% were living in poverty, an estimated one third of the Argentine population took to the streets to voice their discontent with the way they had been governed (North and Huber 2004). Spanning all social classes, the so-called pots and pans demonstrations involved people from all walks of life (Ranis 2004). Unified by the battle cry *¡Que se vayan todos!* (they must all go!), the protest marked a frontal attack on the state, the president and the neoliberal economic model (Colectivo Situaciones 2003). The insurrection opened up a space for a variety of socio-economic experiments, such as the worker-occupied enterprises which form the substantive focus of the following conceptualization.

A conceptual reading of the worker-occupied enterprises

The following reading is based on a conceptual case description of the worker-occupied enterprises. This is then used as a basis for the incremental development of the concept of destituent entrepreneurship. The two concepts destituent power and prefigurative praxis are used to offer a conceptual framework attentive to issues related to disobedience, resistance, self-organized work, democratic decision-making and the commons. The reading will proceed by moving back and forth between historical facts, conceptual analysis, and illustration.

Occupied enterprises and destituent power: disobedience, struggle and resistant entrepreneurs

From the workers' point of view, the political and economic power structures in Argentina were not deemed a pertinent model for securing the well-being of society, since they led to the prioritization of the sectional interests of the owners of big businesses and the affluent strata of Argentine society more generally. During the crisis, the Argentine government had implicitly incentivized owners to file for bankruptcy, thereby allowing them to close their factories without having to bear any of the social costs. Deceitful bankruptcies became a common practice. Examples include the owners of Global S.A. who, after having filed for bankruptcy, precluded bankruptcy procedures by removing all machinery from the building to start a new business (Monteagudo 2008).

Workers felt betrayed by their bosses who, in their view, had abandoned the factories without any consideration of the fate of their employees. Similarly, they lost confidence in a system that permitted the previous owners of the companies they had worked for to act with impunity, despite the fact that they had evidently mislead their creditors and unpaid employees. After thousands of enterprises were closed during the crisis, most workers saw no other option than to seek employment elsewhere. Yet, a small minority refused to accept the close-down of their enterprises. Workers in and outside of Buenos Aires started to occupy and recover abandoned factories. In total, about 200 factories were recovered, totalling approximately 15,000 workers. The worker-occupied enterprises movement included many industries, from the metallurgical, clothing and textile sector to the pharmaceutical, food and beverage industry, as well as schools and hotels (Lavaca Collective 2007).

Occupations as political disobedience

One way of looking at the occupations is to say that they constitute an act of illegality since the enterprises were officially shut down and declared bankrupt in accordance with existing laws. However, instead of seeing workers merely as delinquents, i.e. 'property outlaws' (Peñalver and Katyal 2010), we seek to advance a different appraisal by framing the occupations not as a juridical issue, but as a case of political disobedience. Disobedience has many meanings, but the prevailing interpretation in political theory is that disobedience chiefly tries to challenge sovereign power[2] with the ultimate aim of establishing a new legal constitution or social order which is deemed more adequate (in terms of democracy, equality or freedom). This form of disobedience (referred to in political theory as constituent power; Laudani 2013) does not correspond to the events in Argentina, since the worker-occupied enterprises did not – at least during the initial stages – try to reform the sovereign structures with the aim of creating a better constitution. Quite the contrary, the worker-occupied enterprises symbolize a form of disobedience characterized by a general desire to withdraw from the impeding influence of the neoliberal state by deactivating and suspending its official norms and rules.

This is what Agamben (2014) refers to as destituent power. Central to destituent power is an understanding of disobedience as the outright rejection of the legitimacy of sovereign rule and its politico-juridical apparatus. Destituent power thus describes a revolutionary moment characterized by resistance to official norms and sovereign rule (Laudani 2013). Destituent power attends to 'goals such as outright political independence or the freedom to live with dignity and without the violent imposition of force by the powerful' (Franceschet 2015, 241). The defining moment of destituent power is a kind of disobedience predicated on resistance. Whilst reflected in their slogan 'Occupy, Resist, Produce', which the workers had borrowed from the Brazilian landless movement, moments of resistance became manifest at different levels and during different stages of the occupations.

Resisting bankruptcy orders and reclaiming the right to work

To begin with, resistance in the case of the occupied enterprises was actualized when the workers, who had been excluded from their officially bankrupt enterprises, reopened the enterprises to resume work. The general reasoning of the occupants was that the abandoned enterprises implicitly belonged to society because many of them had received state subsidies, tax exemptions and other forms of government assistance prior to their fraudulent close-downs (Cole 2007). Since the workers construed the enterprises as public assets as they had been supported by taxpayer money, the occupations in their view merely signified the exercise of their right to work. Succinctly put, by taking control of the means of production, workers were effectively 'taking back' what they thought belonged to them already.

Looked at in this way, it becomes clear that the occupations resisted sovereign rule by refusing to accept the bankruptcy orders it had issued. However, resuming work by claiming access to the means of production is by no means a straightforward endeavour. For instance, workers were perpetually struggling to put their factories on a sound footing (Ranis 2006), faced difficulties in gaining access to capital and in establishing relationships with the formal economy which in part had become reluctant to work and trade with the occupants. However, perhaps the main challenge to the liberation of the economic realm was the workers' own sense of identity and self-perception.

The need for new identities: from workers to resistant entrepreneurs

Workers' sense of who they were was so deeply rooted in a wage-labour logic that it was very difficult for many to envision any other life trajectory. Having been used to working for a wage, workers suddenly became part of a revolutionary moment of which they probably never thought they would be part (Marti and Fernandez 2015). As the following extract shows, workers were at times overwhelmed by the revolutionary prospect the occupations had opened up and notably by the inescapable transition from worker to resistant entrepreneurs: 'If they [the bosses] had come to us with 50 pesos and told us to show up for work tomorrow, we would have done just that' (Gibson-Graham 2006, xxxv).

The ability to participate in this revolutionary moment, and to contribute to the widening of the field of economic possibilities, implied a need on the part of the workers to cultivate a new sense of identity which would permit them to resist and transcend norms of authority and hierarchy that had hitherto informed their sense of being. Monteagudo's (2008) ethnographic study of the recovered balloon factory La Nueva Esperanza (The New Hope) is instructive here as it reveals how female workers learned to experience themselves as efficacious beings capable of voicing and asserting their interests and perspectives. The decision to occupy their enterprise literally pushed the female workers into believing in and trusting their own entrepreneurial capabilities. The revolutionary act of occupying their enterprise allowed them to grasp 'the possibility of becoming something other than wages-workers relegated to spending life producing for others within the capital-labor relation' (Vieta 2014, 784). Looked at from the perspective of destituent power, we can see that the workers re-invented themselves as 'resistant entrepreneurs' who refused to endorse normative assumptions of labour, hierarchy and coercion, understanding that cultivating a novel political identity capable of pushing back against sovereign rule was imperative for liberating their economic reality.

Resisting court decisions and ex-proprietors

Perhaps one of the clearest examples of resistance emerged as a reaction to police violence perpetrated in the context of forced evictions. An exemplary case is provided by the workers of Brukman, a textile company in Buenos Aires, who had taken over their enterprise in 2001 after the owners had fled the indebted company (North and Huber 2004). Approximately a year after the workers' occupation, the police took over the enterprise on the authority of a court order to reclaim the machinery. The workers, mainly women, who were present at the enterprise were immediately arrested. According to the theory of destituent power, expelling the workers from their premises signifies attempts to re-establish order within society. However, only a few hours after the arrests, supporters of the Brukman workers as well as various activists and human rights groups arrived on site to protest against the forced eviction and the detention of the female workers. The protests resulted in the withdrawal of the police forces and the release of the arrested workers. And even though various eviction attempts by the police followed, the Brukman workers were ultimately successful in retaining control over the enterprise and even received legal permission to return to their enterprise (Rossi 2015).

While Brukman offers an illuminating example of how workers were able to push back police forces, it cannot be stressed enough that resistance was a collective endeavour that strongly relied upon the support from the communities. As one worker of Chilavert, a book publishing firm, reminds us:

> It [the enterprise] wasn't won merely by its eight workers [...] It was also won by the neighbours, the teacher, the plumber, the grandmother for the neighbourhood who came out and fought off the police, who helped stop the eviction attempt. (Huff-Hannon 2004)

This anecdote draws attention to how destituent power entails the rise of a collective will that refuses to succumb to sovereign rule. This collective will only emerges occasionally during moments of crisis (Agamben 2000).

To summarize, what the concept of destituent power allows us to see is how workers turned into resistant entrepreneurs who, with the support of the community, fought against the debilitating effect of the official order (i.e. courts, governments, the police force and ex-proprietors) and who occupied the abandoned enterprises to reclaim their right to work. The next paragraph complements this image by homing in on how the occupied enterprises were used to prefigure emancipatory working conditions and thriving communities.

Occupied enterprises and the prefiguration of post-capitalist realities

A basic insight that can be gleaned from our analysis so far of the worker occupations is that resistant entrepreneurs based their actions on their own rules and sense of justice. This involved not only the decision to occupy the enterprises on the grounds that they already, if implicitly, belonged to them (cf. above), but also demonstrated their will to recreate the labour process according to a set of new ideals and principles. This self-legislating nature of the worker-occupied enterprises is indicative of the literature on prefigurative praxis.

In broad strokes, prefigurative praxis includes a broad range of activities which are united by a desire to unleash emancipatory, post-capitalist aspirations in the course of everyday life. In prefigurative praxis, emancipatory goals are not projected into the distant future, but recursively built into and activated in the context of everyday life. The basic contention of prefigurative praxis is that a self-determined life under capitalism requires a radical redefinition of the realm of economic practice in the 'here and now'. Popularized in the context of social anarchist works (Graeber 2002) where it formed a critique of revolutionary Marxism[3] (Boggs 1977), prefigurative praxis today is as an inherent part of experiments in alternative politics and 'diverse' economies (Gibson-Graham, Cameron, and Healy 2013) as well as social movements (Maeckelbergh 2011). Buechler (2000) maintains that prefiguration is central to a host of anti-oppressive initiatives that aim to 'work directly from basic values to daily practice' (207). We would like to begin by first revealing and conceptually reflecting on how the occupied enterprises brought about emancipatory effects by rearranging the production process in line with principles of democracy, justice and solidarity. In a second step, we aim to show how the enterprises themselves were used to prefigure a common people by being redefined as part of the commons.

Prefiguring emancipatory working conditions

A conspicuous aspect of the reclaimed factories is that their occupants resumed production, but did so under radically different conditions. After their previous bosses had abandoned the enterprises (Rossi 2015), the workers used their newfound 'liberties' to establish relationships amongst their co-workers characterized by solidarity (Lavaca Collective 2007) and an ethos of mutual support (Monteagudo 2008). This formed a strong contrast with how the hierarchically organized enterprises had previously operated, as worker were often not supposed to talk to each other during their shifts. As Carmen, a member of La Nueva Esperanza, recalls, workers under their previous bosses 'did not even say "hi" to each other' (Monteagudo 2008, 204).

These new practices and ways of relating were mostly made possible through cooperative forms of co-creation, co-ownership and democratic decision-making. Revitalizing the historical struggle for the exercise of control over the means of production, co-operative principles enabled dignified and empowering working conditions by ensuring that everyone would receive the same wage, that basic management decisions were taken democratically by an assembly, and that leaders were elected by the workers (one worker, one vote). Although they loosely followed the example of the cooperative movement around Robert Owen (1771–1858), the occupied factories fostered largely non-oppressive working conditions predicated on values of democracy, justice and equality. Consistent with the literature on cooperative and self-determined organization (Gibson-Graham 2003), accounts of the occupied enterprises show that even though salaries sometimes varied from month to month and most reclaimed enterprises were not working at full capacity, workers were able to carry on production and to do so in a way that was conducive to workers' sense of fulfilment and happiness (Palomino et al. 2010). As one worker at the ceramics factory Zanón commented: 'When we had an owner, I couldn't talk the way we are right now. I couldn't even stop for a couple of minutes. Now I work calmly, with my conscience as my guide, and without a boss yelling that we have to reach the oh-so-important objective' (Lavaca Collective 2007, 60).

These cursory examples of self-managed and cooperative work offer an emblematic example of how the labour process can be used to transcend authoritarian and hierarchical models of organizing which typify the mainstream economy. In this way, the occupied factories support the conclusion that entrepreneurship is not necessarily antithetical to ethics (Longenecker, McKinney, and Moore 1988) for it can be effectively used to implement standards that embrace 'aspects of a post-capitalist world by interlacing alternatives with the ethics, values, and practice that are being struggled over and desired' (Vieta 2014, 784). In this way, prefigurative praxis draws attention to how enterprises achieve a reshaping of capitalism from within by democratizing 'the economic realm at the micro-level of the productive enterprise' (ibid., 796).

Commoning enterprises and the prefiguration of a common people

A key aspect of destituent entrepreneurship involves the transfer of ownership from private owners to the workers. At this decisive point of our argument, it is important to note that many of the formerly investor-owned enterprises were not just taken over by resistant entrepreneurship, but re-appropriated as part of the commons. The commons are understood as the resources that are accessible to all human beings (e.g. water, air, or communal land, but also open-source software or knowledge). The commons form a crucial ingredient of social organizing outside of and against capitalism (Fournier 2013). In the Argentine case, some of the occupied enterprises were transformed into commons in the sense that their premises were used to engage with local communities via the establishment of health clinics and learning centres, or the creation of sites of pedagogical, cultural and artistic production (Ranis 2005).

Consider, as an example, IMPA (Industria Metalúrgica y Plástica de Argentina) which set up a cultural centre for young people providing education to students and a health care centre providing free services to the neighbourhood (Jaramillo, McLaren, and Lazaro 2011). Or think about Zanón which helped set up a health clinic in a poverty stricken neighbourhood (Cole 2007). These are but two illustrations of how the occupied enterprises were used as a shared resource allowing community members to develop new skills and relationships and to satisfy basic human needs. Realizing a broad set of cultural, social, political and economic goals (Palomino 2003), the occupied enterprises as part of the commons became the linchpin of community life in society. Creating circuits between segments of society which were mostly separated by the social division of labour (Jaramillo, McLaren, and Lazaro 2011), the common of the occupied enterprises eventually achieved the prefiguration of a 'common people'. The common people, as Agamben (2000) points out, are not a unified entity, but a heterogeneous assemblage of subjects who previously had no place in the prevailing order. The common people in the case of the occupied enterprises materialized when excluded groups, including the middle class, various groups of street picketers (*picqueteros*), the retired, political activists and human rights groups and many others, were drawn together by a desire to use the enterprises as an openly accessible medium of social organization (Fournier 2013). Through their collective will, they now strove to protect the commons from being annexed, dispossessed or reclaimed by the neoliberal state, its police force or the previous owners (cf. above).

To summarize, the regained enterprises offered resistant entrepreneurs the possibility to recreate reality by their own rule. This involved attempts at redefining the labour process in such a way as to prefigure post-capitalist modes of (co-)existence based on values of democracy, justice and equality. Furthermore, through the use of their premises to establish community centres, schools, hospitals and sites of cultural production, the enterprises were re-appropriated as part of the commons and used to prefigure a common people.

Discussion

Our conceptual reading of worker-occupied enterprises highlights that destituent entrepreneurship involves the simultaneous refusal of sovereign rule as enforced by the neoliberal state on the one hand, and the collective desire to create alternative realities according to one's own rules on the other. Destituent entrepreneurship thus throws light on how disobedience, resistance and struggle but also the affirmation of more democratic and emancipatory modes of economic production all form inherent parts of the mundane experience of entrepreneurship. Testifying to the generative potential of entrepreneurship under conditions of economic hardship and crisis, our conceptualization not only accounts for the creation of new income opportunities under dire circumstances, but, importantly, the imminent transformation of identities (from workers to resistant entrepreneurs), enterprises (from privately owned to collectively managed entities), and communities (from the excluded to the common people). Overall, the concept of destituent entrepreneurship raises interesting, albeit potentially unsettling, questions about the normative role and radical potential of entrepreneurship in society.

To carve out the unique contribution destituent entrepreneurship makes to the further development of entrepreneurship studies, let us accentuate a few points. Evidently enough, the Argentine crisis offers just another example of the destructive effects global neoliberal capitalism ultimately has on the people by putting them out of work. Viewed in this light, one might infer that the reclaimed enterprises form a prototypical example of what entrepreneurship research terms 'necessity entrepreneurship' (Fayolle 2011). This inference is empirically supported by a survey which revealed that 60% of the occupants were not motivated by ideological reasons, but rather by the imperative of putting food on their tables (International Socialist Review 2007). It is here that the parallels end, though. Destituent entrepreneurship is, first and foremost, a political endeavour which uses economic means as a vehicle for prefiguring dignified working conditions and relationships based on solidarity and mutual support. Hence, rather than merely converting a crisis into an economic opportunity (according to the motto: 'never let a crisis go to waste'), destituent entrepreneurship implies that the right to work, dignity and solidarity are accomplishments that need to be reclaimed; destituent entrepreneurship is – to paraphrase Gibson-Graham, Cameron, and Healy (2013) – about 'taking back the economy'. Evidently then, destituent entrepreneurship cannot be reduced to the resumption of work, i.e. making a living in hard times, since it is constitutively based on disobedience, resistance and struggle. To complement the picture, our conceptualization has revealed that the true force of destituent entrepreneurship lies in its ability to actualize immanent collective (rather than individual) possibilities that are available in the present (Gibson-Graham 2006). Perhaps one of the most inspirational insights gained from our conceptual reading is how the occupied enterprises were used to relate to, collaborate with and mobilize their neighbourhoods, thereby contributing to the development of a common people. Destituent entrepreneurship, far from merely being an individual strategy of income creation, self-improvement or coping (Ozarow 2013), represents an eminent fabric of collective life in society.

To the extent that destituent entrepreneurship is primarily a political endeavour, there is seemingly an overlap with the concept of political entrepreneurship. This impression is potentially misleading. The defining feature of political entrepreneurship is that it actively seeks to transform the political system by addressing political goals that are not being met by this system. Political entrepreneurs are 'individuals whose creative acts have transformative effects on politics, policies, or institutions' (Sheingate 2003, 185). What bears emphasizing here is that political entrepreneurship is underpinned by the logic of sovereignty (Colectivo Situaciones 2003) with its fundamental assumption that society must be based on centralized political institutions and clear lines of authority (Franceschet 2015). In Agamben's (2014) view, the logic of sovereignty is deeply problematic due to the way it tends to reproduce structures of repression by simply replacing one constitutional order with another. The logic embodied by destituent entrepreneurship is diametrically opposed to that of sovereignty as it seeks to attain change not through the sovereign structures with their juridical and police apparatus, but outside their influence. As illustrated by the Argentine example, destituent entrepreneurship endeavours to break free from sovereign rule without, however, establishing a new constitutional order. This refusal to seize power and to strive for a new constitution does not, as Laudani (2013) argues necessarily represent an impediment to or weakness of destituent entrepreneurship. Rather, destituent entrepreneurship signifies a conception of politics which engenders radical change by refusing to submit to the norms and rules laid down by sovereign power.

Undoubtedly, our reading of the worker-occupied enterprises casts a positive light on the radical potential of destituent entrepreneurship. An important clarification is in order, though. The looming return of the previous owners of the enterprises, first-hand experience of police violence and of constantly being at the mercy of sovereign rule eventually sparked a desire among some workers to seek protection via inclusion in the legal order. More than sixty occupied factories signed a letter to Congress demanding the establishment of a national law allowing the expropriation of self-managed factories from their former owners (International Socialist Review 2007), thus providing protection from creditor demands based on the previous owner's debts (Ranis 2010). The requests stimulated various legal and quasi-legal reforms, such as the reform of bankruptcy laws with greater stress on workers' right to work (Cole 2007). In 2002, a bankruptcy law was adopted which allowed workers to initiate production in the factories if a majority of the workers agreed to participate in the endeavour (Rossi 2015).

However, legal permissions were only temporary, and even if the enterprises were later expropriated by government, this typically meant that the ownership of the factories was given to government and 'only' the control of the premises to the workers (Cole 2007). Although the new stipulations generally turned workers into public sector employees (Ranis 2006) whose factories remained nationalized property administered by bureaucrats, this aptly illustrates how the more radical aspects of the occupied enterprises, notably the renunciation of the capitalist ownership model,[4] were neutralized. This means that while the legal reforms and the government-led expropriations clearly offered the workers some sense of security by eliminating the threat of evictions, they also undermined the movement's more radical edge in re-defining ownership and the labour process. With the introduction of the 'logic of the state into organizations that were initially conceived as autonomous and collectively self-empowering' (Monteagudo 2008, 193), a noticeable shift in the modus operandi of the regained enterprises occurred as they gradually shifted 'from a political focus to a practical, production focus' (Carroll and Balch 2007).

Workers' reliance on government support exemplifies that destituent entrepreneurship is never completely safe from state capture. Whereas destituent entrepreneurship remains an 'arduous task' (Agamben 2014), since it is always at risk of being eclipsed by the logic of sovereignty (Colectivo Situaciones 2003), we can infer that the power of entrepreneurship as an instrument of political disobedience is related to a large extent to the ability to become ungovernable, and to retain the potential of staying so (Agamben 2014).

In a broader sense, our conceptualization applies to situations where the broader politico-economic order has lost touch with the interests of society. This was the case in Argentina where the state was firmly wedded to financial interests and guided by the policies of transnational organizations such as the IMF. The bold contention destituent entrepreneurship makes is that entrepreneurship is not a key driver of the 'economic destiny' (Baumol 1993, 197), but the very mechanism which disrupts the core values of neoliberal capitalism by transforming the economy from within. The Argentine experience, as an exemplary case of destituent entrepreneurship, offers a powerful example in support of Ostrom's (1990) influential work on the commons which bears out that people are able to collaborate – through entrepreneurship – in such a manner as to share resources in a peaceful and sustainable manner, while at the same time protecting themselves from the risk of being hijacked by sovereign power.

Concluding comments

The starting point of this article was that existing theorizing in entrepreneurship studies offers novel approaches to thinking about the sort of contribution entrepreneurship can make for society under conditions of crisis. Despite its undeniable merits, we have shown that a key shortcoming of this research is that it relegates entrepreneurship to the status of a compensatory force that steps in whenever government has failed. To remedy this shortcoming, we have coined the neologism destituent entrepreneurship to ensure the viability of entrepreneurship as a political concept. Extending canonical interpretations of entrepreneurship during moments of crisis, destituent entrepreneurship makes a significant contribution in that it draws attention to how entrepreneurship forms a vehicle for disrupting and transcending the foundational values of neoliberal capitalism by incorporating the basic values of co-ownership and co-creation as well as the commons into the everyday life of entrepreneurship. In this way, our conceptualization adds a valuable perspective to existing theorizing on entrepreneurship in the context of crisis by revealing that the creation of alternative realities often presupposes the suspension of existing conditions of normative rule.

We cannot, of course, claim originality for having discovered the political thrust and entrepreneurial ingenuity of the Argentine workers. Indeed, the recovered enterprises have been skilfully chronicled by various documentaries, notably *The Take* directed by Naomi Klein and Avi Lewis. These Argentinean enterprises have also stimulated a myriad of inspirational reflections based on concepts such as autogestion (Vieta 2010), horizontalization (Sitrin 2006), and autonomism (Cuninghame 2010), to name but a few. The point to be stressed, however, is that while writing this article it became increasingly obvious that these discussions mainly take place outside of entrepreneurship studies. Although this absence is probably symptomatic of the general political quiescence of entrepreneurship studies (Verduyn et al. 2014), we believe that this situation must change. Thus, we would like to close the article by expressing our hope, the focal motto of this special issue, that the field of entrepreneurship studies will in future become more hospitable to investigations into how entrepreneurial creation involves acts of subversion (Bureau 2013), disruption (Hjorth and Steyaert 2009) and destruction (Jones and Murtola 2012). More specifically, any attempt that purports to capture the radical political possibilities of entrepreneurship must engage, in one way or another, with the complex questions of neoliberal capitalism as the organizing principle of society (Harvey 2005). Neoliberal capitalism is not perforce the superior system of economic organization that many still want it to be, but rather a global process which, albeit uneven, has proven successful in dispossessing ordinary people of their economic rights and their access to common resources. Given this destructive potential of neoliberal capitalism, we must insist on asking if and how entrepreneurship can intervene at this historical conjuncture.

Notes

1. It should be noted that this debate also involves alternative concepts such as 'community-led social venture creation', 'ecopreneurship', or 'sustainable entrepreneurship'.
2. The term denotes all actions taken by the state to govern society, such as the making and executing of laws, collection of taxes, issuing of trade agreements and the application of military or police force.
3. A key distinction from Marxist theorizing is that the transformation of the economic realm in prefiguratve praxis is not predicated on the seizure of power or the takeover of the state (Springer 2014).
4. For instance, the *Programme for Self-Managed Work*, a government instrument for 'institutionalizing' the occupied factories, required that the factories must be transformed from collectively owned into individually owned bodies. Excluding the possibility of collective ownership was exchanged for financial assistance, job preservation and self-managed work (Dinerstein 2007).

Disclosure statement

No potential conflict of interest was reported by the author.

Funding

This work was supported by the Basic Research Fund (GFF) at the University of St. Gallen [grant number 223101].

References

Agamben, G. 2000. *Means without End*. Minneapolis: University of Minnesota Press.
Agamben, G. 2014. "What is a Destituent Power?" *Environment and Planning D: Society and Space* 32: 65–74.
Bailey, N. 2012. "The Role, Organisation and Contribution of Community Enterprise to Urban Regeneration Policy in the UK." *Progress in Planning* 77: 1–35.
Barbero, I. 2015. "When Rights Need to Be (Re)Claimed: Austerity Measures, Neoliberal Housing Policies and Anti-eviction Activism in Spain." *Critical Social Policy* 35: 270–280.

Baumol, W. J. 1993. "Formal Entrepreneurship Theory in Economics: Existence and Bounds." *Journal of Business Venturing* 8: 197–210.

Boggs, C. 1977. "Marxism, Prefiguartive Communism and the Problem of Workers' Control." *Radical America* 6: 99–122.

Buechler, S. M. 2000. *Social Movements in Advanced Capitalism*. Oxford: Oxford University Press.

Bureau, S. 2013. "Entrepreneurship as a Subversive Activity: How Can Entrepreneurs Destroy in the Process of Creative Destruction?" *M@n@gement* 16: 204–237.

Carroll, R., and O. Balch 2007. "Here's the Chocolate Factory, but Where Has Willy Wonka Gone?" *The Guardian*, May 11, 2007.

Clarke, J., and J. Newman. 2012. "The Alchemy of Austerity." *Critical Social Policy* 32: 299–319.

Cole, A. 2007. "You Say You Want a Revolution: Argentina's Recovered Factory Movement." *Hastings International and Comparative Law* 30: 211–230.

Colectivo Situaciones. 2003. *¡Que se vayan todos! Krise und Widerstand in Argentinien* [¡Que se vayan todos! Crisis and resistance in Argentina]. Berlin: Assoziation A.

Cornwall, J. 1998. "The Entrepreneur as Building Block for Community." *Journal of Development Entrepreneurship* 3: 141–148.

Cuninghame, P. 2010. "Autonomism as a Global Social Movement." *Journal of Labor & Society* 13: 451–464.

Daskalaki, M., D. Hjorth, and J. Mair. 2015. "Are Entrepreneurship, Communities, and Social Transformation Related?" *Journal of Management Inquiry* 24: 419–423. doi:10.1177/1056492615579012.

Dey, P., H. Schneider, and F. Maier. 2016. Intermediary Organisations and the Hegemonisation of Social Entrepreneurship: Fantasmatic Articulations, Constitutive Quiescences, and Moments of Indeterminacy. *Organization Studies*. doi: 10.1177/0170840616634133.

Dey, P., and C. Steyaert. 2012. "Social Entrepreneurship: Critique and the Radical Enactment of the Social." *Social Enterprise Journal* 8: 90–107.

Dinerstein, A. C. 2007. "Workers' Factory Takeovers and New State Policies in Argentina: Towards an 'institutionalisation' of Non-governmental Public Action?" *Policy and Politics* 35: 529–550.

Driver, M. 2012. "An Interview with Michael Porter: Social Entrepreneurship and the Transformation of Capitalism." *Academy of Management Learning and Education* 11: 421–431.

Fayolle, A. 2011. "Necessity Entrepreneurship and Job Insecurity." *International Journal of E-Entrepreneurship and Innovation* 2: 1–10.

Fournier, V. 2013. "Commoning: On the Social Organisation of the Commons." *M@N@Gement* 16: 433–453.

Franceschet, A. 2015. "Theorizing State Civil Disobedience in International Politics." *Journal of International Political Theory* 11: 239–256. doi:10.1177/1755088215573092.

Gibson-Graham, J. K. 2003. "Enabling Ethical Economies: Cooperativism and Class." *Critical Sociology* 29: 123–161.

Gibson-Graham, J. K. 2006. *A Postcapitalist Politics*. Minneapolis: University of Minnesota Press.

Gibson-Graham, J. K., J. Cameron, and S. Healy. 2013. *Take Back the Economy: An Ethical Guide to Transforming Our Communities*. Minneapolis: University of Minnesota Press.

Graeber, D. 2002. "The New Anarchists." *The Left Review* 13: 61–73.

Grugel, J., and M. P. Riggirozzi. 2007. "The Return of the State in Argentina." *International Affairs* 83: 87–107.

Harvey, D. 2005. *A Brief History of Neoliberalism*. Oxford: Oxford University Press.

Harvey, D. 2010. *The Enigma of Capital*. Oxford: Oxford University Press.

Harvey, D. 2014. *Seventeen Contradictions and the End of Capitalism*. Oxford: Oxford University Press.

Hjorth, D. 2013. "Public Entrepreneurship: Desiring Social Change, Creating Sociality." *Entrepreneurship and Regional Development* 25: 34–51.

Hjorth, D., and C. Steyaert. 2009. "Entrepreneurship as Disruptive Event." In *The Politics and Aesthetics of Entrepreneurship: A Fourth Movements of Entrepreneurship Book*, edited by D. Hjorth and C. Steyaert, 1–10. Cheltenham: Edward Elgar.

Huff-Hannon, J. 2004. "The Pollen and the Bees." *New Internationalist Magazine: People, Ideas and Action for Global Justice* 368. http://newint.org/features/2004/06/01/factory-occupations/.

International Socialist Review. 2007. "Working Sin Patrón a Perspective on Worker-run Factories." *International Socialist Review* 55: November–December. http://www.isreview.org/issues/55/sinpatron.shtml.

Jameson, F. 1999. "The Theoretical Hesitation: Benjamin's Sociological Predecessor." *Critical Inquiry* 25: 267–288.

Jaramillo, N. E., P. McLaren, and F. Lazaro. 2011. "A Critical Pedagogy of Recuperation." *Policy Futures in Education* 9: 747–758.

Johannisson, B. 1990. "Community Entrepreneurship: Cases and Conceptualization." *Entrepreneurship & Regional Development* 2: 71–88.

Jones, C., and A. M. Murtola. 2012. "Entrepreneurship, Crisis, Critique." In *Handbook of Organizational Entrepreneurship*, edited by D. Hjorth, 116–133. Cheltenham: Edward Elgar.

Laudani, R. 2013. *Disobedience in Western Political Thought: A Genealogy*. Cambridge, MA: Cambridge University Press.

Lavaca Collective. 2007. *Sin Patrón: Stories from Argentina's Worker-run Factories*. Chicago, IL: Haymarket Books.

Longenecker, J. G., J. A. McKinney, and C. W. Moore. 1988. "Egoism and Independence: Entrepreneurial Ethics." *Organizational Dynamics* 16: 64–72.

Maeckelbergh, M. 2011. "Boing is Believing: Prefiguration as a Strategic Practice in the Alterglobalization Movement." *Social Movement Studies* 10: 1–20.

Marti, I., and P. Fernandez. 2015. "Entrepreneurship, Togetherness, and Emotions: A Look at (Postcrisis) Spain." *Journal of Management Inquiry* 24: 424–428. doi:10.1177/1056492615579786.

Mauksch, S., and M. Rowe. 2016. Austerity and Social Entrepreneurship in the United Kingdom: A Community Perspective. In *New Perspectives on Research Policy and Practice in Public Entrepreneurship*, edited by J. Liddle, 173–193. London: Emerald.

Monteagudo, G. 2008. "The Clean Walls of a Recovered Factory: New Subjectivities in Argentina's Recovered Factories." *Urban Anthropology and Studies of Cultural Systems of World Economic Development* 37: 175–210.

Nicholls, A., and A. Murdock. 2011. *Social Innovation: Blurring Boundaries to Reconfigure Markets*. London: Palgrave MacMillan.

North, P., and U. Huber. 2004. "Alternative Spaces of the 'Argentinazo.'" *Antipode* 36: 963–984.

Ostrom, E. 1990. *Governing the Commons: The Evolution of Institutions for Collective Action*. Cambridge: Cambridge University Press.

Ozarow, D. 2013. "Saucepans, Suits and Getting to Know the Neighbours: Resisting Paperisation in Argentina – The 2001-02 Economic Crisis and Its Legacies." Unpublished PhD thesis, Middlesex University, UK.

Palomino, H. 2003. "The Workers' Movement in Occupied Enterprises: A Survey." *Canadian Journal of Latin American and Caribbean Studies* 28: 71–97.

Palomino, H., I. Bleynat, S. Garro, and C. Giacomuzzi. 2010. "The Universe of Worker-recovered Companies in Argentina (2002–2008): Continuity and Changes inside the Movement." *Affinities: A Journal of Radical Theory Culture, and Action* 4: 252–287.

Parra, C., and C. Ruiz, eds. 2014. *Social Entrepreneurship: An Alternative to the Crisis*. Barcelona: J.M. Bosch.

Peñalver, E. M., and S. Katyal. 2010. *Property Outlaws: How Squatters, Pirates, and Protesters Improve the Law of Ownership*. New Haven, CT: Yale University Press.

Peredo, A. M., and J. J. Chrisman. 2006. "Toward a Theory of Community-based Enterprise." *Academy of Management Review* 31: 309–328.

van Praag, C. M., and P. H. Versloot. 2007. "What is the Value of Entrepreneurship? A Review of Recent Research." *Small Business Economics* 29: 351–382.

van Putten II, P., and R. Green 2011. Does It Take an Economic Recession to Advance Social Entrepreneurship? *Research in Business and Economics Journal* 3: 1–10.

Ranis, P. 1999. "The Impact of State and Capital Policies on Argentine Labor: A Comparative Perspective." In *Identities, State and Markets*, edited by J. Havet, 101–123. Toronto: Canadian Scholars' Press.

Ranis, P. 2004. "Rebellion, Class, and Labor in Argentine Society." *Working USA: Journal of Labor and Society* 7: 8–35.

Ranis, P. 2005. "Argentina's Worker-occupied Factories and Enterprises." *Socialism and Democracy* 19: 1–23.

Ranis, P. 2006. To Cccupy, to Resist, to Produce: Argentina's Worker-managed Factories and Enterprises. *Situations: Project of the Radical Imagination* 1: 57–72.

Ranis, P. 2010. "Argentine Worker Cooperatives in Civil Society: A Challenge to Capital-labor Relations." *Working USA: The Journal of Labor and Society* 13: 77–105.

Rindova, V., D. Barry, and D. J. Ketchen. 2009. "Entrepreneuring as Emancipation." *Academy of Management Review* 34: 477–491.

Rossi, F. M. 2015. "Building Factories without Bosses: The Movement of Worker-managed Factories in Argentina." *Societal Movement Studies* 14: 98–107. doi:10.1080/14742837.2013.874525.

Roy, A. 2014. *Capitalism: A Ghost Story*. Chicago, IL: Haymarket Books.

Santos, N. J. C. 2013. "Social Entrepreneurship That Truly Benefits the Poor: An Integrative Justice Approach." *Journal of Management and Global Sustainability* 1: 31–62.

Sassen, S. 2014. *Expulsions: Brutality and Complexity in the Global Economy*. Cambridge, MA: Harvard University Press.

Savaya, R., P. Packer, D. Stange, and O. Namir. 2008. "Social Entrepreneurship: Capacity Building among Workers in Public Human Service Agencies." *Administration in Social Work* 32: 65–86.

Sheingate, A. D. 2003. "Political Entrepreneurship, Institutional Change and American Political Development." *Studies in American Political Development* 17: 185–203.

Sitrin, M. 2006. *Horizontalism: Voices of Popular Power in Argentina*. Oakland, CA: AK Press.

Soederberg, S. 2004. *The Politics of the New International Financial Infrastructure: Reimposing Neoliberal Domination in the Global South*. New York: Zed Books.

Springer, S. 2014. "Human Geography without Hierarchy." *Progress in Human Geography* 38: 402–419.

Steyaert, C., and D. Hjorth. 2006. *Entrepreneurship as Social Change: A Third Movements of Entrepreneurship Book*. Cheltenham: Edward Elgar.

Steyaert, C., and J. Katz. 2004. "Reclaiming the Space of Entrepreneurship in Society: Geographical, Discursive and Social Dimensions." *Entrepreneurship and Regional Development* 16: 179–196.

Teubal, M. 2004. "Rise and Collapse of Neo-Liberalism in Argentina: The Role of Economic Groups." *Journal of Developing Societies* 20: 173–188.

Vail, J. 2010. "Decommodification and Egalitarian Political Economy." *Politics & Society* 38: 310–346.

Verduyn, K., P. Dey, C. Essers, and D. Tedmanson. 2014. "Toward a Critical Agenda of Entrepreneurship Studies: Emancipation and Entrepreneurship." *International Journal of Entrepreneurial Behaviour & Research* 20: 98–107.

Vieta, M. 2010. "The Social Innovation of *Autogestion* in Argentina's Worker-recuperated Enterprises: Cooperatively Organizing Productive Life in Hard times." *Labor Studies Journal* 36: 296–321.

Vieta, M. 2014. "The Stream of Self-determination and *Autogestion*: Prefiguring Alternative Economic Alternatives." *Ephemera: Theory & Politics in Organization* 14: 781–809.

Zahra, S. A., E. Gedajlovic, D. O. Neubaum, and J. M. Shulman. 2009. "A Typology of Social Entrepreneurs: Motives, Search Processes and Ethical Challenges." *Journal of Business Venturing* 24: 519–532.

Zikou, E., P. Gatzioufa, and A. Sarri. 2011. "Social Entrepreneurship in times of Economic Austerity: A Sparkle of Light for the Economies in Crisis." *Scientific Bulletin-Economic Sciences* 11: 53–65.

Entrepreneurial Orientation: do we actually know as much as we think we do?

Kathleen Randerson

ABSTRACT

The focus of this paper is on firm-level entrepreneurial behaviours and the processes that lead to them, known as Entrepreneurial Orientation. Despite the popularity of this construct, we argue that extant EO research suffers from major limitations linked to definitional inconsistencies and measurement issues. We present five distinct conceptualizations of EO in order to frame further research in the positivist mode. Moreover, we show that to gain a holistic and robust understanding of firm-level entrepreneurship, works from other research traditions and philosophies of science are needed. In this respect, the European research tradition and its wide variety of fields of research and research methods can offer a contextualized view of firm-level entrepreneurial behaviours and processes. Works embedded in the social constructionist philosophy of science might also offer an understanding of how, when, and why actors of different levels act do so and the likely outcomes of these actions as well as the interplay and divergence among these actors and levels. Works embedded in the pragmatic approach, illustrated by effectuation, could also contribute to a holistic understanding of the phenomenon. Finally, we call for researchers to be attentive to the need to align their conceptualizations, research methods and philosophies of science.

Introduction

Covin and Lumpkin (2011) state that Entrepreneurial Orientation (EO) is seen as an 'annoying construct', and that 'for every scholar who employs the construct of EO in his or her research, there is another scholar who simply wishes it would exit the scholarly conversation' (Covin and Lumpkin 2011, 859). Our intention is not to see EO exit the scholarly conversation, but rather to demonstrate that it reflects an idea of entrepreneurship that has been institution-alized in a manner that makes it hollow: extant research on firm-level entrepreneurship behaviours has calcified around the EO construct, whereas societies may in fact demonstrate different entrepreneurial behaviours and embrace different meanings of entrepreneurship (Fayolle et al. 2013).

Although EO has been defined in many manners and that many of these definitions are incompatible (George and Marino 2011, 992), the construct is currently used to measure firm-level entrepreneurial behaviours through three to five dimensions (innovation, proactiveness, risk-taking, autonomy and competitive aggressiveness) (Covin and Lumpkin 2011). EO research has contributed to developing the field of entrepreneurship because it was among the pioneers to research entrepreneurial behaviours of organizations rather than individuals (Zahra, Randerson, and Fayolle 2013). We will develop each of these points in the present work.

EO has attracted a great deal of scholarly attention over the past 30 years. Covin and Lumpkin even argue that it has come to eclipse Corporate Entrepreneurship (CE) (Covin and Lumpkin 2011, 855). Covin and Lumpkin note that many scholars consider EO to be an aspect of CE; for others (George and Marino 2011), EO is purely and simply synonymous with CE. In their essay, Zahra, Randerson, and Fayolle (2013) position EO as a component of CE research, arguing that the former reflects 'a firm's disposition to become entrepreneurial in its operations' and the second refers to 'the gamut of informal and formal activities the firm actually undertakes in identifying, evaluating and exploiting opportunities through internal (e.g. the creation of new venture units) and external (e.g. alliances) means' (364). They attribute the EO/CE confusion seen in the work of some authors to the fact that both these branches of the literature are based on the article by Miller (1983). In their essay these authors do not delve into the study of EO or its (dis)connectedness with CE. We adopt the distinction between EO and CE of Zahra, Randerson, and Fayolle (2013) as well as Miller (1983) conceptualization of EO as being revealed through firm-level entrepreneurial behaviour. In the present article, the term 'organisational entrepreneurship' refers to Gartner's (1985) view of entrepreneurial processes as the emergence of new organizations.

Limiting the study of entrepreneurship in organizational settings to EO, be it by confusion (George and Marino 2011) or opportunism (Covin and Lumpkin 2011; Miller 2011), precludes creating knowledge about *how* organizations develop or maintain this disposition to become entrepreneurial. In addition, the manner in which the construct is used in most extant research excludes mining the richness of the entrepreneurial process and its idiosyncrasies (Gartner 1985), whereas the link between entrepreneurial behaviour and individual and organizational processes is actually the heart of the initial debate (Gartner 1985; Miller 1983, 2011). Miller's (1983) article was groundbreaking precisely because it opened up entrepreneurship to firms and was novel because it shifted the focus away from the traditional view (i.e. the identification of entrepreneurship with a dominant organizational personality and the innovative abilities of this entrepreneurial actor) in order to decipher the entrepreneurial activity of the firm (Miller 1983, 770).

To unveil the processes of entrepreneurship and the organizational factors that foster and impede it in different organizational configurations, Miller (1983) creates a dependent 'entrepreneurship' variable defined as the aggregate average of three dimensions, namely risk-taking, innovation, and proactiveness, which best reflect the ideas of some entrepreneurship classics of the day (Miller 2011, 874), until then essentially applied to the individual entrepreneur. In classic theory, an entrepreneur takes risks in order to make great gains, is an agent of innovation, and is quick to act when he or she discovers or identifies an opportunity.

Like most mainstream entrepreneurship research, EO is embedded in a positivist philosophy of science (Covin and Lumpkin 2011; Covin and Wales 2012), in which entrepreneurial phenomena are seen as empirical objects with well-defined descriptive properties and are studied from the perspective of an outsider using methods that emphasize hypothesis testing, inferential statistics, and internal validity (Burg and Romme 2014). On the contrary, seeing organizational entrepreneurship as a form of socially constructed reality offers a way of connecting various entrepreneurship topics (Gartner, Bird, and Starr 1992). The social constructionist perspective considers entrepreneurship to be the fruit of how entrepreneurs and their stakeholders make sense of the world (Burg and Romme 2014; Steyaert and Katz 2004) and mobilizes research methods that are imaginative, critical and reflexive precisely in order to cultivate a critical sensibility to hidden assumptions (Gartner 2007a, 2007b) based on qualitative data such as case studies or grounded theory. This perspective offers other possible entrepreneurial behaviours such as acting 'as if' (Gartner, Bird, and Starr 1992), which begins a cycle of interactions with elements of the surrounding environment.

Academic fields make progress when there is consensus on the key building blocks and constructs (George and Marino 2011), which is the platform for the accumulation of knowledge. However, extant EO research aggregates behaviours at the firm level without capturing the processes that lead to this outcome, whereas firm-level entrepreneurial behaviour is actually the result of (intra)organizational processes (Gartner 1985). Moreover, although there is consensus that researching firm-level entrepreneurial behaviour is important, a number of questions remain unaddressed because of the institutionalization of the dominant paradigm. Outstanding research questions such as 'what behaviours other than innovation, proactiveness, and risk-taking can be considered to be entrepreneurial?' and 'how can other research modes or philosophies of science shed light on firm-level entrepreneurship?' remain unaddressed due to the institutionalization of the dominant paradigm.

To address these issues, we offer a constructive critique of extant EO research and suggest paths for clarifying and expanding research on firm-level entrepreneurship. We begin by highlighting the strengths of EO, related to its popularity and novelty. In the second section, we review the barriers that hinder the construct, which derive from definitional contradictions, measurement issues, and differing conceptualizations. We then identify five conceptualizations of EO that have remained unrecognized. In the fourth section, we identify potential next steps for future research, both on the extant conceptualizations and in terms of bringing other research traditions or philosophies of science to the debate.

The strengths of EO

The popularity of EO is a strength for the construct, the field of entrepreneurship, and beyond

The prevalence of EO has had positive implications for research on firm-level entrepreneurship. Previous studies have established the pertinence of EO constructs composed of three to five common dimensions (innovation, proactiveness, risk-taking, autonomy, competitive aggressiveness). An EO construct can be reflective or formative. It can be used to study the organizational and environmental factors leading to it and its financial and non-financial consequences.

The popularity of EO can be seen through the sheer number of publications devoted to the subject. A Google Scholar search (27 March 2016) shows 356,000 hits, while searching EBSCO Business Source Complete for research with 'entrepreneurial orientation' in the title or keywords yields 510 results. Lumpkin and Dess 1996 paper (Lumpkin and Dess 1996) won the 2009 IDEA Awards Foundational Paper award from the Entrepreneurship Division of the Academy of Management.

The construct has also brought benefits to the field of entrepreneurship. Indeed, despite the present critique, EO research has offered timely, interesting and important contributions to the understanding of firm-level entrepreneurship, such as the theoretical explorations of its antecedents and consequences (Lumpkin and Dess 1996; Zahra 1991, 1993), its relationship with internationalization (Covin and Miller 2014; Slevin and Terjesen 2011), and its influence on organizations (Wales, Monsen, and McKelvie 2011). The popularity of EO research also has broader positive implications, being used in neighbouring fields including human resource management (e.g. Hayton, Hornsby, and Bloodgood 2013), family business (e.g. Sciascia and Bettinelli 2013; Zellweger, Nason, and Nordqvist 2012; Zellweger and Sieger 2012), and supply chain management (e.g. Li, Liu, and Liu 2011).

This popularity in and beyond entrepreneurship research is more related to the ease of use of the construct than to its social utility. The scales often used to measure it are perceived as validated, making EO research 'too easy', with the construct considered to be already legitimized (Miller 2011). However, as we show in this paper, the scales are not as robust as we might hope, particularly in considering their widespread use. Careerist considerations from the pressure to produce research and the relative ease with which this can be achieved using the EO construct(s) have come to overshadow the social utility of the original conceptualization, which is related to the shift in the focus of entrepreneurship research from individual to firm-level behaviours and the processes that lead to them.

A firm level construct, based on individual actions

These different conceptualizations share a common point: this firm-level behaviour is the consequence of individual or team actions. For Miller (1983, 770), the entrepreneurial role can be performed not only by a traditional entrepreneur, but also by 'planning' or 'ventures' offices, or even at lower levels of the hierarchy in R&D, engineering, marketing, or production departments. Miller's work aimed to identify the underlying mechanisms or structures that shape firm-level entrepreneurship, moving beyond the focus on the firm or individual to unveil the processes that cut across departments and individuals. Identifying firm-level entrepreneurship as a multi-level phenomenon is important, because individuals act according to their motivations and environment (Gartner 1985), and because dynamic actions/reactions determine the processes and outcomes at different levels of organizational hierarchy: top-managers, managers or non-managerial employees.

Miller was not alone in his quest to look beyond the figure of the entrepreneur to disclose the processes involved (e.g. Burgelman 1983, 1996; Gartner 1985; Kanter et al. 1990). However, other approaches have received much less scholarly attention than the 'extension' of Miller's work by Covin and Slevin (1989, 1991) (Zahra, Randerson, and Fayolle 2013). Notwithstanding the widespread use of the concept in entrepreneurship and other fields, previous research thus presents important lacunae.

The limitations of EO

We now identify issues related to definitional inconsistencies, measurement tools and research design, which allow us to assert that there are at least five different conceptualizations of EO.

Definitional inconsistencies

These inconsistencies are the fruit of the misunderstanding of Miller's initial work. The popularity of EO curtailed scholarly debate about what firm-level entrepreneurship can be instead of inducing it.

EO: the fruit of the misunderstanding

The focus of Miller's (1983) work was not the definition of firm-level entrepreneurship, but the identification of the underlying mechanisms, in different types of organizations, that lead to entrepreneurship being defined ad hoc (innovation, risk-taking, and proactiveness). In his commentary on this seminal article Miller (2011, 874) stresses:

> Indeed, table III of the 1983 article demonstrated that the firm types differed significantly in the extent to which they exhibited each of the three component variables, and Appendix I showed that these components had rather different sources even within a given type – so, for example, in the simple firm, proactiveness and risk were associated with scanning activity, whereas innovation was not. Such discrepancies were the rule, not the exception, and now I am sorry I did not stress that point more.

The aggregate dependent variable (which has become EO) has been taken out of its initial context (designed as a dependent variable to identify the organizational properties that lead to this result) to become an independent variable explaining firm performance (Covin and Slevin 1991), and employed in multiple attempts to model firm-level entrepreneurial behaviour (e.g. Covin and Slevin 1991; Ireland, Covin, and Kuratko 2009; Jennings and Lumpkin 1989; Kuratko et al. 1993; Lumpkin and Dess 1996; Zahra 1991, 1993).

EO is most often measured by using a variation of the initial scales (George and Marino 2011; Rauch et al. 2009); however, these scales are misused. Covin and Wales (2012, 691) admit that 'the Miller/Covin and Slevin (1989) scale was intended to operationalize the construct of EO as originally discussed by Miller (1983), the scale as it's commonly employed does not do this'. We push this analysis even further: when Covin and Slevin (1989) move innovativeness, proactiveness and risk-taking from dependent variables to independent variables, they ignore Miller (1983) fundamental assumptions. They use an adapted version of Miller's scales to measure entrepreneurship as a means of achieving firm performance, whereas the construct and the scales were conceived to identify the processes that lead to this result. In so doing, they create a new conceptualization of the construct. This is also the case for the Lumpkin and Dess (1996) 'clarification' in which they maintain the status of the independent variable and add two dimensions (autonomy and competitive aggressiveness). The haste of both sets of authors (Covin and Slevin, Lumpkin and Dess) blinded them to the pitfalls of importing, extending and modifying the aggregate entrepreneurship variable (Zahra and Newey 2009, 1068).

It is important to emphasize that the term 'Entrepreneurial Orientation' has been subject to a wide range of definitions, many of which are mutually incompatible (George and Marino 2011, 992). Although EO was coined by Lumpkin and Dess in 1996, the term has been used to refer to different conceptualizations (e.g. Anderson et al. 2015; Covin and Slevin 1989, 1991; Kreiser, Marino, and Weaver 2002; Lumpkin and Dess 1996; Miller 1983). George and Marino (2011, 994) use the work of Chimezie and Osigweh (1989) and Satori (1970) to demonstrate that the EO concept suffers from a lack of precision because its extension or breadth of application has increased (i.e. it has been applied to other domains), while its intension, or collection of encompassed properties, has decreased (e.g. by defining EO research as mobilizing fewer than three dimensions; see Avlonitis and Salavou 2007; Knight 1997; Merz and Sauber 1995). It has also been stretched: this involves increasing a concept's extension without a concurrent decrease in its intension, resulting in a concept that is extremely broad and difficult to distinguish from other concepts in any meaningful way. However, we show that EO is not one broad concept, and that there are in fact multiple conceptualizations. As a consequence, it has become extremely difficult to contribute to a specific body of knowledge because scholars use the empirical results from one conceptualization in studies investigating another. We need to be attentive to the conceptualization we embrace, and respect its fundamental assumptions and measurement method (Covin and Wales 2012; Wales 2016).

Alternative definitions of firm-level entrepreneurship are unexplored

The definition of entrepreneurship based on innovation, proactiveness and risk-taking is derived from a behavioural perspective. Other perspectives would imply the use of other, adapted variables. For example, to investigate the psychological perspective, we could find the variable need for achievement. Adopting a process approach would mean focusing on organizational emergence. In addition, the definition of EO as innovation, proactiveness and risk-taking carries the assumption that firms deploy the same entrepreneurial behaviours as individuals. Spontaneously, scholars could question the behavioural approach. For example, which behaviours can be considered entrepreneurial (Gartner, Bird, and Starr 1992)? Can other behaviours be considered (i.e. are entrepreneurial behaviours culturally bound)? Do entrepreneurs recognize themselves as such through their behaviour (Fletcher 2006; Popp and Holt 2013; Williams and Nadin 2013)? EO, like the majority of mainstream entrepreneurship research, is underpinned by the assumption that entrepreneurship is linked to the entrepreneur and it is universally desirable and beneficial (Miller 2011, 877). In addition, considering that most conceptualizations of EO adopt firm performance as the primary outcome, performance through entrepreneurship is considered desirable; in this deterministic stance, ethics are utilitarian and assumed. These assumptions curtail asking interesting and important research questions such as how the perceived desirability of entrepreneurship varies in different cultures (Dodd, Jack, and Anderson 2013) and what are the manifestations of the 'dark side' of entrepreneurship as well as its consequences (Birkinshaw 2003; Karmann et al. 2016). It also restricts attempts to unveil the underlying processes (Hjorth, Jones, and Gartner 2008).

National cultures embrace different perceptions of entrepreneurship and its desirability (Fayolle, Basso, and Bouchard 2010; Hayton, George, and Zahra 2002; Slevin and Terjesen 2011): entrepreneurship may be valued (e.g. United States, Ireland) or less so (Hungary, Japan). Even more importantly, the behaviours considered to be entrepreneurial may vary according to the national culture. The standard dimensions of risk-taking, innovation and proactiveness may be less relevant than behaviours such as energy, initiative and adaptation (Slevin and Terjesen 2011), 'bricolage' (i.e. creating something from nothing; Baker and Nelson 2005), or effectuation (Sarasvathy 2001).

Understanding those behaviours considered to be entrepreneurial in a specific cultural context matters. Previous researchers have not taken the time to question whether the standard dimensions are the most appropriate for characterizing organizational-level entrepreneurial behaviour, either in each specific culture or globally. In other words, we are comparing companies around the world to a yardstick formulated in the United States (Terjesen and Slevin 2011) and developed in a positivist stance (Covin and Lumpkin 2011;

Covin and Wales 2012). This is problematic because the list of top 100 firms reshaping global industries according to the Boston Consulting Group (2011) includes firms from Argentina, Brazil, Chile, China, Egypt, Hungary, India, Indonesia, Malaysia, Mexico, Russia and Saudi Arabia. Considering that entrepreneurial firms reshape industries and the dearth of research on culturally specific entrepreneurial behaviours, we have no means of knowing which behaviours lead to the success of these firms. Moreover, the paucity of research from other traditions or modes (Burg and Romme 2014; Down 2013) hinders a fine-grained contextualized understanding.

Measurement issues

The measurement of the phenomenon has largely overshadowed the study of EO itself. Pending issues to be addressed include the terms of the scales habitually used to measure EO and the research design that has come to be the norm.

The dominant measurement approach to EO precludes it from achieving its intended goal

Miller's original work focused on identifying the key mechanisms inducing a firm to demonstrate innovative, proactive and risk-taking behaviours, all of which are contextually embedded. Miller (2011, 880) notes that 'it is not just type of entry but context, richly characterized, that may influence the entrepreneurial process'. The measurement tools used in extant EO research preclude gaining an understanding of the variety and potential idiosyncrasies of the processes involved. Indeed, considering that processes are a succession of actions accomplished by individuals or teams, and that these processes influence and are influenced by environmental, individual and organizational factors (Gartner 1985), entrepreneurial processes are diverse and distinctive.

Although EO has been defined as the 'processes, practices, and decision-making activities that lead to new entry' (Lumpkin and Dess 1996, 136), the way in which it is currently used prevents us from gaining an understanding of these processes. In fact, there is a divergence between the starting notion of the process and its subsequent operationalization. The process (EO) is treated as a fixed entity (independent variable) where the dimensions are used to represent the process and link the independent variable (EO) to the outcome of interest, here firm performance (McMullen and Dimov 2013). Setting EO as an independent variable places the processes in the proverbial black box, obscuring important nuances in the processes, structures and underlying mechanisms as well as the 'time' element. This is problematic since the initial goal of firm-level entrepreneurial behaviour research was precisely to unveil these idiosyncrasies; moreover, consensus formed around the initial dimensions, which were assumed to represent firm-level entrepreneurial behaviour, despite the scarcity of scholarly debate on this issue. Indeed, the debate has focused on the measurement of EO than on the actual principle itself or its components, as we discuss below.

The Miller/Covin and Slevin scale

Until recently, EO research has focused on dimensionality and measurement, or EO's relationship with performance. However, significant issues cloud the so-called the Miller/Covin and Slevin scales. Several scholars (Hansen et al. 2011; Knight 1997; Kreiser, Marino, and Weaver 2002; Kreiser et al. 2010) worked to establish the validity and dimensionality of the scale. Yet, their use of different versions or approaches prevented them from validating one scale and one conceptualization, instead inadvertently creating new conceptualizations.

Of these works, Knight (1997) establishes the overall validity of an eight-item scale in terms of the consistency, pattern of facture structure, internal consistency, and convergent and discriminant validity of Covin and Slevin's co-varying conceptualization of EO, finding that double-loadings pose a problem for only one item of the proactiveness dimension. Kreiser, Marino, and Weaver (2002) study a different eight-item version of this scale and conclude that the scale achieves a better fit when modelled with three sub-dimensions that display significant *independent* variance. To establish cross-cultural validity, the authors choose countries that are culturally close to each other as well as to US culture. The 'cross-cultural validity' of their measure therefore suffers from serious bias. They rectify this caveat in their 2010 study (Kreiser et al. 2010), where the between-country analysis provides evidence of the important differences in levels of risk-taking and proactiveness between countries and links these differences to the unique attributes of the institutional environment: national culture does indeed matter.

Lumpkin, Cogliser, and Schneider (2009) investigate the Lumpkin and Dess conceptualization further. In their comparative study, they use the nine-item Covin and Slevin scale and a scale under development and include additional items for innovation (2), proactiveness (1) and risk (1) as well as a set used to measure autonomy (an additional dimension). Their findings indicate, 'either problems in the conceptual definitions of the EO construct or problems with scale items used quite often in measuring EO, or both' (Lumpkin, Cogliser, and Schneider 2009, 4).

The common trend in these works is the reduction in the number of items used to measure the construct, the use of different versions of the scale, and the use of the same scale to measure different conceptualizations. Along with Anderson et al. (2015), we point out the general under-exploitation of negative results or limitations, which could have helped advance research on the topic. For example, Kreiser, Marino, and Weaver (2002) explicitly indicate that the three sub-dimensions should be used to observe differential relationships between themselves and other variables. In their meta-analysis of the relationship between EO and performance (i.e. independently varying), Rauch and colleagues (2009) note that of the 51 studies included, 37 use a summated concept of EO (co-varying). Finally, in their examination of empirical studies of EO, George and Marino (2011) show that 54 of the 61 studies examined use a summated scale (co-varying) of one form or another.

The issues commonly identified with these scales include that (i) the items only question top managers, leading to results with a 'sole respondent' bias; (ii) it is unclear whether several of the items assess individual or group behaviours; and (iii) the question of whether certain items assess behaviours or attitudes remains. Beyond these shortcomings, we note that the Anderson et al. (2015) conceptualization is the only approach to address the issue of attitudes versus behaviours, leading these authors to create the lower order dimensions of attitude and behaviour, and incidentally an additional conceptualization. Through the above developments, we see that works aiming to validate measurement tools contribute to the creation of the five conceptualizations of EO now presented in detail.

Five conceptualizations of EO

According to George and Marino (2011) there is only one EO construct, whereas Covin and Lumpkin (2011, 859) and Wales (2016) suggest two principal conceptualizations: the first is based on the works of Miller (1983) and Covin and Slevin (1989), while the second is based on the findings of Lumpkin and Dess (1996). Wales (2016) suggests taking the 'Miller/Covin and Slevin' conceptualization as the reference point of future conceptualizations. However, we show the existence of at least five conceptualizations of EO, all of which are benchmarked against that of Miller. These conceptualizations display important differences in terms of their dimensions, species, the way in which they are used, the relationship between EO and its dimensions, dimensionality, the possible evolution of the dimensions, and the possible levels of analysis. We summarize the key characteristics of each conceptualization in Table 1.

The original conceptualization of Miller is widely misunderstood. By identifying Miller's construct as a separate, unique conceptualization (instead of groundwork leading to alternative conceptualizations) offers interesting research perspectives. For example, it allows us to identify the organizational, contextual and motivational factors that lead to firm-level entrepreneurial behaviours qualified by the three initial dimensions of EO or establish strategic configurations (Randerson, Bettinelli, and Fayolle 2014). As an outcome, this conceptualization leaves room for independent study of the antecedents (differing processes, practices, and decision-making activities) but does not replace (is not a proxy for) the study of these organizational factors, as is the case of the four other conceptualizations. It also admits only one possible organizational outcome and thus challenges scholars to identify others.

The works of Kreiser, Marino, and colleagues come closest to continuing this stream in that they develop a three-dimensional, independently varying construct, establishing partial cross-cultural validity (Hansen et al. 2011; Kreiser, Marino, and Weaver 2002; Kreiser et al. 2010) as well as a theoretical model of the EO–environment–structure–performance relationship (Kreiser and Davis 2010). This work creates a distinct EO construct because although they adopt Miller's dimensions of innovation, proactiveness and risk-taking, which can vary independently, these dimensions represent the strategic decision-making processes (independent variable) leading to firm performance (dependent variable). In Miller's conceptualization, these dimensions represent firm-level entrepreneurial behaviour (dependent variable), which can be explained by individual and organizational factors (see Table 1).

The works of Covin and Slevin (1991), which aim to operationalize Miller's conceptualization, inadvertently create an alternative conceptualization for two reasons. First, to be qualified as entrepreneurial (having an entrepreneurial strategic posture), the three dimensions co-vary and represent a strategic orientation per se – the 'ultimate dependent variable is firm performance' (Covin and Slevin 1991, 9). As noted previously, this conceptualization has received the greatest scholarly attention to establish measure validity and as well as a relationship with performance.

The Lumpkin and Dess (1996, 137) five-dimensional, independently varying construct represents the 'processes, practices and decision-making activities that lead to new entry' and ultimately performance. This conceptualization differs from the initial construct in three ways: it is directly a proxy for these organizational activities (instead of trying to identify

Table 1. Comparison of the different conceptualizations of EO.

	Original	Unidimensional	Multidimensional	Three independently varying dimensions	Two lower-order dimensions
Seminal work	Miller (1983)	Covin and Slevin (1991)	Lumpkin and Dess (1996)	Kreiser, Marino, and Weaver (2002)	Anderson et al. (2015)
Dimensions	Innovation Proactiveness Risk-taking	Innovation Proactiveness Risk-taking	Innovation Proactiveness Risk-taking Autonomy Competitive aggressiveness	Innovation Proactiveness Risk-taking	Two lower-order dimensions: entrepreneurial behaviour (innovativeness and proactiveness) and managerial attitude towards risk
Species	Quantitative measure of entrepreneurial intensity created as an independent variable to identify what leads to this result in different organizational contexts (Miller 2011)	Strategic posture	Processes, practices, and decision-making activities that lead to new entry (Lumpkin and Dess 1996, 137), and ultimately performance	Strategic decision-making process (2002, 72)	Decision-making practices, managerial philosophies, and strategic behaviours that are entrepreneurial in nature (2015, 1581)
Usage	Dependent variable	Independent variable	Independent variable	Independent variable	Independent variable
Relationship between EO and its dimensions	Formative	Reflective	Formative	Formative	Formative
Dimensionality	Dimensions may vary separately according to context (Miller 2011, 875)	Dimensions co-vary. EO only exists if the three dimensions are present (Covin and Lumpkin 2011, 862)	Dimensions may vary independently. EO is a superordinate construct with the dimensions of risk-taking, innovativeness, proactiveness, competitive aggressiveness, and autonomy being the constructs that function as specific manifestations of EO (Covin and Lumpkin 2011, 863)	Dimensions may vary independently (Kreiser, Marino, and Weaver 2002, 84) according to the structure (Kreiser and Davis 2010)	Positive co-variance between the two dimensions; both dimensions are fundamentally necessary for EO to exist
Possible evolution of dimensions	N/A	Dimensions may be added or substituted	Dimensions fixed	N/A	No, dimensions are not interchangeable
Levels of analysis possible	Individual, business unit/spin-off, firm, country	Business unit	Business unit	N/A	Firm level (2015, 1593)

Source: the authors. Based upon Anderson et al. (2015); Covin and Lumpkin (2011); Covin and Slevin (1989); Kreiser and Davis (2010); Kreiser, Marino, and Weaver (2002); Lumpkin and Dess (1996); Miller (1983).

them), it concerns only the activities leading to new entry, and it admits only these five dimensions.

Finally, the Anderson et al. conceptualization, grounded in measurement theory, defines two lower order dimensions: entrepreneurial behaviours (comprising innovativeness and proactiveness) and managerial attitude towards risk. Their conceptualization represents 'decision-making practices, managerial philosophies, and strategic behaviours that are entrepreneurial in nature' (2015, 1581), and is designed as an independent variable. For an organization to be considered entrepreneurial both types of dimensions are necessary and co-variance is required. This conceptualization does not support any alternative dimensions.

Identifying these different frameworks is important because if our endeavour as scholars is to encourage dialogue and debate (Zahra and Dess 2001), we should also ensure that we are rigorous in our work by identifying the precise conceptual framework for our study, respect its fundamental assumptions (Zahra and Newey 2009), and design our research methods accordingly. We figure in Table 1 the five conceptualizations that we sketch out with the present work and the characteristics of each conceptualization.

Future research can use our work to identify the conceptualization within which it is embedded, to respect the framework's basic assumptions about the number and possible evolution of the dimensions, to understand the relationship between the construct and its dimensions, to adopt proper research methods and measurement tools to operationalize the concept, and ultimately to build cumulative bodies of knowledge (Zahra and Newey 2009). As an illustration, research aiming to contribute to EO à la Lumpkin and Dess would mobilize all five dimensions to assume the position of EO as a proxy for processes and use EO as an independent variable at the business unit level only. Researchers developing EO à la Lumpkin and Dess would be attentive to draw upon the literature relative to this conceptualization in order to progressively build a solid body of cumulative knowledge. We delineate the conceptualizations by comparing them with the initial work of Miller; our work can contribute to the identification of other potential conceptualizations.

Firm-level entrepreneurship behaviour research: now what?

The popularity of EO has had positive implications for the construct as well as for the field of entrepreneurship and beyond. In this section, we suggest ways in which to either develop the extant research streams or to boldly open new ways of researching firm-level entrepreneurial behaviour.

Clarifying and developing the extant conceptualizations

Clarifying the EO construct(s) is necessary to build knowledge of this topic. Indeed, EO research can take several paths. The different conceptualizations may develop separately. Each stream of research could construct its own body of the literature, common assumptions, and distinctive traits (including a name enabling it to be distinguished from the other conceptualizations). Conversely, the research community could agree on what constitutes EO by adopting one conceptualization. Finally, George and Marino (2011) suggest viewing EO as a family of research, articulated around the three-dimensional, independently varying conceptualization of firm-level entrepreneurial behaviour. Concurring with Wales (2016), we advocate this last option and hope that the present work will serve as a reference for distinguishing the different conceptualizations and pave the way to building distinct, robust bodies of cumulative knowledge as well as providing a framework for identifying or creating alternative conceptualizations. Keeping these five conceptualizations in mind, we develop below opportunities for challenging the status quo.

First, while considerable effort has been spent on quantifying the construct(s), very little attention has been paid to qualitative methods. Short and colleagues (2010) use computer-aided text analysis techniques in an effort to establish the construct validity of EO based on Lumpkin and Dess's conceptualization. Considering the original design of Miller's conceptualization, qualitative research designs are desperately needed in order to capture the variety and idiosyncrasies of the processes, uncover and explain the time factor (McMullen and Dimov 2013), and shed light on the interaction of the different levels (e.g. individual, team, organization). Indeed, for the other four conceptualizations, qualitative-based research designs would capture the detailed and contextualized content of the dimensions (Miller 2011), especially given the discrepancy between the way in which these dimensions are presented in the literature and their actual manifestations. For example, Barbat, Hlady Rispail, and Randerson (2014) show that in the context of exporting established sub-contracting SMEs, risk-taking does not relate to a potentially costly failure but to the psychical distance between the domestic market and the target export market. Here, innovation is not manifested through the creation and improvement of products and/or their adaptation to foreign markets, but rather by focusing on quality to adapt the firm's offer to the needs of its client. Finally, in this context, proactiveness is not reflected in anticipating and acting on future wants and needs in the market but in the search for export information, presence at trade fairs, and networking. Early research in firm level entrepreneurship was qualitative (e.g. Burgelman 1983, 1996; Kanter et al. 1990) and capital to the initial understanding of the phenomenon. More research aiming at a deeper understanding of firm level entrepreneurship and the variety of behaviours which can be qualified as entrepreneurial is greatly needed and qualitative methods are better suited to support this type of research.

Second, for any of the five conceptualizations, the dimensions could be investigated by means other than the scales usually used (Covin and Wales 2012; Lyon, Lumpkin, and Dess 2000; Miller 2011). For example, Miller (2011, 879) suggests calling on secondary data such as on share price fluctuations (as a proxy of unsystematic risk), R&D expenditure, patents and patent citations (for innovation), and sales in new markets (new market initiatives). Third, for any of the five conceptualizations, further research could adapt the variables to the specific context or desired outcome to generate cumulative and stable insights (e.g. risk-taking in resource accession or financing, proactiveness in global resource leveraging, and clearly defined types of innovation; Miller 2011, 879).

Fourth, according to the conceptualization of EO adopted, additional or alternative dimensions could be added. Covin and Lumpkin (2011, 868) suggest exploring dimensions related to change or adaptation. Since the behaviours (dimensions) valued as entrepreneurial can differ according to the context, researchers could also draw upon the frameworks suggested in recent research (Welter 2011; Zahra 2007; Zahra and Wright 2011) to structure their investigations in particular geographical contexts (Fayolle, Basso, and Bouchard 2010; Hayton, George, and Zahra 2002; Slevin and Terjesen 2011).

Finally, the study of firm-level entrepreneurial behaviours also carries a specific challenge in terms of the multiple levels to be studied. The firm-level phenomenon is the consequence of the actions of individuals or teams, which differ according to the conceptualization of EO espoused. We should therefore also focus scholarly attention on the identification of these actors and the dynamics of action (i.e. the interaction with the firm level). The framework offered by Gartner (1985) to describe the phenomenon of new venture creation could support such research. This framework was devised to unveil the idiosyncrasies of organizational emergence for both independent and organizational entrepreneurship (Gartner 1985, 700). It comprises four dimensions: (1) the individual or person(s) involved in creating a new organization, (2) the organization or type of venture started, (3) the environment or situation surrounding and influencing the new organization, and (4) the process or actions undertaken by the individual to start the venture. The dimensions together provide a canvas for understanding the phenomena and specificity of each occurrence.

More importantly, opening the scientific study of firm-level entrepreneurial behaviours, the original purpose of EO, to other research modes and traditions would allow a more holistic approach.

Opening up the debate to other research modes and traditions

Entrepreneurship (and thus organizational entrepreneurship) is a multidimensional and multiparadigmatic phenomenon that cannot be fully understood or captured through a single philosophy of science or research tradition (Burg and Romme 2014; Gartner 2013). Extant research studying firm-level entrepreneurial behaviours focuses on EO and EO is embedded in a positivist philosophy of science (Covin and Lumpkin 2011; Covin and Wales 2012). Moreover, as demonstrated in the previous section, EO as it is currently researched precludes unveiling important facets of firm-level entrepreneurial behaviours and unravelling the processes that can lead to them. Other research traditions (e.g. the European tradition) or philosophies of science (e.g. social constructivism and pragmatism) could offer new and fresh perspectives, and more importantly provide the contextualized, multi-level, and longitudinal approaches currently missing. These alternative traditions should not be understood as either/or approaches, but as a means of completing and complementing each other (Gartner 2013).

The European tradition of entrepreneurship research
The European tradition of entrepreneurship research (Down 2013; Gartner 2013) draws on a broad base of social sciences that includes, but is not restricted to economics. In this research tradition, contextualization is innate because scientific universalism and positivism are avoided. This opens the door to a wider set of research questions (Hjorth, Jones, and Gartner 2008, 82), and is particularly appropriate for the study of firm-level entrepreneurship because it aims to explicitly link socio-economic, historical and cultural contexts to real-life practices (Down 2013). In other words, the European tradition allows us to move from the question of how EO relates to firm performance, where EO is universally recognized as the sole manifestation of firm-level entrepreneurial behaviour, to asking which behaviours can be considered to be entrepreneurial in specific contexts. The answer to this would enable us to understand, for example, how firms that 'reshape global industries' (Boston Consulting Group 2011) actually do so. This is important because EO is a strategic posture (Covin and Slevin 1991) that focuses on competing in a given industry (Lumpkin and Dess 1996) rather than reshaping or creating new ones. Considering that entrepreneurial behaviours are

culturally embedded at the national level (Dodd, Jack, and Anderson 2013), as well as at the industry and organizational levels (Fayolle, Basso, and Bouchard 2010), the diversity of the fields of science upon which the European tradition draws would provide a more holistic view than the economic approach currently developed through EO. This would allow us to examine which processes can lead to such behaviours: the idiosyncrasies of entrepreneurial processes and their evolution over time can be understood by observing the process of organizational emergence (Gartner 1985, 1990). The European tradition of entrepreneurship research welcomes research from different philosophies of science.

The social constructionist philosophy of science

Research embedded in a social constructionist perspective allows for multiple 'truths' related to different cultural, historical and ideological directions and understandings (Ogbor 2000), which affect the construction of entrepreneurial processes. The key question in the social constructionist philosophy of science is 'how entrepreneurial activities are constructed through dialogic, social structural and relational processes' (Fletcher 2007, 165). This is well suited to organizational entrepreneurship research because 'entrepreneurship, like everything else people "know", is a socially constructed reality or concept' (Steyaert and Katz 2004, 186), and is always ongoing, emerging and becoming (Fletcher 2007). Coviello and Jones (2004), for example, characterize this approach (emic) as culturally specific, whereas an etic approach (positivist) is culturally ubiquitous. It is concerned with linguistic representations, mean-ing-making and sense-making processes at the individual and inter-personal level and is inferred from the relationality between individuals, institutions, objects, entities and lan-guage (Fletcher 2006, 422). Social constructionism focuses on the social/relational meanings, interactions, conversations, and discourses at the level of teams, partnerships, and joint acts, admitting the existence of, and allowing us to grasp, multiple perspectives (Fletcher 2007). It is relationally aware when constructing and analysing entrepreneurial accounts, firstly by focusing on the social context of these practices and secondly by showing how, why, and in what ways. Relevant research methods include ethnography, discourse analysis, partici-pant observation, narrative, and biography (Fletcher 2007) and relevant frameworks include 'bricolage' (Baker and Nelson 2005).

A specific illustration would be to extend Spigel's (2013) framework to firm-level entre-preneurship, which is bound by culture on three levels: nation, industry and organization (Fayolle, Basso, and Bouchard 2010). Spigel builds on Bourdieu's (1977, 1990) sociology of practice, which views entrepreneurial actions as emerging from actors' comprehension of the social rules around them, specifically the 'values' of the forms of capital (economic, cul-tural and social) they possess or want to obtain. Bourdieu calls upon three conceptual tools to describe the emergence of practices: field, habitus and capital. Fields are historically pro-duced social spaces of rules (Bourdieu 1977), the 'rules of the game', in which practices take place, which can help us understand the 'rules' in the three levels of culture. The habitus is how actors develop an understanding of the rules as well as their applicability according to the actor's power or status in the field (Bourdieu 1990), which can help us understand the behaviours of institutions (in the nation), competitors (in the industry), and individuals and teams (in the organization). The field becomes the context in which practices influenced by the habitus are acted out. This provides an environment in which certain practices make sense. Understanding how these actors identify which practices to enact in relation to multiple fields is crucial to understanding the development of unique entrepreneurial behaviours and their development over time.

More generally, the social constructionist approach allows us to flush out new and interesting research questions to unveil idiosyncratic and holistic portraits of firm-level entrepreneurial behaviours and the mechanisms that induce and hinder them. Considering that this perspective leverages on dialogic, social structural, and relational processes to understand how entrepreneurial activities are constructed (Fletcher 2007), this approach is better apt to capture the interplay and divergence among the actors and levels of analysis proper to the organizational entrepreneurial process, which the normative approach to the phenomenon (EO) does not grasp. For a firm to behave entrepreneurially, individuals inside the organization must take action; however, EO sheds very little light on the individual level of action or the interplay between the individual, team, and organizational levels. For example, in an organizational context, individuals and teams undertake risky projects, many of which fail (Shepherd, Kuratko, and Covin 2009). Whereas EO has neglected the 'dark side' of entrepreneurship (Birkinshaw 2003), by looking only at how the mechanism of risk and reward mediates an individual's willingness to undertake an entrepreneurial project in an organization (Monsen, Patzelt, and Saxton 2010) or by identifying that risk leads to unethical behaviours (Karmann et al. 2016), the social constructionist perspective can shed light on how a project fails and grasp the dynamics of failure at different levels as well as the precise levers that lead to unethical behaviours. The model by Ireland, Covin, and Kuratko (2009) analyse the antecedents, elements and outcomes of a CE strategy, which can be best explored from a social constructionist perspective because it offers the research methods and broader theoretical base needed to understand the actions and interactions among actors and levels.

The pragmatic philosophy of science

Developing research in a pragmatic perspective, which recognizes both the relevance of social construction processes and the presence of a 'real world', can usefully contribute to enriching and expanding the sphere of firm-level entrepreneurship research. The focus is on the entrepreneurial actions and processes in which people engage in particular contexts and times. As Watson (2013) notes, pragmatism is based on the acceptance that there is no proper, fully realized theory of any aspect of life and that scientific knowledge should inform human actions in the world rather than tell us 'what the case is' (positivism). The role of pragmatic research is to facilitate learning, offering different 'how to' practices (in this case, individual and collective actions leading to firm-level entrepreneurship), where the 'how to' constitutes the reality of the situation in a pragmatic worldview. To identify the 'how to' researchers rely on methods such as ethnography, interviews, documentaries, and even surveys as long as they are contextualized to field investigation (Watson 2013).

Effectuation (Sarasvathy 2001) includes pragmatic elements (Watson 2013) or represents the pragmatic approach in entrepreneurship research (Burg and Romme 2014). Watson (2013) laments the fact that effectuation, as a non-linear process, has been labelled as 'entrepreneurial', whereas a Pragmatist would say 'this is part of the way the social world works' (Watson 2013, 26). In the present work we take effectuation as an application of pragmatism. 'Corporate Effectuation' scales are used to establish a specific outcome (e.g. R&D performance; Brettel et al. 2012). With this research design, we do not gain insights into the specificities of the effectual entrepreneurial process; they are considered to be fixed

(McMullen and Dimov 2013). Effectuation has also been used to understand internal corporate venturing in SMEs (Evald and Senderovitz 2013) as well as opportunity creation and identification (Randerson, Degeorge, and Fayolle 2016). The last two studies although using qualitative methods, also consider effectuation to be fixed (independent variable) and seek to identify a specific outcome (internal corporate venturing or opportunity identification or creation): the idiosyncrasies of the processes are overlooked.

Effectuation can contribute to the EO debate in at least three ways. First, it can be considered to be firm-level entrepreneurial behaviour per se, aiming to reshape environments rather than to act within existing ones (Dew et al. 2008), which could help explain how some firms reshape industries (Boston Consulting Group 2011). Such firm-level behaviours relate to accumulating stakeholder commitments under goal ambiguity, achieving control through non-predictive strategies, and demonstrating a predominately exaptive orientation (Sarasvathy 2001). Such research would create new and valuable knowledge because EO embraces only a causal approach to entrepreneurship, aiming to 'beat the competitor to the punch' (Miller 1983, 771) rather than creating new industries.

A second avenue would be to research effectuation (the set of principles) as a method for solving the problems organizations face and the process and levels of problem solving involved (Sarasvathy and Venkataraman 2011). Miller (1983) adopts EO as the dependent variable (firm-level entrepreneurial behaviours) to unveil the processes and mechanisms that induce or hinder it. Researching firm-level entrepreneurship by using effectuation as the independent variable would thus greatly enrich our knowledge of this entrepreneurial phenomenon and ultimately lead to qualifying behaviours other than innovation, proactiveness, risk-taking autonomy, and competitive aggressiveness.

A third avenue of research concerns organizational design. Effectuation, as a science of the artificial, sees human artefacts as the interface between the inner and outer environments. Organizations are thus human artefacts. Organizational design occurs at both the founder(s)–organizational firm interface and the organization–environment interface. Little is known about how the principles of effectuation affect organizational design and how organizations affect environments (Sarasvathy et al. 2008). Researching this would therefore contribute to the EO debate on the levels to include in the analysis of firm level entrepreneurship. Aligning the philosophy of science, conceptual domain, research methods, and measurement tools is crucial for developing a sound knowledge base. Diversifying the approaches adopted would thus help widen the scope and relevance of the research.

Conclusion

In the present work, we alert scholars of the shortcomings of extant EO research and profile the five distinct conceptualizations of EO that can ground future research around clearly identified constructs as well as their definition, use, and fundamental assumption. This work also facilitates the identification of other conceptualizations. We embed EO within the organizational entrepreneurship literature, the first concerning firm-level entrepreneurial behaviours and the second being the entire gamut of activities an organization undertakes, to demonstrate that the important aspects of firm-level entrepreneurial behaviours remain understudied. Important questions such as what behaviours can be qualified as entrepreneurial, and which processes can lead to such behaviours remain unanswered. Researchers must thus look to traditional EO research as well as other research traditions or philosophies of science to address these outstanding issues.

We show that the European tradition of research can contribute to this debate: the broad array of fields and methods on which this tradition leverages as well as its aim to bridge the gap between real life practices (here, EO) and socio-economic, historical and cultural contexts sets the stage for multiple responses to the question of which behaviours can be considered to be entrepreneurial. We show that the processes of organizational emergence shed light on those processes leading to firm-level behaviours.

We also demonstrate how research under alternative philosophies of science can complete the normative/positivist (EO) approach. First, the social constructionist approach is particularly useful for disentangling actions at different levels (individual, team, organization and environment) and, in this regard, we offer an extension of Spigel's model (based on Bourdieu's sociology of practice) to firm-level entrepreneurial behaviours. Moreover, we show how this perspective can clarify the interplay and divergence among the actors and levels of action suitable to firm-level entrepreneurship, which the normative approach to EO currently puts in a black box. Second, the pragmatic approach, illustrated by effectuation, can also contribute to building a holistic view of firm-level entrepreneurial behaviours. The principles of effectuation can be studied as entrepreneurial behaviours per se (as the dependent variable), as the processes leading to firm-level entrepreneurial behaviours (independent variables), and as organizational design to cast a net on the different levels of actors to analyse.

Our suggestions are made with the aim of enhancing the completeness of research into firm-level entrepreneurial behaviour and of increasing its impact. We hope that our work is useful to structure positivist (normative) EO research around the five conceptualizations described herein, thereby allowing scholars to identify others, and triggering a renewal of this scholarly debate. Furthermore, we hope that our work creates awareness that very little is known about which firm-level behaviours can be qualified as 'entrepreneurial' or which processes can lead to such behaviours EO is only one tightly focused approach; hence, to gain a holistic understanding of this phenomenon, contributions from other research traditions and philosophies of science are greatly needed.

Disclosure statement

No potential conflict of interest was reported by the author.

References

Anderson, B. S., P. M. Kreiser, D. F. Kuratko, J. S. Hornsby, and Y. Eshima. 2015. "Reconceptualizing Entrepreneurial Orientation." *Strategic Management Journal* 36 (10): 1579–1596.

Avlonitis, G. J., and H. E. Salavou. 2007. "Entrepreneurial Orientation of SMEs, Product Innovativeness, and Performance." *Journal of Business Research* 60 (5): 566–575.

Baker, T., and R. E. Nelson. 2005. "Creating Something from Nothing: Resource Construction through Entrepreneurial Bricolage." *Administrative Science Quarterly* 50 (3): 329–366.

Barbat, V., M. Hlady Rispail, and K. Randerson. 2014. "Disentangling the Roles of International Entrepreneurial Orientation and Networking in the Internationalisation Process of SESBs." *International Journal of Entrepreneurship and Small Business* 23 (3): 363–384.

Birkinshaw, J. 2003. "The Paradox of Corporate Entrepreneurship." *Strategy and Business* 30 (Spring): 46–57.

Boston Consulting Group 2011. *Companies on the Move: Rising Stars from Rapidly Developing Economies Are Reshaping Global Industries (White Paper)*. Boston, MA: BCG.

Bourdieu, P. 1977. *Outline of a Theory of Practice*. Cambridge: Cambridge University Press.

Bourdieu, P. 1990. *The Logic of Practice*. Stanford: Stanford University Press.

Brettel, M., R. Mauer, A. Engelen, and D. Küpper. 2012. "Corporate Effectuation: Entrepreneurial Action and Its Impact on R&D Project Performance." *Journal of Business Venturing* 27 (2): 167–184.

Burgelman, R. A. 1983. "A Process Model of Internal Corporate Venturing in the Diversified Major Firm." *Administrative Science Quarterly* 28 (2): 223–244.

Burgelman, R. A. 1996. "A Process Model of Strategic Business Exit: Implications for an Evolutionary Perspective on Strategy." *Strategic Management Journal* 17: 193–214.

Burg, E., and A. L. Romme. 2014. "Creating the Future Together: Toward a Framework for Research Synthesis in Entrepreneurship." *Entrepreneurship: Theory & Practice* 38 (2): 369–397.

Chimezie, A., and B. Osigweh. 1989. "Concept Fallibility in Organizational Science." *Academy of Management Review* 14 (4): 579–594.

Coviello, N. E., and M. V. Jones. 2004. "Methodological Issues in Entrepreneurship Research." *Journal of Business Venturing* 19 (4): 485–508.

Covin, J. G., and G. T. Lumpkin. 2011. "Entrepreneurial Orientation Theory and Research: Reflections on a Needed Construct." *Entrepreneurship: Theory & Practice* 35 (5): 855–872.

Covin, J. G., and D. P. Slevin. 1989. "Strategic Management of Small Firms in Hostile and Benign Environments." *Strategic Management Journal* 10 (1): 75–87.

Covin, J. G., and D. P. Slevin. 1991. "A Conceptual Model of Entrepreneurship as Firm Behavior." *Entrepreneurship: Theory & Practice* 16 (1): 7–25.

Covin, J. G., and W. J. Wales. 2012. "The Measurement of Entrepreneurial Orientation." *Entrepreneurship: Theory & Practice* 36 (4): 677–702.

Covin, J. G., and D. Miller. 2014. "International Entrepreneurial Orientation: Conceptual Considerations, Research Themes, Measurement Issues, and Future Research Directions." *Entrepreneurship: Theory & Practice* 38 (1): 11–44.

Dew, N., S. Read, S. D. Sarasvathy, and R. Wiltbank. 2008. "Outlines of a Behavioral Theory of the Entrepreneurial Firm." *Journal of Economic Behavior & Organization* 66 (1): 37–59.

Dodd, S. D., S. Jack, and A. R. Anderson. 2013. "From Admiration to Abhorrence: The Contentious Appeal of Entrepreneurship across Europe." *Entrepreneurship & Regional Development* 25 (1/2): 69–89.

Down, S. 2013. "The Distinctiveness of the European Tradition in Entrepreneurship Research." *Entrepreneurship & Regional Development* 25 (1/2): 1–4.

Evald, M. R., and M. Senderovitz. 2013. "Exploring Internal Corporate Venturing in SMEs: Effectuation at Work in a New Context." *Journal of Enterprising Culture* 21 (3): 275–299.

Fayolle, A., O. Basso, and V. Bouchard. 2010. "Three Levels of Culture and Firms' Entrepreneurial Orientation: A Research Agenda." *Entrepreneurship & Regional Development* 22 (7/8): 707–730.

Fayolle, A. P., H. Riot, K. Berglund Landström, and W. B. Gartner. 2013. "The Institutionalization of Entrepreneurship: Questioning the Status Quo and Re-gaining Hope for Entrepreneurship Research." *Entrepreneurship & Regional Development* 29 (9/10): 889–890.

Fletcher, D. E. 2006. "Entrepreneurial Processes and the Social Construction of Opportunity." *Entrepreneurship & Regional Development* 18 (5): 421–440.

Fletcher, D. E. 2007. "Social Constructionist Thinking: Some Implications for Entrepreneurship Research and Education." In *Handbook of Research in Entrepreneurship and Education*. Vol. 1, edited by A. Fayolle, 160–172. Cheltenham (UK): Edward Elgar Publishing.

Gartner, W. B. 1985. "A Conceptual Framework for Describing the Phenomenon of New Venture Creation." *Academy of Management Review* 10 (4): 696–706.

Gartner, W. B. 1990. "What Are We Talking about When We Talk about Entrepreneurship?" *Journal of Business Venturing* 5: 15–28.

Gartner, W. B. 2007a. "Is There an Elephant in Entrepreneurship? Blind Assumptions in Theory Development." *Entrepreneurship Theory and Practice* 25 (4): 27–39.

Gartner, W. B. 2007b. "Entrepreneurial Narrative and a Science of the Imagination." *Journal of Business Venturing* 22 (5): 613–627.

Gartner, W. B. 2013. "Creating a Community of Difference in Entrepreneurship Scholarship." *Entrepreneurship & Regional Development* 25 (1/2): 5–15.

Gartner, W. B., B. J. Bird, and J. A. Starr. 1992. "Acting as If: Differentiating Entrepreneurial from Organizational Behavior." *Entrepreneurship: Theory & Practice* 16 (3): 13–31.

George, B. A., and L. Marino. 2011. "The Epistemology of Entrepreneurial Orientation: Conceptual Formation, Modeling, and Operationalization." *Entrepreneurship: Theory & Practice* 35 (5): 989–1024.

Hansen, J. D., G. D. Deitz, M. Tokman, L. D. Marino, and K. M. Weaver. 2011. "Cross-national Invariance of the Entrepreneurial Orientation Scale." *Journal of Business Venturing* 26 (1): 61–78.

Hayton, J. C., G. George, and S. A. Zahra. 2002. "National Culture and Entrepreneurship: A Review of Behavioral Research." *Entrepreneurship: Theory & Practice* 26 (4): 33–53.

Hayton, J. C., J. S. Hornsby, and J. Bloodgood 2013. "Part II: The Contribution of HRM to Corporate Entrepreneurship: A Review and Agenda for Future Research." *M@N@Gement* 16 (4): 381–409.

Hjorth, D., C. Jones, and W. B. Gartner. 2008. "Introduction for Recreating/Recontextualising Entrepreneurship." *Scandinavian Journal of Management* 24 (2): 81–84.

Ireland, R. D., J. G. Covin, and D. F. Kuratko. 2009. "Conceptualizing Corporate Entrepreneurship Strategy." *Entrepreneurship: Theory & Practice* 33 (1): 19–46.

Jennings, D. F., and J. R. Lumpkin. 1989. "Functioning Modeling Corporate Entrepreneurship: An Empirical Integrative Analysis." *Journal of Management* 15 (3): 485–502.

Kanter, R. M., J. North, A. P. Bernstein, and A. Williamson. 1990. "Engines of Progress: Designing and Running Entrepreneurial Vehicles in Established Companies." *Journal of Business Venturing* 5 (6): 415.

Karmann, T., R. Mauer, T. Flatten, and M. Brettel. 2016. "Entrepreneurial Orientation and Corruption." *Journal of Business Ethics* 133 (2): 223–234.

Knight, G. A. 1997. "Cross-cultural Reliability and Validity of a Scale to Measure Firm Entrepreneurial Orientation." *Journal of Business Venturing* 12 (3): 213–225.

Kreiser, P. M., and J. Davis. 2010. "Entrepreneurial Orientation and Firm Performance: The Unique Impact of Innovativeness, Proactiveness, and Risk-taking." *Journal of Small Business & Entrepreneurship* 23 (1): 39–51.

Kreiser, P. M., L. D. Marino, P. Dickson, and M. K. Weaver. 2010. "Cultural Influences on Entrepreneurial Orientation: The Impact of National Culture on Risk Taking and Proactiveness in SMEs." *Entrepreneurship: Theory & Practice* 34 (5): 959–983.

Kreiser, P. M., L. D. Marino, and K. M. Weaver. 2002. "Assessing the Psychometric Properties of the Entrepreneurial Orientation Scale: A Multi-country Analysis." *Entrepreneurship: Theory & Practice* 26 (4): 71–95.

Kuratko, D. F., J. S. Hornsby, D. W. Naffziger, and R. V. Montagno. 1993. "Implement Entrepreneurial Thinking in Established Organizations." *SAM Advanced Management Journal (07497075)* 58 (1): 28–35.

Li, Y., Y. Liu, and H. Liu. 2011. "Co-opetition, Distributor's Entrepreneurial Orientation and Manufacturer's Knowledge Acquisition: Evidence from China." *Journal of Operations Management* 29 (1/2): 128–142.

Lumpkin, G. T., C. C. Cogliser, and D. R. Schneider. 2009. "Understanding and Measuring Autonomy: An Entrepreneurial Orientation Perspective." *Entrepreneurship: Theory & Practice* 33 (1): 47–69.

Lumpkin, G. T., and G. G. Dess. 1996. "Clarifying the Entrepreneurial Orientation Construct and Linking It to Performance." *Academy of Management Review* 21 (1): 135–172.

Lyon, D. W., G. T. Lumpkin, and G. G. Dess. 2000. "Enhancing Entrepreneurial Orientation Research: Operationalizing and Measuring a Key Strategic Decision Making Process." *Journal of Management* 26 (5): 1055–1085.

McMullen, J. S., and D. Dimov. 2013. "Time and the Entrepreneurial Journey: The Problems and Promise of Studying Entrepreneurship as a Process." *Journal of Management Studies* 50 (8): 1481–1512.

Merz, G. R., and M. H. Sauber. 1995. "Profiles of Managerial Activities in Small Firms." *Strategic Management Journal* 16 (7): 551–564.

Miller, D. 1983. "The Correlates of Entrepreneurship in Three Types of Firms." *Management Science* 29 (7): 770–791.

Miller, D. 2011. "Miller (1983) Revisited: A Reflection on EO Research and Some Suggestions for the Future." *Entrepreneurship: Theory & Practice* 35 (5): 873–894.

Monsen, E., H. Patzelt, and T. Saxton. (2010). Beyond Simple Utility: Incentive Design and Trade Offs for Corporate Employee-Entrepreneurs. *Entrepreneurship: Theory and Practice* 34 (1), 105–130.

Ogbor, J. O. 2000. "Mythicizing and Reification in Entrepreneurial Discourse: Ideology-critique of Entrepreneurial Studies." *Journal of Management Studies* 37 (5): 605–635.

Popp, A., and R. Holt. 2013. "Entrepreneurship and Being: The Case of the Shaws." *Entrepreneurship & Regional Development* 25 (1/2): 52–68.

Randerson, K., C. Bettinelli, and A. Fayolle. 2014. "A Taxonomic Approach to Entrepreneurial Orientation." In *Entrepreneurship, People and Organisations: Frontiers in European Entrepreneurship Research*, edited by R. Blackburn, F. Delmar, A. Fayolle and F. Welter, 51–73. Cheltenham: Edward Elgar.

Randerson, K., J. M. Degeorge, and A. Fayolle. 2016. "Entrepreneurial Opportunities: How Do Cognitive Styles and Logics of Action Fit in?" *International Journal of Entrepreneurship and Small Business* 27 (1): 19–39.

Rauch, A., J. Wiklund, G. T. Lumpkin, and M. Frese. 2009. "Entrepreneurial Orientation and Business Performance: An Assessment of past Research and Suggestions for the Future." *Entrepreneurship: Theory & Practice* 33 (3): 761–787.

Sarasvathy, S. D. 2001. "Causation and Effectuation: Toward a Theoretical Shift from Economic Inevitability to Entrepreneurial Contingency." *Academy of Management Review* 26 (2): 243–263.

Sarasvathy, S. D., N. Dew, S. Read, and R. Wiltbank. 2008. "Designing Organizations That Design Environments: Lessons from Entrepreneurial Expertise." *Organization Studies* 29 (3), 331–350.

Sarasvathy, S. D., and S. Venkataraman. 2011. "Entrepreneurship as Method: Open Questions for an Entrepreneurial Future." *Entrepreneurship: Theory & Practice* 35 (1), 113–135.

Satori, G. 1970. "Concept Misformation in Comparative Politics." *American Political Science Review* 64: 1033–1053.

Sciascia, S., and C. Bettinelli. 2013. "Part III: Corporate Entrepreneurship in Context: 1. Corporate Entrepreneurship in Family Businesses: Past, Present and Future Research." *M@N@Gement* 16 (4), 422–432.

Shepherd, D. A., D. F. Kuratko, and J. G. Covin. 2009. "Project Failure from Corporate Entrepreneurship: Managing the Grief Process." *Journal of Business Venturing* 24: 588–600.

Short, J. C., J. C. Broberg, C. C. Cogliser, and K. H. Brigham. 2010. "Construct Validation Using Computer-Aided Text Analysis (CATA): an Illustration Using Entrepreneurial Orientation." *Organizational Research Methods* 13 (2): 320–347.

Slevin, D. P., and S. A. Terjesen. 2011. "Entrepreneurial Orientation: Reviewing Three Papers and Implications for Further Theoretical and Methodological Development." *Entrepreneurship: Theory & Practice* 35 (5): 973–987.

Spigel, B. 2013. "Bourdieuian Approaches to the Geography of Entrepreneurial Cultures." *Entrepreneurship & Regional Development* 25 (9/10): 804–818.

Steyaert, C., and J. Katz. 2004. "Reclaiming the Space of Entrepreneurship in Society: Geographical, Discursive and Social Dimensions." *Entrepreneurship & Regional Development* 16: 179–196.

Wales, W. J. 2016. "Entrepreneurial Orientation: A Review and Synthesis of Promising Research Directions." *International Small Business Journal* 34 (1): 3–15.

Wales, W., E. Monsen, and A. McKelvie. 2011. "The Organizational Pervasiveness of Entrepreneurial Orientation." *Entrepreneurship: Theory & Practice* 35 (5): 895–923.

Watson, T. J. 2013. "Entrepreneurial Action and the Euro-American Social Science Tradition: Pragmatism, Realism and Looking beyond 'the Entrepreneur.'" *Entrepreneurship & Regional Development* 25 (1/2): 16–33.

Welter, F. 2011. "Contextualizing Entrepreneurship-conceptual Challenges and Ways Forward." *Entrepreneurship: Theory & Practice* 35 (1): 165–184.

Williams, C. C., and S. J. Nadin. 2013. "Beyond the Entrepreneur as a Heroic Figurehead of Capitalism: Re-representing the Lived Practices of Entrepreneurs." *Entrepreneurship & Regional Development* 25 (7/8): 552–568.

Zahra, S. A. 1991. "Predictors and Financial Outcomes of Corporate Entrepreneurship: An Exploratory Study." *Journal of Business Venturing* 6 (4): 259.

Zahra, S. A. 1993. "A Conceptual Model of Entrepreneurship as Firm Behavior: A Critique and Extension." *Entrepreneurship: Theory & Practice* 17 (4): 5–21.

Zahra, S. A. 2007. "Contextualizing Theory Building in Entrepreneurship Research." *Journal of Business Venturing* 22 (3): 443–452.

Zahra, S. A., and G. G. Dess. 2001. "Entrepreneurship as a Field of Research: Encouraging Dialogue and Debate." *Academy of Management Review* 26 (1): 8–10.

Zahra, S. A., and L. R. Newey. 2009. "Maximizing the Impact of Organization Science: Theory-building at the Intersection of Disciplines and/or Fields." *Journal of Management Studies* 46 (6): 1059–1075.

Zahra, S. A., K. Randerson, and A. Fayolle. 2013. "Part I: The Evolution and Contributions of Corporate Entrepreneurship Research." *M@N@Gement* 16 (4): 362–380.

Zahra, S. A., and M. Wright. 2011. "Entrepreneurship's Next Act." *Academy of Management Perspectives* 25 (4): 67–83.

Zellweger, T., and P. Sieger. 2012. "Entrepreneurial Orientation in Long-lived Family Firms." *Small Business Economics* 38 (1): 67–84.

Zellweger, T. M., R. S. Nason, and M. Nordqvist. 2012. "From Longevity of Firms to Transgenerational Entrepreneurship of Families: Introducing Family Entrepreneurial Orientation." *Family Business Review* 25 (2): 136–155.

Index

Note: Page numbers in *italics* indicate a figure
Page numbers in **bold** indicate a table
'N' after a page number indicates a note

Timmers, Jeroen 67–71
Tolbert, P. S. 5
Touraine, A. 68
transition theory 80

U.S. Army post office 19–33

Van der Linde, Ilco 67–72
Vieta, M. 94, 96

Wales, W. J. 108, 112, 114
Warnock, Mary 49
Watson, T. J. 118
Watson, Tony J. 41
Weaver, K. M. 111, 112
Weick, K. E. 6
Whitehead, A. 31

Wilson, John 49
worker-occupied enterprises 91–97
world-making 80

Zahra, S. A. 31, 105
Zald, M. N. 68
Zanón ceramics factory 95, 96
Zeitgeist movement **72**, **76**; effectiveness of 82; engagement of activists in 71–73; global context of 64–65; goals of 69; leadership of 69–71; narrative dimensions 75; national context of 63–64; overview of 66–67; selection of, as SE case study 61–62; temporal, spatial, and relational deixis 77, **78–79**; websites 73–75, **74**; *see also* social entrepreneurship (SE) study
Zucker, L. G. 5

*For Product Safety Concerns and Information please contact
our EU representative GPSR@taylorandfrancis.com Taylor & Francis
Verlag GmbH, Kaufingerstraße 24, 80331 München, Germany*

T - #0153 - 160425 - C0 - 246/174/8 - PB - 9780367519193 - Gloss Lamination